Augustine David Crake

Brian Fitz-Count

a story of Wallingford Castle and Dorchester Abbey

Augustine David Crake

Brian Fitz-Count

a story of Wallingford Castle and Dorchester Abbey

ISBN/EAN: 9783741193088

Manufactured in Europe, USA, Canada, Australia, Japa

Cover: Foto ©ninafisch / pixelio.de

Manufactured and distributed by brebook publishing software (www.brebook.com)

Augustine David Crake

Brian Fitz-Count

PREFACE

THE author has accomplished a desire of many years in writing a story of Wallingford Castle and Dorchester Abbey. They are the two chief historical landmarks of a country familiar to him in his boyhood, and now again his home. The first was the most important stronghold on the Thames during the calamitous civil war of King Stephen's days. The second was founded at the commencement of the twelfth century, and was built with the stones which came from the Bishop's palace in Dorchester, abandoned when Remigius in 1092 removed the seat of the Bishopric to Lincoln.

The tale is all too true to mediæval life in its darker features. The reader has only to turn to the last pages of the *Anglo-Saxon Chronicle* to justify the terrible description of the dungeons of the Castle, and the sufferings inflicted therein. Brian Fitz-Count was a real personage. The writer has recorded his dark deeds, but has striven to speak gently of him, especially of his tardy repentance; his faults were those of most Norman barons.

The critic may object that the plot of the story, so far as the secret of Osric's birth is concerned, is too soon revealed—nay, is clear from the outset. It was the writer's intention, that the fact should be patent to the attentive reader, although unknown at the time to the parties most concerned. Many an intricate story is more interesting the second time of reading than the first, from the fact that the reader, having the key, can better understand the irony of fate in the tale, and the bearing of the events upon the situation.

In painting the religious system of the day, he may be thought by zealous Protestants too charitable to the Church of our forefathers; for he has always brought into prominence the evangelical features which, amidst much superstition, ever existed within her, and which in her deepest corruption was still *the salt* which kept society from utter ruin and degradation. But, as he has said elsewhere, it is a far nobler thing to seek points of agreement in controversy, and to make the best of things, than to be gloating over "corruptions" or exaggerating the faults of our Christian ancestors. At the same time the author must not be supposed to sympathise with all the opinions and sentiments which, in consistency with the period, he puts into the mouth of theologians of the twelfth century.

There has been no attempt to introduce archaisms in language, save that the Domesday names of places are sometimes given in place of the modern ones where it seemed appropriate or interesting to use them. The speakers spoke either in Anglo-Saxon or Norman-French: the present diction is simply translation. The original was quite as free from stiffness, so far as we can judge.

The roads, the river, the hills, all the details of the scenery have been familiar to the writer since his youth, and are therefore described from personal knowledge. The Lazar-House at Byfield yet lingers in tradition. Driving by the "Pond" one day years ago, the dreary sheet of water was pointed out as the spot where the lepers once bathed; and the informant added that to that day the natives shrank from bathing therein. A strange instance of the long life of oral tradition—which is, however, paralleled at Bensington, where the author in his youth found traditions of the battle of the year 777 yet in existence, although the fight does not find a place, or did not then, in the short histories read in schools.

The author dedicates this book, with great respect, to the present owner of the site and remains of Wallingford Castle, John Kirby Hedges, Esq., who with great kindness granted him free access to the Castle-grounds at all times for the purposes of the story; and whose valuable work, *The History of Wallingford*, has supplied the topographical details and the special history of the Castle. For the history of Dorchester Abbey, he is especially indebted to the notes of his lamented friend, the late vicar of Dorchester.

A. D. C.

CHRISTMAS 1887.

CONTENTS

CHAP.		PAGE
I.	The Lord of the Castle	1
II.	The Chase	8
III.	Who Struck the Stag?	16
IV.	In the Greenwood	24
V.	Cwichelm's Hlawe	32
VI.	On the Downs	40
VII.	Dorchester Abbey	48
VIII.	The Baron and his Prisoners	56
IX.	The Lepers	64
X.	The New Novice	72
XI.	Osric's first Ride	79
XII.	The Hermitage	87
XIII.	Osric at Home	95

CHAP.		PAGE
XIV.	THE HERMITAGE	104
XV.	THE ESCAPE FROM OXFORD CASTLE	117
XVI.	AFTER THE ESCAPE	131
XVII.	LIFE AT WALLINGFORD CASTLE	141
XVIII.	BROTHER ALPHEGE	150
XIX.	IN THE LOWEST DEPTHS	158
XX.	MEINHOLD AND HIS PUPILS	170
XXI.	A DEATHBED DISCLOSURE	178
XXII.	THE OUTLAWS	189
XXIII.	THE PESTILENCE (AT BYFIELD)	200
XXIV.	THE OPENING OF THE PRISON HOUSE	206
XXV.	THE SANCTUARY	216
XXVI.	SWEET SISTER DEATH	226
XXVII.	FRUSTRATED	234
XXVIII.	FATHER AND SON	244
XXIX.	IN THE HOLY LAND	257

CHAPTER I

THE LORD OF THE CASTLE

It was the evening of the 30th of September in the year of grace 1139; the day had been bright and clear, but the moon, arising, was rapidly overpowering the waning light of the sun.

Brian Fitz-Count, Lord of Wallingford Castle by marriage with the Lady Maude (*Matildis Domina de Walingfort*), the widow of the doughty Baron Milo Crispin, who died in 1107, without issue—was pacing the ramparts of his castle, which overlooked the Thames. Stern and stark was this mediæval baron, and large were his possessions. He was the son of Count Alain of Brittany [1]—a nephew of Hamelin de Baladin, of Abergavenny Castle, from whom he inherited large possessions in Wales: a nephew also of Brian, lord of a manor in Cornwall, which he also inherited.

> "Great his houses, lands, and castles,
> Written in the Domesday Book."

Furthermore, he was an especial favourite with Henry the First, who commanded the Lady of Wallingford to marry his minion—according to the law which placed such widows at the disposal of the crown—he was present at the consecration of the great abbey of Reading, where amongst the co-signatories we read "*Signum Brientii filii comitis, de Walingfort:*" the seal of Brian Fitz-Count of Wallingford.

[1] Anglo-Saxon Chronicle.

He walked the ramparts on this last evening of September, and gazed upon his fair castle, or might have done so had his mind been at rest, but "black care sat on his back."

Still we will gaze, unimpeded by that sable rider, although we fear he is not dead yet.

The town of Wallingford had been utterly destroyed by the Danes in 1006, as recorded in our former story of *Alfgar the Dane*. It was soon afterwards rebuilt, and in the time of Edward the Confessor, was in the hands of the thane, and shire-reeve (sheriff) Wigod de Wallingford, a cupbearer of the pious monarch, and one who shared all that saintly king's Norman proclivities. Hence it is not wonderful that when William the Conqueror could not cross the Thames at Southwark, owing to the opposition of the brave men of London town, he led his army along the southern bank of the great river to Wallingford, where he was assured of sympathy, and possessed an English partisan. Here Wigod received him in his hall—a passable structure for those times—which subsequently formed a part of the castle which the Norman king ordered to be built, and which became one of the strongest fortresses in the kingdom, and the key of the midlands.

The Conqueror was a guest of Wigod for several days, and before he left he witnessed the marriage of the eldest daughter of his host, the English maiden Aldith, to a Norman favourite, Robert d'Oyley, whom he made Lord of Oxford.

Now the grand-daughter of that Wigod, whom we will not call traitor to his country—although some might deem him so—in default of male issue, became the wife of Brian Fitz-Count. The only son of Wigod, who might have passed on the inheritance to a line of English lords—Tokig of Wallingford—died in defence of William the Conqueror [1]

---

[1] William's first wound came from the hand from which a wound is most bitter. Father and son met face to face in the battle; the parricidal spear of Robert pierced the hand of his father, an arrow at the same moment

at the battle of Archenbrai, waged between the father and his son Robert Courthose.

To build the new castle,[1] Robert d'Oyley, who succeeded to the lordship on the death of Wigod, destroyed eight houses, which furnished space for the enlargement, and material for the builders. We are not told whether he made compensation—it is doubtful.

The castle was built within the ancient walls in the north-east quarter of the town, occupying a space of some twenty or thirty acres, and its defence on the eastern side was the Thames.

Within the precincts rose one of those vast mounds thrown up by Ethelfleda, lady of the Mercians, and daughter of the great Alfred, a century and a half earlier. It formed the kernel of the new stronghold, and surmounted by a lofty tower, commanded a wondrous view of the country around, from a height of some two hundred feet.

On the north-east lay the long line of the Chilterns; on the south-west, the Berkshire downs stretching towards Cwichelm's Hlawe, and the White Horse Hill; between the two lay the gorge of the Thames, and in the angle the fertile alluvial plain, chiefly filled at that time by a vast park or chase, or by forest or marsh land.

The Chilterns were covered with vast beech forests, the Berkshire downs were more bare.

There were three bastions to the north and two on the south; within the inner dyke or moat on the east was the

struck the horse on which he rode, and the Conqueror lay for a moment on the earth expecting death at the hands of his own son. A loyal Englishman sped to the rescue—Tokig, the son of Wigod of Wallingford, sprang down and offered his horse to the fallen king—at that moment the shot of a crossbow gave the gallant thane of Berkshire a mortal wound, and Tokig gave up his life for his sovereign.—*Freeman.*

[1] Leland writes—giving his own observations in the sixteenth century (temp. Henry VIII.):—"The castle joineth to the north gate of the town, and hath three dykes, large and deep and well watered; about each of the two first dykes, as upon the crests of the ground, runneth an embattled wall now sore in ruin; all the goodly building with the tower and dungeon be within the three dykes." The dykes or moats were supplied with water from the *Moreton* brook.

"glacis," which sloped abruptly towards the river: the main entrance, on the west, was approached by a series of drawbridges, while beneath the tower a heavy portcullis defended the gateway.

Upon the keep stood two sentinels, who from the summit of their lofty tower scrutinised the roads and open country all day long, until they were relieved by those who watched by night. Beneath them lay the town with its moat, and earthen rampart in compass a good mile and more, joining the river at each extremity. Within the compass were eleven parishes, "well and sufficiently built," with one parish church in each of them, well constructed, and with chaplains and clerks daily officiating, so that people had no lack of spiritual provision.

Beyond, the roads stretched in all directions: the Lower Icknield Street ran by woody Ewelme along the base of the downs, towards distant Stokenchurch and Wycombe; while on the opposite side, it ran across the wild moor land through Aston and Blewbery to the Berkshire downs, where it joined the upper way again, and continued its course for Devizes. Our readers will know this road well by and by.

Another road led towards the hills, called "Ye Kynge's Standynge," where it ascended the downs, and joining the upper Icknield Street, stretched across the slopes of Lowbury Hill, the highest point on the eastern downs, where the remains of a strong Roman tower formed a conspicuous object at that date. Another road led directly to the west, and to distant Ffaringdune, along the southern side of the twin hills of Synodune.

Now we will cease from description and take up our story.

"Our lord looks ill at ease," said Malebouche, one of the sentinels on the keep, to Bardulf, his companion.

"As well he may on this day!"

"Why on this day?"

"Dost thou not know that he is childless?"

"I suppose that is the case every day in the year."

"Ah, thou art fresh from fair Brittany, so I will tell thee the tale, only breathe it not where our lord can hear of my words, or I shall make acquaintance with his dog-whip, if not with gyves and fetters. Well, it chanced that thirteen years agone he burnt an old manor-house over on the downs near Compton, inhabited by a family of English churls who would not pay him tribute; the greater part of the household, unable to escape, perished in the flames, and amongst them, the mother and eldest child. In a dire rage and fury the father, who escaped, being absent from home, plotted revenge. Our lord had a son then, a likely lad of some three summers, and soon afterwards, on this very day, the child was out with scanty attendance taking the air, for who, thought they, would dare to injure the heir of the mighty baron, when some marauders made a swoop from the woods on the little party, slew them all and carried off the child—at least the body was never found, while those of the attendants lay all around, male and female."

"And did not they make due search?"

"Thou mayst take thy corporal oath of that. They searched every thicket and fastness, but neither the child nor any concerned in the outrage were ever found. They hung two or three poor churls and vagrants on suspicion, but what good could that do; there was no proof, and the wretches denied all knowledge."

"Did not they try the 'question,' the *'peine forte et dure?'*"

"Indeed they did, but although one poor vagrant died under it, he revealed nothing, because he had nothing to reveal, I suppose."

"What ho! warder! dost thou see nought on the roads?" cried a stern, loud voice which made both start.

"Nought, my lord."

"Keep a good look-out; I expect guests."

And Brian Fitz-Count resumed his walk below—to and fro, communing with his own moody thoughts.

An hour had passed away, when the sentinel cried aloud—

"A party of men approaches along the lower Ickleton Way from the west."

"How many in number?"

"About twenty."

"Where are they?"

"They cross the moor and have just left the South Moor Town."

"Canst thou make out their cognisance?"

"The light doth not serve."

"Order a troop of horse: I ride to meet them; let the banquet be prepared."

In another quarter of an hour a little party dashed over the lowered drawbridges and out on the western road; meanwhile the great hall was lighted, and the cooks hurried on the feast.

In less than another hour the blast of trumpets announced the return of the Lord of the Castle with his guest. And Brian Fitz-Count rode proudly into his stronghold: on his right hand rode a tall knight, whose squires and attendants followed behind with the Wallingford men.

"Welcome, Sir Milo of Gloucester, to my castle," exclaimed the Lord of Wallingford, as he clasped the hand of his visitor beneath the entrance tower.

"By'r ladye, a fine stronghold this of yours; that tower on the keep might rival in height the far-famed tower of Babel."

"We do not hope to scale Heaven, although, forsooth, if the Masses said daily in Wallingford are steps in the ladder, it will soon be long enough."

And they both laughed grimly in a way which did not infer implicit belief in the power of the Church.

"The bath, then the board—prepare the bath for our guest."

So they led him to the bathroom, for the Normans washed themselves, for which the natives charged them with effeminacy; and there they brought towels, and perfumed waters, and other luxuries. After which two pages conducted the guest to the great hall, which was nearly a hundred feet in length. The high table stood at the one end upon a platform, and there the Lord of Wallingford seated himself, while upon his left hand sat the Lady Maude, a lady of middle age, and upon his right a seat of state was prepared, to which the pages led his visitor.

Fully two hundred men banqueted in the hall that night, boards on trestles were distributed all along the length at right angles to the high table, with space between for the servers to pass, and troops of boys and lower menials squatted on the rushes, while the men-at-arms sat at the board.

A gallery for the musicians projected above the feasters on one side of the hall, and there a dozen performers with harps and lutes played warlike songs, the while the company below ate and drank. The music was rough but seemed to stir the blood as its melody rose and fell.

And when at last the banquet was ended, a herald commanded silence, and Brian Fitz-Count addressed the listening throng:

"My merry men all, our guest here bringeth us news which may change our festal attire for helm and hauberk, and convert our ploughshares and pruning-hooks into swords and lances; but nought more of this to-night, the morrow we hunt the stag, and when we meet here on to-morrow night I may have welcome news for all merry men who love war and glory better than slothful ease."

A loud burst of applause followed the speech, the purport of which they fully understood, for the long peace had wearied them, and they were all eager for the strife as the beasts of prey for rapine, so in song and wassail they spent the evening, while the Baron and his guest withdrew to take secret council in an inner chamber.

CHAPTER II

THE CHASE

> Hail, smiling morn,
> That tips the hills with gold."

THE merry sound of horns blowing the *reveillée* greeted the sleepers as they awoke, lazily, and saw the morning dawn shining through their windows of horn, or stretched skin, or through the chinks of their shutters in the chambers of Wallingford Castle, and in a very short space of time the brief toilettes were performed, the hunting garb donned, and the whole precincts swarmed with life, while the clamour of dogs or of men filled the air.

Soon the doughty Baron with his commanding voice stilled the tumult, as he gave his orders for the day; the *déjeuner* or breakfast of cold meats, washed down with ale, mead, or wine, was next despatched, a hunting Mass was said in "St. Nicholas his Chapel"—that is, a Mass shorn of its due proportions and reduced within the reasonable compass of a quarter of an hour—and before the hour of Prime (7 A.M.) the whole train issued from the gates, Milo, Sheriff of Gloucester,[1] riding by the side of his host.

It was a bright, bracing morning that First of October, the air keen but delicious—one of those days when we hardly regret the summer which has left us and say we like autumn best; every one felt the pulses of life beat the more healthily, as the hunting train rode up by the side of the Moreton brook, towards distant Estune or East-town, as Aston was then called.

[1] Sir Milo was Sheriff of Gloucester, and was afterwards created Earl of Hereford by the Empress Maude.

They were now approaching a densely-wooded district, for all that portion of the "honour" of Wallingford which lay beneath the downs, was filled with wood and marsh nourished by many slow and half stagnant streams, or penetrated by swiftly running brooks which still follow the same general course through the district in its cultivated state.

At length they reached a wide open moor covered with gorse or heather; gay and brilliant looked the train as it passed over the spot. The hunters generally wore a garb familiar to some of us by pictorial representations, a green hunting tunic girded by a belt with silver clasps, a hunting knife in the girdle, a horn swung round the shoulder dependent from the neck; but beneath this gay attire the great men wore suits of chain mail, so flexible that it did not impede their movements nor feel half so uncomfortable as some present suits of corduroy would feel to a modern dandy. There were archers a few, there were also spearmen who ran well and kept up with the mounted company at a steady swinging trot, then there were fine-looking dogs of enormous size, and of wondrous powers of strength and motion. The very thought of it is enough to make the modern hunter sigh for the "good old times."

Onward! onward! we fly, the moor is past, the hunting train turns to the right and follows the course of the brook towards the park of Blidberia (or Blewbery), the wood gets thicker and thicker; it is a tangled marsh, and yet a forest; tall trees rise in endless variety, oaks that might have borne mistletoes for the Druids; huge beeches with spreading foliage, beneath which Tityrus might have reclined nor complained of want of shade; willows rooted in water; decaying trunks of trees, rotting in sullen pools of stagnant mire; yet, a clear, fresh spring rushes along by the side of the track.

And at intervals the outline of the Bearroc hills, the Berkshire downs, rises above the forest, and solemnly in the distance looms the huge tree-covered barrow, where Cwichelm, the last King of Wessex, sleeps his long sleep while his subjugated descendants serve their Norman masters in the country around his hill-tomb.

And now a gallant stag is roused—a stag of ten branches. He scents the dogs as the wind blows from them to him, he shakes the dewdrops from his flanks, he listens one moment to the clamour of the noisy pack of canine foes, he shakes his head disdainfully, and rushes on his headlong course. The dogs bark and bay, the horns ring out, the voices of men and boys, cheering and shouting as they spur their willing steeds, join the discord. Hark! hark! Halloa! halloa! Whoop! whoop! and onward they fly. The timid hares and rabbits rush away or seek their burrows. The hawks and birds of prey fly wildly overhead in puzzled flight, as the wild huntsmen rush along.

But now the natural obstacles retard their flight, and the stag gains the downs first, and speeds over the upper plains. A mile after him, the hunt emerges just above the tangled maze of Blewbery. Now all is open ground, and the stag heads for Cwichelm's Hlawe.

Swiftly they sweep along; the footmen are left far behind. The wind is blowing hard, and the shadows of fleecy clouds are cast upon the downs, but the riders outstrip them, and leave the dark outlines behind them. The leaves blow from many a fading tree, but faster rush the wild huntsmen, and Brian Fitz-Count rides first.

They have left the clump on Blewbery down behind: the sacred mound on which St. Birinus once stood when he first preached the Gospel of Christ to the old English folk of Wessex, is passed unheeded. When lo! they cross a lateral valley and the stag stops to gaze, then as if mature reflection teaches him the wood and tangled marsh are safer for him, descends again to the lower ground.

What a disappointment to be checked in such a gallant run, to leave the springy turf and have again to seek the woods and abate their speed, and what is worse, when they enter the forest they find all the dogs at variance of purpose; a fox, their natural enemy, has crossed the track but recently, and nearly all the pack are after him, while the rest hesitate and rush wildly about. The huntsmen strive to restore order, but meanwhile the stag has gained upon his pursuers. The poor hunted beast, panting as though its heart would break, is safe for a while.

Let us use a tale-teller's privilege and guide the reader to another scene.

Not many furlongs from the spot where the hunters stopped perplexed, stood a lonely cot in a green islet of ground, amidst the mazy windings of a brook, which sprang from the hills and rising from the ground in copious streams, inundated the marsh and gave protection to the dwellers of this primæval habitation.

It was a large cottage for that period, divided into three rooms, the outer and larger one for living, the two inner and smaller for bedchambers. Its construction was simple and not unlike those raised by the dwellers in the wild parts of the earth now. Larches or pines, about the thickness of a man's leg, had been cut down, shaped with an axe, driven into the earth at the intervals of half a yard, willow-twigs had been twined round them, the interstices had been filled with clay, cross beams had been laid upon the level summits of the posts, a roof of bark supported on lighter timber placed upon it, slightly shelving from the ridge, and the outer fabric was complete. Then the inner partitions had been made, partly with bark, partly with skins, stretched from post to post; light doors swung on hinges of leather, small apertures covered with semi-transparent skin formed the windows, and a huge aperture in the roof over a hearth, whereon rested a portable iron grate, served for chimney.

A table, roughly made, stood upon trestles, two or three seats, like milking-stools, supplied the lack of chairs —such was the furniture of the living room.

Over the fire sat the occupants of the house—whom we must particularly introduce to our readers.

The first and most conspicuous was an old man, dressed mainly in vestments of skin, but the one impression he produced upon the beholder was "fallen greatness." Such a face, such noble features, withered and wrinkled though they were by age; long masses of white hair, untouched by barber or scissors, hung down his back, and a white wavy beard reached almost to his waist.

By his side, attentive to his every word, sat a youth of about sixteen summers, and he was also worthy of notice—he seemed to combine the characteristic features of the two races, Norman and English—we will not use that misnomer "Saxon," our ancestors never called themselves by other name than English after the Heptarchy was dissolved. His hair was dark, his features shapely, but there was that one peculiarity of feature which always gives a pathetic look to the face—large blue eyes under dark eyebrows.

The third person was evidently of lower rank than the others, although this was not evident from any distinction of dress, for poverty had obliterated all such tokens, but from the general manner, the look of servitude, the air of submission which characterised one born of a race of thralls. In truth she was the sole survivor of a race of hereditary bondsmen, who had served the ancestors of him whom she now tended with affectionate fidelity amidst poverty and old age.

Let us listen to their conversation, and so introduce them to the reader.

"And so, grandfather," said the boy in a subdued voice of deep feeling, "you saw him, your father, depart for the last time—the very last?"

"I remember, as if it were but yesterday, when my father gathered his churls and thralls[1] around him at our house at Kingestun under the downs to the west: there

---

[1] Otherwise ceorls and theowes, tenant farmers and labourers, the latter, bondsmen, "*adscripti glebæ*," bought with the land, but who could not be sold apart from it.

were women and children, whose husbands and fathers were going with him to join the army of Harold at London; they were all on foot, for we had few knights in those days, but ere my father mounted his favourite horse —'Whitefoot'—he lifted me in his arms and kissed me. I was but five years old, and then he pressed my mother to his bosom, she gave one sob but strove to stifle it, as the wife of a warrior should. Then all tried to cry— 'Long live Thurkill of Kingestun.'

"'Come, my men,' said my father, 'we shall beat these dainty Frenchmen, as our countrymen have beaten the Danes at Stamford, so the 'bode' here tells me. We go to fill the places of the gallant dead who fell around our Harold in the hour of victory—let there be no faint hearts amongst us,'tis for home and hearth; good-bye, sweethearts,' and they rode away.

"They rode first to the Abbey town (Abingdon), and there made their vows before the famous 'Black Cross' of that ancient shrine; then all bent them for the long march to London town, where they arrived in time to march southward with the hero king, the last English king, and seventy-three years ago this very month of October the end came; blessed were the dead who fell that awful day on the heights of Senlac, thrice blessed— and cursed we who survived, to lose home, hearth, altar, and all, and to beget a race of slaves."

"Nay, not slaves, grandfather; thou hast never bent the knee."

"Had I been ten years older, I had been at Senlac and died by my father's side."

"But your mother, you lived to comfort her."

"Not long; when the news of our father's death came, she bore up for my sake—but when our patrimony was taken by force, and we who had fought for our true king were driven from our homes as rebels and traitors, to herd with the beasts of the field; when our thralls became the bondsmen of men of foreign tongues and hard hearts—her heart broke, and she left me alone, after a few months of privation."

"But you fought against the Norman."

"I fought by the side of the last Englishman who fought at all, with Hereward and his brave men at the 'Camp of Refuge'; and spent the prime of my life a prisoner in the grim castle of the recreant Lords of Wallingford."

And he lifted up his eyes, suffused with tears, to heaven.

"Why do you call the Lords of Wallingford Castle recreant?"

"Because they were false to their country, in submitting to the Norman invader. When the Conqueror came to Southwark, the brave men of the city of London, guarded by their noble river and Roman walls, bade him defiance. So he came up the south bank of the stream to Wallingford, where the shire-reeve (the sheriff), Wigod, was ready, like a base traitor, to receive him. There Wigod sumptuously entertained him, and the vast mound which told of English victory in earlier days, became the kernel of a Norman stronghold. The Conqueror gave the daughter of Wigod in marriage to his particular friend, Robert d'Oyley, of Oxford Castle; and when men afterwards saw men like Wigod of Wallingford and Edward of Salisbury glutted with the spoils of Englishmen, better and braver than themselves, they ate their bread in bitterness of spirit, and praised the dead more than the living."

Just then a rustling in the branches attracted their attention.

"Oh, grandfather, there is a gallant stag! may I go and take him?—it will replenish our larder for days. We have been so hungry."

"It is death to kill the Baron's deer."

"When he can catch us!—that!—for him," and the boy snapped his fingers.

"Hist! I hear the sound of hound and horn—be cautious, or we may get into dire trouble."

"Trust me, grandfather. Where are my arrows? Oh, here they are. Come, Bruno."

And a large wolf-hound bounded forth, eager as his young master.

CHAPTER III

WHO STRUCK THE STAG?

"It was a stag, a stag of ten,
Bearing his branches sturdily."

WE left the grandson of the recluse setting forth in quest of the stag.

Forth he and his dog bounded from the thick covert in which their cottage was concealed, and emerging from the tall reeds which bordered the brook, they stood beneath the shade of the mighty beech-trees, whose trunks upbore the dense foliage, as pillars in the solemn aisles of cathedrals support the superstructure; for the woods were God's first temples, and the inhabitants of such regions drew from them the inspiration from which sprang the various orders of Gothic architecture.

Here Osric, for such was his name, paused and hid in a thicket of hazel, for he spied the stag coming down the glade towards him, he restrained the dog by the leash: and the two lay in ambush.

The hunted creature, quite unsuspecting any new foes, came down the glen, bearing his branches loftily, for doubtless he was elate, poor beast, with the victory which his heels had given him over his human and canine foes. And now he approached the ambush: the boy had fitted an arrow to his bow but hesitated, it seemed almost a shame to lay so noble an animal low; but hunger and want are stern masters, and men must eat if they would live.

Just then the creature snuffed the tainted air, an instant, and he would have escaped; but the bow twanged, and the arrow buried itself in its side, the stag bounded in the death agony towards the very thicket whence the fatal dart had come; when Osric met it, and drawing his keen hunting-knife across its throat, ended its struggles and its life together.

He had received a woodland education, and knew what to do; he soon quartered the stag, whose blood the dog was lapping, and taking one of the haunches on his shoulders, entered the tangled maze of reeds and water wherein lay his island-home.

"Here, grandfather, here is one of the haunches, what a capital fat one it is! truly it will be a toothsome morsel for thee, and many tender bits will there be to suit thy aged teeth; come, Judith, come and help me hang it on the tree; then I will go and fetch the rest, joint by joint."

"But stop, Osric, what sound, what noise is that?" and the old man listened attentively—then added—

"Huntsmen have driven that stag hitherwards, and are following on its trail."

The breeze brought the uproarious baying of dogs and cries of men down the woods. It was at that moment, that, as stated in our last chapter, the fox had crossed the track, and baffled them for the moment.

Alas for poor Osric, only for the moment, for the huntsmen had succeeded in getting some of the older and wiser hounds to take up the lost trail, and the scent of their former enemy again greeting their olfactory organs, they obeyed the new impulse—or rather the old one renewed, and were off again after the deer.

And as we see a flock of sheep, stopped by a fence, hesitating where to go, until one finds a gap and all follow; so the various undecided dogs agreed that venison was better than carrion, and the stag therefore a nobler quarry than the fox; so, save a few misguided young puppies, they resumed the legitimate chase.

The huntsmen followed as fast as the trees and bushes allowed them, until, after a mile or two, they all came to a sudden stand, where the object of the chase had already met its death at the hands of Osric.

Meanwhile the unhappy youth had heard them drawing nearer and nearer. He knew that it would be impossible to escape discovery, unless the intricacies of their retreat should baffle the hunters, whom they heard drawing nearer and nearer. The dogs, they knew, would not pursue the chase beyond the place of slaughter. Oh! if they had but time to mangle it before the men arrived, so that the manner in which it had met its death might not be discovered—but that was altogether unlikely. And in truth clamorous human cries mingled with wild vociferous barkings, howlings, bayings, and other canine clamour, showed that the hunt was already assembled close by.

"I will go forth and own the deed: then perhaps they will not inquire further———"

"Nay, my son, await God's Will here."

And the old man restrained the youth.

At length they heard such words as these—

"He cannot be far off."

"He is hidden amongst the reeds."

"Turn in the dogs."

"They have tasted blood and are useless."

"Fire the reeds."

"Nay, grandfather, I must go, the reeds are dry, they will burn us all together. They may show me mercy if I own it bravely."

"Nay, they love their deer too well; they will hang thee on the nearest beech."

"Look! they have fired the reeds."

"It may be our salvation: they cannot penetrate them when burning, and see, if the smoke stifle us not, the fire will not reach us; there is too much green and dank vegetation around the brook between us and the reeds."

"Ah! the wind blows it the other way; nay, it eddies— see that tongue of flame darting amongst the dry fuel— now another: that thick smoke—there it is changed to flame. Oh, grandfather, let us get off by the other side—at once—at once."

"Thou forgettest I am a cripple; but there may be time for you and Judith to save yourselves."

"Nay," said Osric, proudly, "we live or die together."

"Judith will stay with her old master," said the poor thrall, "and with her young lord too."

They were yet "lords" in her eyes, bereft although they were of their once vast possessions.

"Perhaps we are as safe here; their patience will wear out before they can penetrate the island. See, they are firing the reeds out yonder. Normans love a conflagration," said the old man.

In fact, it was as much with that inherent love of making a blaze, which had marked the Normans and the Danes from the beginning, when church, homestead, barn, and stack, were all kindled as the fierce invaders swept through the land; that the mischievous and vindictive men-at-arms had fired the reeds, wherein they thought the slayer of the deer had taken refuge, when they found that the dogs would not enter after him. There was little fear of any further harm than the clearing of a few acres. The trees were too damp to burn, or indeed to take much harm from so hasty and brief a blaze: so they thought, if they thought at all.

But the season had been dry, the material was as tinder, and the blaze reached alarming proportions—several wild animals ran out, and were slain by the bystanders, others were heard squeaking miserably in the flames; but that little affected the hardened folk of the time, they had to learn mercy towards men, before the time came to start a society for the prevention of cruelty to animals.

"He cannot be there or he would have run out by this time."

"He has escaped the other side."

"Nay, Alain and his men have gone round there to look out."

"But they cannot cross the brook on foot, and even a horse would get stuck in the mire."

"They will do their best."

The three in the cottage saw the flames rise and crackle all round them, and the dense clouds of smoke were stifling. Osric got water from the brook and dashed it all over the roof and the more inflammable portions of their dwelling, lest a spark should kindle them, and worked hard at his self-imposed task, in the intense heat.

But the conflagration subsided almost as rapidly as it arose from sheer want of fuel, and with the cessation of the flames came the renewal of the danger of discovery.

Other voices were now heard, one loud and stern as befitted a leader :—

"What meaneth this? Who hath kindled the reeds without my order?"

"The deer-slayer lurketh within."

"What deer-slayer? Who struck the stag?"

"We know not. It could not have been many minutes before we arrived; the carcase was still warm."

"He must be caught; thou shalt not suffer a poacher to live, is the royal command, and mine too; but did you not set the dogs after him?"

"They had tasted blood, my lord."

"But if he were hidden herein, he must have come forth. If the bed of reeds were properly encircled—it seems to cover some roods of forest."

"A shame for so fine a beast to be so foully murdered."

"It was a stag of ten branches."

"And he gave us good sport."

"We will hang his slayer in his honour."

"A fine acorn for a lusty oak."

"When we catch him."

"He shall dance on nothing, and we will amuse ourselves by his grimaces."

"Nothing more laughable than the face a *pendu* makes with the rope round his neck."

"Has anybody got a rope?"
"Has anybody found the poacher?"
A general laugh.
"Silence, listen."

A dry old oak which had perhaps seen the Druids, and felt the keen knife bare its bosom of the hallowed mistletoe, had kindled and fallen; as it fell sending forth showers upon showers of sparks.

The fall of the tree opened a sort of vista in the flames, and revealed——

"Look," said the Baron, "I see something like the roof of a hut just beyond the opening the tree has made."

"I think so too," said Sir Milo of Gloucester.

"Very well, wait here awhile, my men; these reeds are all burnt, and the ground will soon cool, then you may go in and see what that hut contains: reserve them for my judgment. Here, Tristam, here, Raoul, hold our horses."

Two sprightly-looking boy pages took the reins, and Brian and Milo, if we may presume to call them by such familiar appellations, walked together in the glade.

Deep were their cogitations, and how much the welfare of England depended upon them, would hardly be believed by our readers. We would fain reveal what they said, but only the half can be told.

"It can be endured no longer!"
"Soon no one but he will be allowed to build a castle!"
"But to lay hands upon two anointed prelates."
"The Bishops of Sarum and Lincoln."
"Arrested just when they were trusting to his good faith."
"The one in the king's own ante-chamber, the other in his lodgings eating his dinner."
"The Bishop of Ely only escaped by the skin of his teeth."
"And he, too, was forced to surrender his castle, for the king vowed that the Bishop of Salisbury should have

no food until his nephew of Ely surrendered, and led poor Roger, pale and emaciated, stretching forth his skinny hands, and entreating his nephew to save him from starvation, to and fro before the walls, until he gained his ends, and the castle was yielded."

"He is not our true king, but a foul usurper."

"Well, my good cousin, a few hours may bring us news. But, listen; can our folk have caught the deer-slayers? let us return to them."

In the absence of their leaders, the men-at-arms, confiding in the goodness of their boots and leggings, had trodden across the smoking soil in the direction where their leader had pointed out the roof of a hut amidst leafy trees, and had quickly discovered their victims, crossed the brook, and surrounded the house.

"Come forth, Osric, my son," said the old man, "whatever befalls, let us not disgrace our ancestry; let nothing become us in life more than the mode of leaving it, if die we must."

"But must we die? what have we done?"

"Broken their tyrannical laws. Judith, open the door."

A loud shout greeted the appearance of the old man, his beard descending to his waist, as he issued forth, leading Osric by the hand.

"What seek ye, Normans? wherefore have ye surrounded my humble home, whither tyranny has driven me?"

A loud shout of exultation.

"The deer—give up the deer—confess thy guilt."

"Search for it"—"a haunch was gone"—"if in the house, we need no further trial"—"to the nearest tree."

The house was rudely entered—but the haunch, which had been removed from the tree and hidden by Judith, could not be found.

"Ye have no proof that we have offended."

They searched a long while in vain, they opened cupboard and chest, but no haunch appeared.

"Examine them by torture: try the knotted cord."

"One should never go out without thumbscrews in this vile country; they would fit that young poacher's thumbs well."

Just then the Baron was seen returning from his stroll with his guest.

"Bring them to the Baron! bring them to the Baron!"

"And meanwhile fire the house."

"Nay, not till we have orders; our master is stern and strict."

CHAPTER IV

IN THE GREENWOOD

"What shall he have who killed the deer?"

THE return of Brian Fitz-Count and his companion from their stroll in the woods probably saved our aged friend Sexwulf and his grandson from much rough treatment, for although in the presence of express orders from their dread lord, the men-at-arms would not attempt aught against the *life* of their prisoners, yet they might have offered any violence and rudeness short of that last extremity, in their desire to possess proof of the slaughter of the deer.

Poor beast, the cause of so much strife: it had behoved him to die amongst the fangs of the hounds, and he had been foully murdered by arrow and knife! It was not to be endured.

But no sooner did the Baron return, than the scene was changed.

"What means this clamour? Shut your mouths, ye hounds! and bring the deer-slayers before me; one would think Hell had broken loose amongst you."

He sat deliberately down on the trunk of a fallen tree, and called Milo to be his assessor (*amicus curiæ*), as one might have said.

A circle was immediately formed, and the old man and boy, their arms tied behind them, were placed before their judge.

He looked them sternly in the face, as if he would read their hearts.

"Whose serfs are ye?"

"We were never in bondage to any man."

"It is a lie—all Englishmen are in serfdom."

"Time will deliver them."

"Do you dare to bandy words with me; if so, a short shrift and a long halter will suffice: you are within my jurisdiction, and your lives are as much in my power as those of my hounds."

This was not said of hot temper, but bred of that cool contempt which the foreign lords felt for the conquered race with which, nevertheless, they were destined to amalgamate.

"Your names?"

"Sexwulf, son of Thurkill, formerly thane of Kingestun."

"Whose father fell in the fight at Senlac (Hastings), by the side of the perjured Harold; and is this thy son? brought up doubtless to be a rebel like thyself."

"He is my grandson."

"And how hast thou lived here, so long unknown, in my woods?"

"The pathless morass concealed us."

"And how hast thou lived? I need not ask, on my red deer doubtless."

"No proof has been found against us," said the old man, speaking with that meek firmness which seemed to impress his questioner.

"And now, what hast thou done with the haunch of this deer?"

"I have not slain one."

"But the boy may have done so—come, old man, thou lookest like one who would not lie even to save his neck; now if thou wilt assure me, on the faith of a Christian, and swear by the black cross of Abingdon that thou knowest nought of the deer, I will believe thee."

A pause—but Brian foresaw the result of his appeal.

"I cannot," said the captive at length; "I did not slay it, yet if, according to your cruel laws, a man must die for a deer: I refuse not to die—I am weary of the world."

"Nay, the father shall not bear the iniquity of the son; that were contrary to Scripture and to all sound law."

"Grandfather, thou shalt not die," interrupted the boy; "Baron, it was I; but must I die for it? we were so hungry."

"Oh my lord, crush not the young life in the spring-time of youth. God has taken all my children in turn from me, He has deprived me of home and kin: but He is just. He has left this boy to comfort my old age: take not away the light of the old man's eyes. See I, who never asked favour of Norman or foreign lord before, bow my knees to thee; let the boy live, or if not, let both die together."

"One life is enough for *one* deer."

"Nay, then let me die."

"Who slew the deer?"

"I, my lord, and I must die, not my grandfather."

"It was for me, and I must die, as the primal cause of the deed," said the old man.

"By the teeth of St. Peter, I never saw two thralls contending for the honour of a rope before," said Milo.

"Nor I, but they have taken the right way to escape. Had they shown cowardice, I should have felt small pity, but courage and self-devotion ever find a soft place in my heart; besides, there is something about this boy which interests me more than I can account for. Old man, tell the truth, as thou hopest for the life of the boy. Is he really thy grandson?"

"He is the son of my daughter, now with the Saints."

"And who was his sire?"

"An oppressed Englishman."

"Doubtless: you all think yourselves oppressed, as my oxen may, because they are forced to draw the plough, but the boy has the face of men of better blood, and I should have said there was a cross in the breed: but hearken! Malebouche, cut their bonds, take a party of six, escort them to the castle, place them in the third story of the

North Tower, give them food and drink, but let none have access to them till I return."

Further colloquy was useless; the Baron spoke like a man whose mind was made up, and his vassals had no choice but to obey.

Therefore the party broke up, the rest of the train to seek another stag, if they could find one, but Brian called the Sheriff of Gloucester aside.

They stood in a glade of the forest near a tree blown down by the wind, where they could see the downs beyond.

"Dost see that barrow, Sir Milo?"

"I do."

"It is called Cwichelm's Hlawe; there an old king of these English was buried; they say he walks by night."

"A likely place."

"Well, I have a curiosity to test the fact, moreover the hill commands a view unrivalled in extent in our country; I shall ride thither."

"In search of ghosts and night scenery, the view will be limited in darkness."

"But beacon fires will show best in the dark."

"I comprehend; shall I share thy ride?"

"Nay, my friend, my mind is ill at rest, I want solitude. Return with the hunting train and await my arrival at the castle; and the Baron beckoned to his handsome young page Alain, to lead the horse to him.

"Well, Alain, what didst thou think of the young Englishman? He confronted death gallantly enough."

"He is only half an Englishman; I am sure he has Norman blood, *noblesse oblige*," replied the boy, who was a spoiled pet of his stern lord, stern to others.

"Well, the old man feared the cord as little."

"He has not much life left to beg for: one foot in the grave already."

"How wouldst thou like that boy for a fellow-page?"

"Not at all, my lord."

"And why not?"

"Because I would like my companions to be of known lineage and of gentle blood on both sides."

"The great Conqueror himself was not."

"And hence many despised him."

"They did not dare tell him so."

"Then they were cowards, my lord; I hope my tongue shall never conceal what my heart feels."

"My boy, if thou crowest so loudly, I fear thou wilt have a short life."

"I can make my hands keep my head, at least against my equals."

"Art thou sorry I pardoned the lad then?"

"No, I like not to see the brave suffer; had he been a coward I should have liked the sport fairly well."

"Sport?"

"It is so comical to see deer-stealers dance on nothing, and it serves them right."

Now, do not let my readers think young Alain unnatural, he was of his period; pity had small place, and the low value set on life made boys and even men often see the ridiculous side of a tragedy, and laugh when they should have wept: yet courage often touched their sympathies, when entreaty would have failed.

But the Lord of Wallingford was in a gentle frame of mind, uncommon in him: he had not merely been touched by the strife, which of the two should die, between the ill-assorted pair, but there had been something in every tone and gesture of the boy which had awakened strange sympathy in his heart, and the sensation was so unprecedented, that Brian longed for solitude to analyse it.

In truth, the prisoners had not been in great danger, for although their judge was pleased to try their courage, he had not the faintest intention of proceeding to any extremities with either grandsire or grandson—not at least after he had heard the voice of the boy.

The party broke up, the Baron rode on alone towards the heights, the sheriff, attended by young Alain, returned down the course of the stream towards the castle. The rest separated into divers bands, some to hunt for deer or smaller game, so as not to return home with empty hands, to the great wrath of the cooks and others also. Malebouche with six archers escorted the prisoners. They rode upon one steed, the boy in front of his sire.

"Old man, what is the stripling's name?"

"Osric."

"And you will not tell who his sire was?"

"If I would not tell your dread lord, I am not likely to tell thee."

"Because I have a *guess:* a mere suspicion."

"'Thoughts are free;' it will soon be shown whether it be more."

"Which wouldst thou soonest be in thy heart, boy, English or Norman?"

"English," said the boy firmly.

"Thou preferrest then the deer to the lion?"

"I prefer to be the oppressed rather than the oppressor."

"Well, well, each man to his taste, but I would sooner be the wolf who eats, than the sheep which is eaten; of the two sensations I prefer the former. Now dost thou see that proud tower soaring into the skies down the brook? it is the keep of Wallingford Castle. Stronger hold is not in the Midlands."

"I have been there before," said old Sexwulf.

"Not in my time."

Our readers may almost have forgotten the existence of the poor thrall Judith during the exciting scene we have narrated.

She loved her masters, young and old, deeply loved them did this hereditary slave, and her anxiety had been extreme during the period of their danger: she skipped in and out of the hut, for no one thought her worth molesting, she peered through the bushes, she acted like a hen partridge whose young are in danger, and when they bound Osric, actually flew at the men-at-arms, but they thrust her so roughly aside that she fell; little recked they. An English thrall, were she wife, mother, or daughter, was naught in their estimation.

Yet she did not feel the same anxiety in one respect, which Sexwulf felt. "I can save him yet," she muttered; "they shall never put a rope around his bonnie neck, not even if I have to betray the secret I have kept since his infancy."

So she listened close at hand. Once or twice she seemed on the point of thrusting herself forward, when the fate of her dear boy seemed to hang in the balance, but restrained herself.

"I promised," she said, "I promised, and *he* will grieve to learn that I was faithless to my word. The old woman has a soul, aged crone though she be: and I swore by the black cross of Abingdon. Yet black cross or white one, I would risk the claws of Satan, sooner than allow the rope to touch his neck: bad enough that it should encircle his fair wrists."

When at last the suspense was over, and the grandsire and grandson were ordered to be taken as prisoners to the castle, she seemed content.

"I must see him," she said, "and tell him what has chanced: he will know what to do."

Just then she heard a voice which startled her.

"Shall we burn the hut, my lord?"

A moment of suspense: then came the stern reply.

"He that doth so shall hang from the nearest oak."

She chuckled.

"The spell already works," she said; "I may return to the shelter which has been mine so long. He will not harm them."

The time of the separation of the foe had now come; the Baron rode off to his midnight watch on Cwichelm; Malebouche conducted the two captives along the road to the distant keep; the others, men and dogs, circulated right and left in the woods.

The woods and reeds were still smoking, the atmosphere was dense and murky, as Judith returned to the hut.

She sat by the fire which still smoked on the hearth, and rocked herself to and fro, and as she sat she sang in an old cracked voice—

> "They sought my bower one murky night,
> They burnt my bower, they slew my knight;
> My servants all for life did flee,
> And left me in extremitie:
> But vengeance yet shall have its way,
> When shall the son the sire betray?"

The last line was very enigmatical, like a Delphic response; perhaps our tale may solve it.

Then at last she arose, and going to a corner of the hut, opened a chest filled with poor coarse articles of female attire, such as a slave might wear, but at the bottom wrapped in musty parchment was something of greater value.

It was a ring with a seal, and a few articles of baby attire, a little red shoe, a small frock, and a lock of maiden's hair.

She kissed the latter again and again, ere she looked once more at the ring: it bore a crest upon a stone of opal, and she laughed weirdly.

The crest was the crest of Brian Fitz-Count.

CHAPTER V

CWICHELM'S HLAWE

IT was a wild and lonely spot, eight hundred feet above sea level, the highest ground of the central downs of Berkshire, looking northward over a vast expanse of fertile country, as yet but partially tilled, and mainly covered with forest.

A tumulus or barrow of huge dimensions arose on the summit, no less than one hundred and forty yards in circumference, and at that period some fifty feet in height; it had been raised five hundred years earlier in the history of the country over the remains of the Saxon King Cwichelm, son of Cynegils, and grandson of Ceol, who dwelt in the Isle of Ceol—or Ceolseye—and left his name to Cholsey.

A wood of firs surrounded the solemn mound, which, however, dominated them in height; the night wind was sighing dreamily over them, the heavens were alternately light and dark as the aforesaid wind made rifts in the cloud canopy and closed them again—ever and anon revealing the moon wading amidst, or rather beyond, the masses of vapour.

An aged crone stood on the summit of the mound clad in long flowing garments of coarse texture, bound around the waist with a girdle of leather; her hair, white as snow, streamed on the wind. She supported her strength by an ebony staff chased with Runic figures. Any one who gazed might perchance have thought her a sorceress, or at least a seer of old times raised again into life.

"Ah, he comes!"

Over the swelling ridges of the downs she saw a horseman approaching; heard before she saw, for the night was murky.

The horseman dismounted in the wood, tied his horse to a tree, left it with a huge boar-hound, as a guard, and penetrating the wood, ascended the mound.

"Thou art here, mother: the hour is come; it is the first day of the vine-month, as your sires called it."

"Yes, the hour is come, the stars do not lie, nor did the mighty dead deceive me."

"The dead; call them not, whilst I am here."

"Dost thou fear them? We must all share their state some day."

"I would sooner, far sooner, not anticipate the time."

"Yet thou hast sent many, and must send many more, to join them."

"It is the fortune of war; I have had Masses said for their souls. It might have chanced to me."

"Ha! ha! so thou wouldst not slay soul and body both?"

"God forbid."

"Well, once I believed in Priest and Mass—I, whom they call the witch of 'Cwichelm's Hlawe': now I prefer the gods of war, of storm, and of death; Woden, Thor, and Teu; nay, even Hela of horrid aspect."

"Avaunt thee, witch! wouldst worship Satan!"

"Since God helped me not: listen, Brian Fitz-Count. I, the weird woman of the haunted barrow, was once a Christian, and a nun."

"A nun!"

"Yea, and verily. A few of us had a little cell, a dozen were we in number, and we lived under the patronage—a poor reed to lean on we found it—of St. Etheldreda.[1] Now a stern Norman like thyself came into those parts after the conquest; he had relations abroad who 'served God'

---

[1] See a similar instance in Thierry's *Norman Conquest*, vol. i.

after another rule; he craved our little home for them; he drove us out to perish in the coldest winter I remember. The abbess, clinging to her home and refusing to go, was slain by the sword: two or three others died of cold; we sought shelter in vain, the distress was everywhere. I roamed hither—I was born at the village of Hendred below—my friends were dead and gone, my father had followed Thurkill of Kingestun, and been killed at Senlac. My mother, in consequence, had been turned out of doors by the new Norman lord, and none ever learned what became of her, my sweet mother! my brothers had become outlaws; my sisters—well, I need tell thee no more. I lost faith in the religion, in the name of which, and under the sanction of whose chief teacher, the old man who sits at Rome, the thing had been done. They say I went mad. I know I came here, and that the dead came and spoke with me, and I learned mysteries of which Christians dream not, yet which are true for good or ill."

"And by their aid thou hast summoned me here, but I marvel thou hast not perished as a witch amidst fire and faggot."

"They protect me!"

"Who are they?"

"Never mind; that is my secret."

"Thou didst tell me that if I came to-night I should see the long-expected signal to arm my merrie men, and do battle for our winsome ladie."

"Cry havoc, and let slip the dogs of war. Well, I told thee truly: the hour is nigh, wait and watch with me; fix thine eyes on the south."

Dim and misty the outlines of the hills looked in that uncertain gloaming; here and there a light gleamed from some peasant's hut, for the hour of eight had not yet struck, when, according to the curfew law, light and fire had to be extinguished. But our lone watchers saw them all disappear at last, and still the light they looked for shone not forth.

"Why does not the bale-fire blaze?"

"Baleful shall its influence be."

"Woman, one more question I have. Thou knowest my family woes, that I have neither kith nor kin to succeed me, no gallant boy for whom to win honour: two have I had, but they are dead to the world."

"The living death of leprosy."

"And one—not indeed the lawful child of my spouse—was snatched from me in tender infancy; one whom I destined for my heir: for why should that bar-sinister which the Conqueror bore sully the poor child. Thou rememberest?"

"Thou didst seek me in the hour of thy distress, and I told thee the child lived."

"Does it yet live? tell me." And the strong man trembled with eagerness and emotion as he looked her eagerly in the face.

"They have not told me; I know not."

"Methinks I saw him to-day."

"Where?"

"In the person of a peasant lad—the grandson of an old man, who has lived, unknown, in my forest, and slain my deer."

"And didst thou hang him, according to thy wont?"

"No, for he was brave, and something in the boy's look troubled me, and reminded me of her I once called my 'Aimée.' She was English, but Eadgyth was hard to pronounce, so I called her 'Aimée.'"

"Were there any marks by which you could identify your boy? Pity such a race should cease."

"I remember none. And the grandfather claims the lad as his own. Tell me, is he mine?"

"I know not, but there is a way in which thou canst inquire."

"How?"

"Hast thou courage?"

"None ever questioned it and lived."

"But many could face the living, although girt in triple mail, who fear the dead."

"I am distracted with hope."

"And thou canst face the shrouded dead?"

"I would dare their terrors."

"Sleep here, then, to-night."

"Where?"

"In a place which I will show thee, ha! ha!"

"Is it near?"

"Beneath thy feet."

"Beneath my feet?"

"It is the sepulchre of the royal dead."

"Of Cwichelm?"

"Even he."

"May I see it? the bale-fire blazes not, and it is cold waiting here."

"Come."

"Lead on, I follow."

She descended the sloping sides of the mound, he followed. At the base, amidst nettles and briars, was a rude but massive door. She drew forth a heavy key and opened it. She passed along a narrow passage undeterred by a singular earthy odour oppressive to the senses, and the Baron followed until he stood by her side, in a chamber excavated in the very core of the huge mound.

There, in the centre, was a large stone coffin, and within lay a giant skeleton.

"It is he, who was king of this land."

"Cwichelm, son of Ceol, who dwelt in the spot they now call Ceolseye."

"And the son of the Christian King of Wessex—they mingled Christian and Pagan rites when they buried him here. See his bow and spear."

"But who burrowed this passage? Surely they left it not who buried him?"

"Listen, and your ears shall drink in no lies. Folk said that his royal ghost protected this spot, and that if the heathen Danes came where the first Christian king lay, guarding the land, even in death, they should see the sea no more. Now, in the Christmas of the year 1006, aided by a foul traitor, Edric Streorn, they left the Isle of Wight, where they were wintering, and travelling swiftly, burst upon the ill-fated, unwarned folk of this land, on the very day of the Nativity, for Edric had removed the guardians of the beacon fires.[1] They burnt Reading; they burnt Cholsey, with its church and priory; they burned Wallingford; they slew all they met, and left not man or beast alive whom they could reach, save a few most unhappy captives, whom they brought here after they had burned Wallingford, for here they determined to abide as a daring boast, having heard of the prophecy, and despising it. And here they revelled after the fashion of fiends for nine days and nights. Each day they put to death nine miserable captives with the torture of the Rista Eorn, and so they had their fill of wine and blood. And as they had heard that treasures were buried with Cwichelm, they excavated this passage. Folk said that they were seized with an awful dread, which prevented their touching his bones or further disturbing his repose. At length they departed, and each year since men have seen the ghosts of their victims gibbering in the moonlight between Christmas and Twelfth Day."

"Hast thou?"

"Often, but covet not the sight; it freezes the very marrow in the bones. Only beware that thou imitate not these Danes in their wickedness."

"I?"

"Yes, even thou."

"Am I a heathen dog?"

"What thou art I know, what thou wilt become I think I trow. But peace: wouldst thou invoke the dead king to learn thy future path? I can raise him."

Brian Fitz-Count was a brave man, but he shuddered.

[1] I have told the story of this Danish invasion in *Alfgar the Dane*.

"Another time; besides, mother, the bale-fire may be blazing even now!"

"Come and see, then. I foresee thou wilt return in time of sore need."

They reached the summit of the mound. The change to the open air was most refreshing.

"Ah! the bale-fire!!"

Over the rolling wastes, far to the south, arose the mountainous range now called Highclere. It was but faintly visible in the daytime, and under the uncertain moonlight, only those familiar with the locality could recognise its position. The central peak was now tipped with fire, crowned with a bright flickering spot of light.

And while they looked, Lowbury caught the blaze, and its beacon fire glowed in the huge grating which surmounted the tower, whose foundations may yet be traced. From thence, Synodune took up the tale and told it to the ancient city of Dorchester, whose monks looked up from cloistered hall and shuddered. The heights of Nettlebed carried forward the fiery signal, and blazing like a comet, told the good burgesses of Henley and Reading that evil days were at hand. The Beacon Hill, above Shirburne Castle, next told the lord of that baronial pile that he might buckle on his armour, and six counties saw the blaze on that beacon height. Faringdon Clump, the home of the Ffaringas of old, next told the news to the distant Cotswolds and the dwellers around ancient Corinium; and soon Painswick Beacon passed the tidings over the Severn to the old town of Gloucester, whence Milo came, and far beyond to the black mountains of Wales. The White Horse alarmed Wiltshire, and many a lover of peace shook his head and thought of wife and children, although but few knew what it all meant, namely, that the Empress Maud, the daughter of the Beauclerc, had come to claim her father's crown, which Stephen, thinking it right to realise the prophecy contained in his name,[1] had put on his own head.

[1] "Stephanus" signifies "a crown."

And from Cwichelm's Hlawe the curious ill-assorted couple we have portrayed beheld the war beacons' blaze.

She lost all her self-possession, she became entranced; her hair streamed behind her in the wind; she stretched out her aged arms to the south and sang—did that crone of ninety years—

> "Come hither, fatal cloud of death,
> O'er England breathe thy hateful breath;
> Breathe o'er castles, churches, towns,
> Brood o'er flat plain, and cloud-flecked downs,
> Until the streams run red with gore,
> From eastern sea to western shore.
> Let mercy frighted haste away,
> Let peace and love no longer stay,
> Let justice outraged swoon away,
> But let revenge and bitter hate
> Alone control the nation's fate;
> Let fell discord the chorus swell,
> Let every hold become a hell——
> Let——"

"Nay, nay, mother, enough! Thou ravest. Every hold a hell! not at least Wallingford Castle!"

"That worst of all, Brian Fitz-Count. There are possibilities of evil in thee, which might make Satan laugh! Thy sword shall make women childless, thy torch light up——"

"Nay, nay, no more, I must away. My men will go mad when they see these fires. I must home, to control, advise, direct."

"Go, and the powers of evil be with thee. Work out thy curse and thy doom, since so it must be!"

CHAPTER VI

ON THE DOWNS

WE fear that Brian Fitz-Count must have sunk in the reader's estimation. After the perusal of the last chapter, it is difficult to understand how a doughty warrior and belted knight could so demean himself as to take an old demented woman into his consultations, and come to her for guidance.

Let us briefly review the phases of mind through which he had passed, and see whether we can find any rational explanation of his condition.

The one great desire of Brian's life was to have a son to whom he could bequeath his vast possessions, and his reflected glory. Life was short, but if he could live, as it were, in the persons of his descendants, it seemed as if death would be more tolerable. God heard his prayer. He had two sons, fine lads, by his Countess, and awhile he rejoiced in them, but the awful scourge of leprosy made its appearance in his halls. For a long time he would not credit the reality of the infliction, and was with difficulty restrained from knocking down the physician who first announced the fact. By degrees the conviction was forced upon him, and the law of the time—the unwritten law especially—forced him to consign them to a house of mercy for lepers, situated near Byfield in Northamptonshire. Poor boys, they wept sore, for they were old enough to share their father's craving for glory and distinction; but they were torn away and sent to this living tomb, for in the eyes of all men it was little better.

Brian wearied Heaven with prayers; ho had Masses innumerable said on their behalf; he gave alms to all the churches of Wallingford for the poor; he made benefactions to Reading Abbey and the neighbouring religious houses; he helped to enrich the newly-built church of Cholsey, built upon the ruins of the edifice the Danes had burnt. But still Heaven was obdurate, the boys did not recover, and he had to part with the delight of his eyes.

And then ensued a sudden collapse of faith. He ceased to pray. God heard not prayer: perhaps there was no God; and he ceased from his good deeds, gave no alms, neglected Divine service, and became a sceptic in heart—secretly, however, for whatever a man might think in his heart in those days of ecclesiastical power, the doughtiest baron would hesitate to avow scepticism; men would condone, as, alas, many do now, an irreligious life, full of deeds of evil, if only the evil-doer *professed* to believe in the dominant Creed.

When a man ceases to believe in God, he generally comes to believe in the Devil. Men must have a belief of some sort; so in our day, men who find Christianity too difficult, take to table turning, and like phenomena, and practise necromancy of a mild description.

So it was then. Ceasing to believe in God, Brian Fitz-Count believed in witches.

The intense hatred of witchcraft, begotten of dread, which kindled the blazing funeral pyres of myriads of people, both guilty—at least in intention—and innocent of the black art, had not yet attained its height.

Pope Innocent had not yet pronounced his fatal decree. The witch inquisitors had not yet started on their peregrinations, Hopkins had yet to be born, and so the poor crazed nun who had done no one any harm, whom wise men thought mad, and foolish ones inspired, was allowed to burrow at Cwichelm's Hlawe.

And many folk resorted to her, to make inquiries about lost property, lost kinsfolk, the present and the future.

Amongst others, a seneschal of Wallingford, who had lost a valuable signet ring belonging to his lord.

"On your return to the castle seize by the throat the first man you meet after you pass the portals. He will have the ring."

And the first man the seneschal met was a menial employed to sweep and scour the halls; him without fear he seized by the throat. "Give me the ring thou hast found," and lo, the affrighted servitor, trembling, drew it forth and restored it.

Brian heard of the matter; it penetrated through the castle. He gave orders to hang the servitor, but the poor wretch took sanctuary in time; and then he rode over to Cwichelm's Hlawe himself.

What was his object?

To inquire after his progeny.

One son, a beautiful boy, had escaped the fatal curse, but it was not the child of his wife. Brian had loved a fair English girl, whom he had wooed rather by violence than love. He carried her away from her home, a thing too common in those lawless days to excite much comment. She died in giving birth to a fair boy, and was buried in the adjacent graveyard:

After he lost his other two children by leprosy, Brian became devoted to this child; the reader has heard how he lost him.

And to inquire whether, perchance, the child, whose body had never been found, yet lived, Brian first rode to Cwichelm's Hlawe.

"Have I given the fruit of my body for the sin of my soul?" was his bitter cry. "Doth the child yet live?"

The supposed sorceress, after incantations dire, intended to impress the mind, replied in the affirmative.

"But where?"

"Beware; the day when thou dost regain him it will be the bitterest of thy life."

"But where shall he be found?"

"That the dead have not told me."

"But they may tell."

"I know not, but thou shalt see him again in the flesh. Come again in the vine-month, when the clouds of war and rapine shall begin to gather over England once more, and I will tell thee all I shall have learned."

"The clouds of war and rapine ?"

"Yes, Brian Fitz-Count. Dost thou, the sworn ally of the banished Empress, mistake my words ?"

And we have seen the result of that last interview—in the second visit.

. . . . .

When Brian rode from the barrow—out on the open downs—he gazed upon the beacons which yet blazed, and sometimes shouted with exultation, for like a war-horse he sniffed the coming battle, and shouted ha! ha! He gave his horse the reins and galloped along the breezy ridge—following the Icknield way—his hound behind him.

And then he saw another horseman approaching from the opposite direction, just leaving the Blewbery down. In those days when men met it was as when in a tropical sea, in days happily gone by, sailors saw a strange sail: the probability was that it was an enemy.

Still Brian feared not man, neither God nor man, and only loosing his sword in its sheath, he rode proudly to the *rencontre*.

"What ho! stranger! who? and whence ?"

"Thy enemy from the grave, whither thou hast sent my kith and kin."

"Satan take thee; when did I slay them ? If I did, must I send thee to rejoin them ?"

"Try, and God defend the right. Here on this lonely moor, we meet face to face. Defend thyself."

"Ah! I guess who thou art: an outlaw!"

"One whom thou didst make homeless."

"Ah! I see, Wulfnoth of Compton. Tell me, thou English boar, what thou didst with my child."

"And if I slew him, as thou didst mine, what then ?"

A mighty blow was the reply, and the two drawing their swords, fell to work—the deadly work.

And by their sides a canine battle took place, a wolfhound, which accompanied the stranger, engaged the boarhound of the Baron.

Oh! how they strove; how blow followed blow; how the horses seemed to join in the conflict, and tried to bite and kick each other with their rampant fore-feet; how the blades crashed; how thrust, cut, and parry, succeeded each other.

But Norman skill prevailed over English strength, and the Englishman fell prone to the ground, with a frightful wound on the right shoulder, while his horse galloped round and round in circles.

And meanwhile the opposite result took place in the struggle between the quadrupeds: the wolf-hound had slain the boar-hound. Brian would fain have avenged his favourite, but the victor avoided his pursuit, and bow and arrows had he none, nor missile of any kind, for he had accidentally left his hunting spear behind.

He looked at his foe who lay stretched on the turf, bleeding profusely. Then dismounting, he asked sternly—

"Say what thou didst with my boy!"

"Strike; thou shalt never know."

And Brian would have struck, but his opponent fell back senseless, and he could not strike him in that condition: something restrained his hand.

"Poor Bruno," he said, as he gave his gallant hound one sigh. "Less fortunate than thy lord; that mongrel cur hath slain thee: but I may not stay to waste tears over thee," and remounting, he rode away unscathed from the struggle, leaving the horse of the vanquished one to roam the downs.

And as he rode, his thoughts were again on his lost child, and on the boy whom he had seen on the previous day, and sent before him in durance. Was it possible this was his son? Nay, the old man, who would not lie to save his life, had affirmed the contrary. Still he would make further inquiries, and keep the lad in sight, if not assured of his birth and parentage.

A thought struck him: should he threaten the torture to the aged Englishman, and so strive to wring the secret —if there were one—from him. Yet he hesitated, and debated the question with its pros and cons again and again, until the greater urgency of the coming struggle extinguished all other thoughts in his mind.

He had enemies, yes, bitter ones, and now that the dogs of war were allowed to be unchained, he would strike a blow for himself, as well as for Maud. Why, there was that hated rival, the Lord of Shirburne, who boasted that he kept the Key of the Chilterns in his hand—there was his rival of Donnington Castle over the downs—what splendid opportunities for plunder, vainglory, and revenge.

In such meditations did the Lord of Wallingford ride home through the forest, and adown the Moreton brook.

. . . . .

Meanwhile his defeated foe, upon whom the victor had scarcely bestowed a passing thought, lay stiff and stark upon the ground.

The night wind sang a dirge over him, but no human being was there to see whether the breath was yet in him. But a canine friend was there—his poor wolf hound— mangled by the teeth of his foe, but yet alive and likely to live. And now he came up to the prostrate body of his master and licked his face, while from time to time he raised his nose in the air, and uttered a plaintive howl, which floated adown the wind an appeal for help.

Was it a prayer for the living or the dead?

Surely there were the signs of life, the hues of that bloodless cheek are not yet those of death; see, he stirs! only just a stir, but it tells of life, and where there is life there is hope.

But who shall cherish the flickering spark?

The aspect of nature seems all merciless. Is there mercy yet in man?

A faint beating of the heart; a faint pulsation of the wrist—it might be quickened into life.

Is it well that he should live?

A typical Englishman, of Saxon lineage, stout, thickset. Did we believe in the transmigration of souls, we should say he had been a bull in some previous state of existence. Vast strength, great endurance, do find their incarnations in that frame: he might have felled an ox, but yet he went down before the subtlety of Norman fence.

Is it good that he should live, an outlaw, whose life any Norman may take and no questions asked? Look at that arm; it may account for many a Norman lost in solitary wayfaring. Oh! what memories of wrong sleep within that insensible brain!

Happily it is for a wiser power to decide.

Listen, there is a tinkling of small bells over there in the distance. It draws nearer; the dog gives a louder howl—now the party is close.

Five or six horses, a sumpter mule, five or six ecclesiastics in sombre dress, riding the horses, the hoods drawn back over the heads, the horses richly caparisoned, little silver bells dependent here and there from their harness.

"What have we here, brother Anselm? why doth the dog thus howl?"

"There hath been a fray, brother Laurentius. Here is a corpse; pray for his soul."

"Nay, he yet liveth," said a third, who had alighted. "I feel his heart beat; he is quite warm. But, oh! Saint Benedict! what a wound, what a ghastly gash across the shoulder."

"Raise him on the sumpter mule; we must bear him home and tend him. Remember the good Samaritan."

"But first let me bind up the wound as well as I can, and pour in oil and wine. I will take him before me.

Sancta Maria! what a weight! No, good dog, we mean thy master no harm."

But the dog offered no opposition; he saw his master was in good hands. He only tried as well as his own wounds would let him to caper for joy.

"Poor dog, he hath been hurt too. How chanced it? What a mystery."

Happily the good brothers never travelled without medicinal stores, and a little ointment modifies pain.

So in a short time they were on their road again, carrying the wounded with them.

They were practical Christians, those monks.

CHAPTER VII

DORCHESTER ABBEY

THE Abbey of Dorchester stood on the banks of the river Tame, a small stream arising near the town of the same name, and watering the finest pasture land of the county of Oxfordshire, until, half a mile below the Abbey, it falls into the Isis, which thence, strictly speaking, becomes the Thames (Tamesis).

This little town of Dorchester is not unknown to fame; it was first a British town, then a Roman city. Destroyed by the Saxons, it rose from its ashes to become the Cathedral city of the West Saxons, and the scene of the baptism of Cynegils, son of Ceol, by the hands of St. Birinus. The see was transferred to Winchester, but afterwards it became the seat of the great Mercian bishopric, and as its jurisdiction had once reached the Channel, so now it extended to the Humber and the Wash.

Cruelly destroyed by the Danes, it never regained its importance, and on account of its impoverished state,[1] the see was again removed by Remigius, the first Norman Bishop, to Lincoln, in the year 1092. But although the ancient city was thus deserted, the Bishop strove to make it some amends. He took care that an abbey should be created at Dorchester, lest the place should be ruined, or sunk in oblivion; and some say the Abbey was built with the stones which came from the Bishop's palace, the site of which is still marked by a farm called "Bishop's Court."

But the earlier buildings must have been of small extent,

[1] "Quæ urbs propter parvitatem Remigio displicebat."—JOHN OF BROMPTON.

for at the time of our story, Alexander, Bishop of Lincoln, was busy with a more magnificent structure, and he had already removed into the buildings, as yet but incomplete, a brotherhood of Black Canons, or Augustinians, under the rule of Abbot Alured.

The great church which had been the cathedral—the mother church of the diocese—had been partially rebuilt in the Norman style,[1] and around stood the buildings of the Abbey, west and north of the church.

In the scriptorium, overlooking the Tame, sat Abbot Alured. The Chapter Mass, which followed Terce (9 A.M.), had been said, and he was busy with the librarian, arranging his books. Of middle stature, with dark features, he wore an air of asceticism, tempered by an almost feminine suavity, and his voice was soft and winning.

He was the son of a Norman knight by an English wife, who had brought the aforesaid warrior an ample dowry in lands, for thus did the policy of the Conqueror attempt the reconciliation of conflicting interests and the amalgamation of the rival races of conquerors and conquered. For a long time the pair were childless, until the mother—like Hannah, whose story she had heard in church—vowed, if God would grant her a child, to dedicate it to God. Alured was born, and her husband, himself weary of perpetual fighting and turmoil, allowed her to fulfil her vow. The boy was educated at Battle Abbey, and taught monastic discipline; sent thence to Bec, which the fame of Lanfranc and Anselm—both successively translated to Canterbury—had made the most renowned school of theology in Northern Europe. There he received the tonsure, and passed through the usual grades, until, attracting the attention of Bishop Alexander, during a visit of that

[1] It consisted of the present nave, exclusive of the south aisle, and extended some distance beyond the chancel arch, including the north aisle as far as the present door. The cloister extended northward, covering the small meadow which separates the manor-house grounds from the church. The latter were probably the gardens of the abbey.

prelate to Bec, he was selected to be the new Abbot of Dorchester.

And now he was in the library, or scriptorium—the chamber he loved best in his Abbey. What books, forsooth, had he there in those dark ages!

First there were all the books of the Old Testament in several volumes and in the Latin tongue; then the New Testament in three volumes; there were all the works of St. Augustine, in nineteen large tomes, with most of the books of the other fathers of the Western Church; the lives of the great monastic Saints, and the martyrology or acts of the Martyrs. There were books of ecclesiastical history, and treatises on Church music, with various liturgical works. Of light reading there was none, but the lives of the Saints and Martyrs furnished the most exciting reading, wherein fact was unintentionally blended with fiction.

"What a wonderful mine of wealth we have here in this new martyrology! Truly, my brethren, here we have the patience and faith of the Saints to encourage us in our warfare," said the Abbot, opening a huge volume bound in boar's hide, and glancing round at the scribes, who, pen in hand and ink-horn at their girdles, with clear sheets of vellum before them, prepared to write at his dictation.

"This book was lent us by the Abbot of Abingdon, now six months ago, and before Advent it must be returned thither—not until every letter has been duly transcribed into our new folios. Where didst thou leave off yesterday?"

"At the 'Acts of St. Artemas.'"

And the Abbot read, while they wrote down his words: "Artemus was a Christian boy, who lived at Puteoli, and who was sent, at the instigation of heathen relations, to the school of one Cathageta, a heathen. But the little scholar could not hide his faith, although bidden to do so, lest he should suffer persecution. But what is deep in the heart comes out of the mouth, and he converted two or three school-fellows, so that at the next festival, in honour of Diana, they omitted to place the customary garlands on her image. This aroused inquiry, and the young athlete of Christ was discovered. The master, bidding him renounce his faith in vain, severely scourged him, but the boy said: 'The more you scourge me the more you whip my religion into me.' Whereupon Cathageta, turning to the other scholars, said: 'Perhaps your endeavours will be more successful than mine in wiping out this disgrace from the school;' and he departed, leaving him to the mercies of the other boys, who, educated in the atrocities of the arena, stabbed him to death with their stili or pointed iron pens."[1]

"Poor boy," murmured the youngest copyist—himself but a boy—when the dictation was finished.

"Nay; glorious Martyr, you mean. He has his reward now. You have heard me speak of the martyrdom of St. Euthymius; that was a harder one. It follows here.

"St. Euthymius was a Bishop of the African Church, who, being taken by his persecutors, and refusing to offer sacrifice to the idols, was shut up in a close stone cell with a multitude of mice. A wire, attached to a bell outside, was placed near his hand, and he was told that if he were in distress he might ring it, and should obtain immediate assistance; but that his doing so would be taken as equivalent to a renunciation of Christ. No bell was heard, and when on the third day they opened the cell, they found nought but a whitened skeleton and a multitude of fattened mice."

Every one drew in his breath, some in admiration, some in horror.

The young novice had suspended his labours to listen.

"Benedict, you are neglecting your gradual," said the Abbot. "The music must be completed for the coming festival of All Saints; it is the chant of Fescamp—somewhat softer to our ears than the harsher Gregorian strains.

---

[1] This true story is the foundation of *The Victor's Laurel*, a tale of school life in Italy, by the same author.

Yet many love the latter well; as did the monks of Glastonbury."

Here he paused, and waited until he saw they were all open-mouthed for his story; for such was monastic discipline, that no one ventured to say: "Tell us the story."

"Well," he said, "the English monks of Glastonbury had endured much unmerited severity at the hands of Thurstan, their Norman Abbot, but they bore all, until he bade them leave off their crude Gregorian strains, and chant the lays of William of Fescamp. Then they stoutly refused; and he sent for a troop of men-at-arms. The monks rushed to the great church and barred themselves in, but the men-at-arms forced a way into the church, and slew the greater part of the monks with their arrows. So thick was the storm of piercing shafts, that the image of the Christ on the rood was stuck full of these sacrilegious missiles."

"And what became of Thurstan?" asked one of the elder brethren.

"The king deposed him, as unfit to rule; suggesting that a shepherd should not flay his sheep."

"And that was all?" said an indignant young novice, whose features showed his English blood.

"Hush! my son Wilfred. Novices must hear—not speak. Speech is silver; silence is golden."

At that moment the Prior made his appearance in the doorway.

"My father Abbot, the brethren have returned from our poor house at Hermitage, and they bring a wounded man, whom they found on the downs."

"English or Norman?"

"The former, I believe, but he has not yet spoken."

"Send for the almoner and infirmarer. I will come and look at him myself."

Leaving the scriptorium, the Abbot traversed the pleasant cloisters, which were full of boys, learning their lessons under the superintendence of certain brethren—some declining Latin nouns or conjugating verbs; some reading the scanty leaves of parchment which served as lesson books, more frequently repeating passages *viva voce* after a master, while seated upon rude forms, or more commonly standing. So were the cloisters filled—the only schools for miles around. They looked upon an inner quadrangle of the monastery, with the great church to the south. Passing through a passage to the west of the nave, the Abbot reached the gateway of the abbey, somewhere near the site of the present tower, which is modern. The view to the south from this point stretched across the Thames to Synodune; nearer at hand rose to left and right the towers of two parish churches,[1] the buildings of the town (or city, as it had hitherto been), poor and straggling as compared with the ecclesiastical dwellings, lay before them; the embankment of the Dyke hills then terminated the town in this direction, and beyond rose the stately clumps of Synodune.

Inside the porch rested the wayfarers; their beasts had been led to the stables, and on a sort of hand-bier before them, resting on tressels, lay the prostrate form of the victim of the prowess of Brian Fitz-Count.

"Where didst thou find him?" asked the Abbot.

"Near the spot on the downs where once holy Birinus preached the Evangel."

"And this dog?"

"Was with him, wounded by teeth as the master by sword. It was his moans and howls which attracted us."

The Abbot bent over the prostrate form.

"Has he spoken since you found him?"

"No, my lord; only moans and gasps."

"I see he is much hurt; I fear you have only brought him hither to die."

"Houselled, anointed and annealed?"

---

[1] Leland thus marks their site—three in all besides the abbey church—one a little by south from the abbey, near the bridge; one more south above it (nearer the Dyke); and "there was the 3 Paroch Chirch by south-west" (towards Wittenham).

"If he recover his senses sufficiently."

Just then a moan, louder than before, made them all start, then followed a deep, hollow, articulate voice.

"Where am I?"

"At the Abbey of Dorchester."

"Who brought me hither?"

"Friends."

He gazed wildly round, then sank with a deep groan back on the bier.

"Take him to the infirmary, and on the morrow we will see him."

A chance medley on the downs—a free fight between two who met by chance—was so common, that the Abbot thought far less of the matter than we may imagine.

"Insooth, he is ghastly," he said, "but in the more need of our aid. I trust we shall save both soul and body. Let the dog also have food and shelter."

But the dog would not leave his master's side, and they were forced to move both into the same cell, where the poor beast kept licking the hand which dropped pendent from the couch.

"My lord Abbot, there are weightier matters to consider than the welfare of one poor wounded wayfarer, who has fallen among thieves."

"What are they?"

"Didst thou mark the bale-fire on Synodune last night?"

"We did, and marvelled what it could mean."

"They were lighted all over the country: Lowbury, Highclere, White Horse, Shirburne Beacon—all sent their boding flames heavenward."

"What does it portend?"

"There were rumours that Matilda, the Empress Queen, had landed somewhere in the south."

"Then we shall have civil war, and every man's hand will be against his brother, which God forbid. Yet when Stephen seized our worthy Bishop in his chamber, eating his dinner of pulse and water——"

"Pheasant, washed down with malmsey, more likely," muttered a voice.

The Abbot heard not, but continued—

"And shut him in a dungeon—the anointed of the Lord—and half starved him——"

"Making him fast for once, in earnest!"

"Until he should deliver his castles of Newark and Sleaford——"

"Pretty sheepfolds for a shepherd to keep!"

"Such a king has little hold of his people; and it may be, God's just judgments are impending over us. And what shall we do if we cannot save the poor sheep committed to our charge; for be the one party or the other victorious, the poor will have to suffer. Therefore, my dear brethren, after Sext, we will hold a special chapter before we take our meridiana" (noontide nap, necessitated when there was so much night rising), "and consider what we had best do. Haste ye, my brother Ambrose; take thy party to the cellarer, and get some light refreshment. This is the day when he asks pardon of us all for his little negligencies, and in return for the Miserere we sing in his name, we get a better refection than usual. So do not spoil your appetites now. Haste, and God be with you. The sacristan has gone to toll the bell for Sext."

CHAPTER VIII

THE BARON AND HIS PRISONERS

WHEN Brian Fitz-Count returned to his castle it was buried in the silence and obscurity of night; only the sentinels were awake, and as they heard his password, they hastened to unbar the massive gates, and to undraw the heavy bolts, and turn the ponderous keys which gave admittance to his sombre castle.

The fatigue of a long day had made even the strong man weary, and he said nought to any man, but sought his inner chamber, threw himself on his pallet, and there the man of strife slept, for he had the soldier's faculty of snatching a brief nap in the midst of perplexity and toil.

In vain did the sentinels look for some key to the meaning of the bale-fires, which had blazed all round; their lord was silent. "The smiling morn tipped the hills with gold," and the *reveillée* blew loud and long; the busy tide of life began to flow within the walls; men buckled on their armour, to try if every rivet were tight; tried the edge of their swords, tested the points of their lances; ascended the towers and looked all round for signs of a foe; discussed, wondered, argued, quarrelled of course, but all without much result, until, at the hour of *déjeûner* (or breakfast), their dread lord appeared, and took his usual place at the head of the table in the great hall.

The meal—a substantial one of flesh, fish, and fowl, washed down by ale, mead and wine—was eaten amid the subdued murmur of many voices, and not till it was ended, and the Chaplain had returned thanks—for such forms did Brian, for policy's sake, if for no better motive, always observe—than he rose up to his full height and spoke—

"Knights and pages, men-at-arms all! I have good news for you! The Empress—our rightful Queen—has landed in Sussex, and this very day I go to meet her, and to aid in expelling the fell usurper Stephen. Who will follow in my train?"

Every hand was upraised, amidst a clamour of voices and cheers, for they sniffed the battle afar, like the war-horse in Job, and delighted like the vulture in the scent of blood.

"It is well. I would sooner have ten free-hearted volunteers than a hundred lagging retainers, grudgingly fulfilling their feudal obligations. Let every man see to his horse, armour, sword, shield, and lance, and at noontide we will depart."

"At what time," asked the Chaplain, "shall we have the special Mass said, to evoke God's blessing on our efforts to dethrone the tyrant, who has dared to imprison our noble Bishop, Alexander?"

"By all means a Mass, it will sharpen our swords: say at nine—a hunting Mass, you know." (That is, a Mass reduced to the shortest proportions the canons allowed.)

When the household had dispersed, all save the chief officers who waited to receive their lord's orders about the various matters committed severally to their charge, Brian called one of them aside.

"Malebouche, bid Coupe-gorge, the doomster, be ready with his minions in the torture-chamber, and take thither the old man whom we caught in the woods yestere'en. I will be present myself, and give orders what is to be done, in half an hour."

Malebouche departed on the errand, and Brian hastened to accomplish various necessary tasks, ere the time to which he looked forward with some interest arrived. It came at last, and he descended a circular stone staircase in the interior of the north-west tower, which seemed to lead into the bowels of the earth.

Rather into a vaulted chamber, curiously furnished with divers chains and pulleys, and hooks, and pincers, and other quaint instruments of mediæval cruelty. In one corner hung a thick curtain, which concealed all behind from view.

In the centre there was a heavy wooden table, and at the head a massive rude chair, wherein the Baron seated himself.

Before the table stood the prisoner—the aged Sexwulf—still preserving his composure, and gazing with serene eye upon the fierce Baron—the ruthless judge, in whose hands was his fate.

Two lamps suspended from the roof shed a lurid light upon the scene.

"Sexwulf, son of Thurkill, hearken, and thou, Malebouche, retire up the stairs, and wait my orders on the landing above."

"My lord, the tormentor is behind the curtain," whispered Malebouche, as he departed.

Brian nodded assent, but did not think fit to order the departure of the doomster, whose horrible office made him familiar with too many secrets, wrung from the miserable victims of his art, and who was, like a confessor, pledged to inviolable secrecy. A grim confessor he!

"Now, old man," said the Baron, "I am averse to wring the truth from the stammering lips of age. Answer me, without concealment, the truth—the whole truth!"

"I have nought to conceal."

"Whose son is the boy I found in thy care?"

"My daughter's son."

"Who was his father?"

"Wulfnoth of Compton."

"Now thou liest; his features proclaim him Norman."

"He has no Norman blood."

"And thou dost persist in this story?"

"I have none other to tell."

"Then I must make the tormentor find thee speech. What ho! Coupe-gorge!"

The curtain was drawn back with a clang, and revealed the rack and a brasier, containing pincers heated to a gray heat, and a man in leathern jerkin with a pendent mask of black leather, with two holes cut therein for the eyes, and two assistants similarly attired—one a black man, or very swarthy Moor.

The old man did not turn his head.

"Look," said Brian.

"Why should I look? I have told thee the very truth; I have nought to alter in my story. If thou dost in thy cruelty misuse the power which God has given thee, and rend me limb from limb, I shall soon be beyond thy cruelty. But I can tell thee nought."

"We will see," said Brian. "Place him on the rack!"

"It needs not force," said the aged Englishman. "I will walk to thy bed of pain," and he turned to do so.

Again this calm courage turned Brian.

"Man," he said, "thou wouldst not lie before to save thy life; nor now, I am convinced, to save thy quivering flesh, if it does quiver. Tell me what thou hast to tell, without being forced to do so."

"I will. Thou didst once burn a house at Compton—the house of Wulfnoth."

"I remember it too well. The churl would not pay me tribute."

"Tribute to whom tribute is due," muttered the aged one; then, aloud, "One child escaped the flames, in which my daughter and her other poor children perished. A few days afterwards the father, who had escaped, brought me this child and bade me rear it, in ignorance of the fate of kith and kin, while he entered upon the life of a hunted but destroying wolf, slaying Normans."

"And he said the boy was his own?"

"And why should he not be? He has my poor daughter's features in some measure, I have thought."

"She must have been lovely, then," thought Brian, but only said—

"Tormentor, throw aside thy implements; they are for cowards. Old man, ere thou ascend the stairs, know that thy life depends upon thy grandson. Canst thou spare him to me?"

"Have I any choice?"

"Nay. But wilt thou bid him enter my service, and perchance win his spurs?"

"Not for worlds."

"Why refuse so great an opening to fame?"

"I would sooner far follow him to his grave! Thou wouldst destroy the soul."

"Fool! has he a soul? Have I or you got one? What is it? I do not know." Then he repressed these dangerous words—dangerous to himself, even in his stronghold.

"Malebouche!"

Malebouche appeared.

"Take the grandsire away. Bring hither the boy."

He waited in a state of intense but subdued feeling.

The boy appeared at last—pale, not quite so free from apprehension as his grandsire: how could any one expect a real boy, unless he were a phenomenon, to enter a torture chamber as a prisoner without emotion? What are all the switchings, birchings, and canings modern boys have borne, compared with rack, pincer, and thumbscrew—to the hideous sachentage, the scorching iron? The very enumeration makes the hair rise in these days; only they are but a memory from the grim bad past now.

"Osric, whose son art thou?"

"The son of Wulfnoth."

"And who was thy mother?"

The boy flushed.

"I know not—save that she is dead."

"Does thy father live?"

"I know not."
"Art thou English or Norman?"
"English."
"Thou art not telling the truth."
"Not the truth!" cried the boy, evidently surprised.
"No, and I must force it from thee."
"Force it from me!" stammered the poor lad.
"Look!"
Again the curtain opened, and the grisly sight met the eyes of Osric. He winced, then seemed to make a great effort at self-control, and at last spoke with tolerable calmness—

"My lord, I have nought to tell if thou pull me in pieces. What should I hide, and why? I have done thee no harm; why shouldst thou wish to torture me—a poor helpless boy, who never harmed thee?"

The Baron gazed at him with a strange expression.

"Thou knowest thou art in my hands, to do as I please with thee."

"But God will protect or avenge me."

"And this is all thou hast to say? Dost thou not fear the rack, the flame?"

"Who can help fearing it?"

"Wouldst thou lie to escape it?"

"No, God helping me. That is, I would do my best."

The Baron drew a long breath. There was something in the youth which fascinated him. He loved to hear him speak; he revelled in the tones of his voice; he even liked to see the contest between his natural courage and truthfulness and the sense of fear. But he could protract it no longer, because it pained while it pleased.

"Boy, wilt thou enter my service?"

"I belong to my grandsire."

"Wouldst thou not wish to be a knight?"

"Nay, unless I could be a true knight."

"What is that?"

"One who keeps his vow to succour the oppressed, and never draw sword save in the cause of God and right."

Again the Baron winced.

"Wilt thou be my page?"

"No."

Brian looked at him fixedly.

"Thou must!"

"Why?"

"Thy life is forfeit to the laws; it is the only avenue of escape."

"Then must I die."

"Wouldst thou sooner die than follow me?"

"I think so; I do not quite know."

"And thy grandsire, too? Ye are both deer-stealers, and I have hanged many such."

"Oh, not my grandsire—not my poor grandfather!" and the boy knelt down, and raised his hands joined in supplication. "Hang me, if thou wilt, but spare him."

"My boy, neither shalt hang, if thou wilt but hear me—be my page, and he shall be free to return to his hut, with permission to kill one deer per month, and smaller game as he pleases."

"And if I will not promise?"

"Thou must rot in a dungeon till my return, when I will promise thou wilt be glad to get out at any price, and *he* must hang to-day—and thou wilt know thou art his executioner."

The boy yielded.

"I *must* give way. Oh! must I be thy page?"

"Yes, foolish boy—a good thing for thee, too."

"If I must, I will—but only to save his life. God forgive me!"

"God forgive thee? For what?"

"For becoming a Norman!"

"Malebouche!" called Brian.

The seneschal descended.

"Take this youth to the wardrobe, and fit him with a page's suit; he rides with me to-day. Feed the old man, and set him free."

He sent for Alain, the chief and leader amongst his pages—a sort of cock of the walk.

"Alain, that English boy we found in the woods rides with us to-day. Mark me, neither tease, nor bully him thyself, nor allow thy fellows to do so. Thou knowest that I will be obeyed."

"My lord," said the lad, "I will do my best. What is the name of our new companion?"

"'Fitz-urse'—that is enough."

"I should say Fitz-daim," muttered the youngster, as soon as he was outside.

CHAPTER IX

THE LEPERS

THE scene was the bank of a large desolate pond or small lake in Northamptonshire. It was on high table-land, for the distant country might be seen through openings in the pine-trees on every side: here and there a church tower, here and there a castle or embattled dwelling; here and there a poverty-stricken assemblage of huts, clustering together for protection. In the south extended the valley of the Cherwell, towards the distant Thames; on the west the high table-land of North Oxfordshire sank down into the valley of the Avon and Severn.

It was a cold windy autumnal morning, the ground yet crisp from an early frost, the leaves hung shivering on the trees, waiting for the first bleak blast of the winter wind to fetch them down to rot with their fellows.

On the edge of a pond stood two youths of some fifteen and thirteen years. They had divested themselves of their upper garments—thick warm tunics—and gazed into the water, here deep, dark, and slimy. There was a look of fixed resolution, combined with hopeless despair, in their faces, which marked the would-be suicides.

They raised their pale faces, their eyes swollen with tears, to heaven.

"O God," said the elder one, "and ye, ye Saints—if Saints there be—take the life I can bear no longer: better trust to your mercies than those of man—better Purgatory, nay, Hell, than earth. Come, Richard, the rope!"

The younger one was pale as death, but as resolved as

the elder. He took up a rope, which he had thrown upon the grass, and gave it mechanically, with hands that yet trembled, to his brother.

"One kiss, Evroult—the last!"

They embraced each other fervently.

"Let us commend ourselves to God; He will not be hard upon us, if He is as good as the Chaplain says—He knows it all."

And they wound the rope around them, so as to bind both together.

"We shall not be able to change our minds, even if the water be cold, and drowning hard."

The younger shivered, but did not falter in his resolution. What mental suffering he must have gone through; for the young naturally cling to life.

But the dread secret was all too visible.

From the younger boy two fingers had fallen off—rotted away with the disease. The elder had a covering over the cheek, a patch, for the leprosy had eaten through it. There was none of the spring and gladness of childhood or youth in either; they carried the tokens of decay with them. They had the sentence of physical death in themselves.

Now they stood tottering on the brink. The wind sighed hoarsely around them; a raven gave an ominous croak-croak, and flew flapping in the air. One moment—and they leapt together.

There was a great splash.

Was all over?

No; one had seen them, and had guessed their intent, and now arrived panting and breathless on the brink, with a long rope, terminated by a large iron hook, in his hand. Behind him came a second individual in a black cassock, but he had girded up his loins to run the better.

The man threw the rope just as the bodies rose to the surface—it missed and they disappeared once more. He watched—a moment of suspense—again they rose; he threw once more. Would the hook catch? Yes; it is entangled in the cord with which they have bound themselves, and they are saved! It is an easy task now to draw them to the land.

"My children! my children!" said the Chaplain, "why have ye attempted self-murder; to rush unsummoned into the presence of your Judge? Had we not been here ye had gone straight to eternal misery."

The boys struggled on the shore, but the taste of the cold water had tamed them. The sense of suffocation was yet upon them; they could not speak, but their immersion was too brief to have done them much harm, and after a few minutes they were able to walk. No other words were said, and their rescuers led them towards a low building of stone.

It was a building of great extent—a quadrangle enclosing half an acre, with an inner cloister running all round. In the centre rose a simple chapel of stern Norman architecture; opening upon the cloister were alternate doors and unglazed windows, generally closed by shutters, in the centre of which was a thin plate of horn, so that when the weather necessitated their use, the interiors might not be quite destitute of light. On one side of the square was the dining-hall, on the other the common room; these had rude cavernous chimneys, and fires were kindled on the hearths; there was no upper story. In each of the smaller chambers was a central table and three or four rough wooden bedsteads.

In the cloisters were scores of hapless beings, men and boys, some lounging about, some engaged in games now long forgotten; some talking and gesticulating loudly. All races which were found in England had their representatives—the Norman, the Saxon, the Celt.

It was the recreation hour, for they were not left in idleness through the day; the community was mainly self-supporting. Men wrought at their own trades, made their own clothes and shoes, baked their own bread, brewed their own beer, worked in the fields and gardens within the outer enclosure. The charity of the outside world did the rest, upon condition that the lepers never strayed beyond their precincts to infect the outer world of health. The Chaplain, himself also enclosed, belonged to an order of brethren who had devoted themselves to this special work throughout Europe—they nearly always took the disease.[1] Father Ambrose quite understood, when he entered upon his self-imposed task, that he would probably die of the disease himself, but neither priests, physicians, nor sisters were ever wanting to fulfil the law of Christ in ministering to their suffering brethren, remembering His words: "Inasmuch as ye have done it to the least of these My brethren, ye have done it unto Me."

The day was duly divided: there was the morning Mass, the service of each of the "day hours" in the chapel, the hours of each meal, the time of recreation, the time of work; all was fixed and appointed in due rotation, and could the poor sufferers only have forgotten the world, and resigned themselves to their sad fate, they were no worse off than the monks in many a monastery.

But the hideous form of the disease was always there; here an arm in a sling, to hide the fact the hand was gone;

---

[1] The disease of leprosy has been deemed incurable, and so practically it was; but it was long before it proved fatal; it ordinarily ran its course in a period not less than ten, nor exceeding twenty, years.

The first symptoms were not unlike those of malarious disease; perhaps leprosy was not so much contagious as endemic, bred of foul waters, or the absence of drainage, or nourished in stagnant marshes; but all men deemed it highly contagious.

The distinctive symptoms which next appeared were commonly reddish spots on the limbs; these by degrees extended, until, becoming white as snow in the centre, they resembled rings; then the interior became ulcerous, and as the ulcer ate into the flesh, the latter presented the tuberous or honey-combed appearance which led to the disease being called *leprosa tuberosa*. Especially did the disease affect the joints of the fingers, the wrists, and the elbows; and limbs would sometimes fall away—or "slough off," as it is technically called.

By degrees it spread inward, and attacking the vital organs, particularly the digestive functions, the sufferer died, not so much from the primary as from the secondary effects of the disease—from exhaustion and weakness.

here a footless man, here an eyeless one; here a noseless one, there another—like poor Evroult—with holes through the cheek; here the flesh livid with red spots or circles enclosing patches white as snow—so they carried the marks of the most hideous disease of former days.

Generally they were the objects of pity, but also of abhorrence and dread. The reader will hardly believe that in France, in the year 1341, the lepers were actually burnt alive throughout the land, in the false plea that they poisoned the waters, really in the cruel hope to stamp out the disease.[1]

Outside the walls were all the outhouses, workshops, and detached buildings, also an infirmary for the worst cases; within the enclosure also the last sad home when the fell destroyer had completed his work—the graveyard, God's acre; and in the centre rose a huge plain cross, with the word PAX on the steps.

It was a law of the place that no one who entered on any pretence might leave it again: people did not believe in cures; leprosy was incurable—at least save by a miracle, as when the Saviour trod this weary world.

The Chaplain took the poor boys to his own chamber, a little room above the porch of the chapel, containing a bed, over which hung the crucifix, a chair, a table, and a few MS. books, a gospel, an epistle, a prophetical book, the offices, church services; little more.

He made them sit in the embrasure of the window, he did not let them speak until he had given each a cup of hot wine, they sat sobbing there a long time, he let nature have its way. At length the time came and he spoke.

"Evroult, my dear child, Richard, how could you attempt self-murder? Know you not that your lives are God's, and that you may not lay them down at your own pleasure."

"Oh, father, why did you save us? It would have been all over now."

"And where would you have been?"

[1] *Chronicle of St. Evroult* in loco.

The boy shuddered. The teaching about Hell, and the horrors of the state of the wicked dead, was far too literal and even coarsely material, at that time, for any one to escape its influence.

"Better a thousand times to be here, only bear up till God releases you, and He will make up for all this. You will not think of the billows past when you gain the shore."

"But, father, anything is better than this—these horrid sights, these dreadful faces, and my father a baron."

"Thou art saved many sins," said and felt the priest; "war is a dreadful thing, strife and bloodshed would have been thy lot."

"But I loved to hunt, to *fight;* I long to be a man, a knight, to win a name in the world, to win my spurs. Oh, what shall I do, how can I bear this?"

"And do *you* feel like this, Richard," said the priest, addressing the younger boy.

"Indeed I do, how can I help it? Oh, the green woods, the baying of the hounds, the delightful gallop, the sweet, fresh air of our Berkshire downs, the hall on winter nights, the gleemen and their songs, their stories of noble deeds of prowess, the——"

"And the tilt-yard, the sword and the lance, the tournament, the *melée*," added the other.

"And Evroult, so brave and expert; oh what a knight thou wouldst have made, my brother."

"And our father loved to see us wrestle and fight, and ride, and jump, and called us his brave boys; and our mother was proud of us—oh, how can we bear the loss of all?"

What could be said: nature was too strong, the instincts of generations were in the boys, the blood of the sea-kings of old ran in their veins.

"Oh, can you not help us? we know you are kind; shall we never get out? is there no hope?"

The tears streamed down the venerable man's cheeks.

"We know you love us or you would not be here; they say you came of your own accord."

He glanced at a glowing circle of red on his right hand, encircling a spot of leprous flesh as white as snow.

"Ah, my dear boys," he said, "I had your feelings once; nay, I was a knight too, and had wife and children."

"Do they live?"

"Yes, but not here; a neighbour, Robert de Belesme, you may have heard of him——"

"As a cruel monster, a wicked knight."

"Stormed my castle in my absence, and burnt it with all therein."

"And did you not avenge them?"

"I was striving to do so, when the hand of God was laid upon me, and I woke from a burning fever to learn that He has said, 'Vengeance is Mine, I will repay.'"

"And then?"

"I came here."

"Poor Father Ambrose," said Richard.

"If I could get out *I* would try to avenge him," said Evroult.

"The murderer has gone before his Judge; leave it," said the priest; "there the hidden things shall be made clear, my boys, *noblesse oblige*, the sons of a baron should keep their word."

"Have we ever broken it?"

"Not so far as I am aware, and I am sure you will not now."

"What are we to promise?"

"Promise me you will not strive to destroy yourselves again."

They looked at each other.

"It is cowardly, unworthy of gentlemen."

"*Cowardly!*" and the hot blood rose in their faces.

"Base cowardice."

"None ever called me coward before; but you are a priest."

"My children, will you not promise? Then you shall not be confined as you otherwise must be——"

"Let them confine us; we can dash our heads against the walls!"

"For my sake, then; they hurt me when they hurt you."

They paused, looked at each other, and sighed.

"Yes, Evroult?" said Richard.

"Yes, be it then, father; we promise."

But there was another thought in Evroult's mind which he did not reveal.

The bell then rang for chapel, but we fear the boys did not take more than their bodies there; and when they were alone in their own little chamber—for they were treated with special distinction (their father "subscribed liberally to the charity")—the hidden purpose came out.

"Richard," said Evroult, "we must escape."

"What shall we do? where can we go?"

"To Wallingford."

"But our father will slay us."

"Not he; he loves us too well. We shall recover then. Old Bartimœus here told me many do recover when they get away, and live, as some do, in the woods. It is all infection *here ;* besides, I *must* see our mother again, if it is only once more—MUST see her, I long for her so."

"But do you not know that the country people would slay us."

"They are too afraid of the disease to seize us."

"But they keep big dogs—mastiffs, and would hunt us if they knew we were outside."

"We must escape in the night."

"The gates are barred and watched."

"A chance will come some evening, at the last hour of recreation before dark, we will hide in the bushes, and as soon as the others go in make for the wall; we can easily get over; now, Richard, are you willing?"

"Yes," said the younger, who always looked up to his elder brother with great belief, "I am willing, but do not make the attempt yet; let us wait a day or two; we are watched and suspected now."

CHAPTER X

THE NEW NOVICE

IT was the day of St. Calixtus, the day on which, seventy-three years earlier in the history of England, the Normans had stormed the heights of Senlac, and the brave Harold had bitten the dust in the agonies of death with the despairing cry, "Alas for England."

Of course it was ever a high day with the conquering race, that fourteenth of October, and the reader will not be surprised that it was observed with due observance at Dorchester Abbey, and that special thanksgiving for the victory was offered at the chapter Mass, which took place at nine of the clock.

Abbot Alured had just divested himself of the gorgeous vestments, in which he had officiated at the high altar, when the infirmarer craved an audience—it was granted.

"The wounded guest has partially recovered, his fever has abated, his senses have returned, and he seems anxious to see thee."

"Why does he wish to see me particularly?"

"Because he has some secret to communicate."

"And why not to thee?"

"I know not, save that he knows that thou art our father."

"Dost think he will ever fight again?"

"He will lay lance in rest no more in this world."

"Nor in the next either, I presume, brother. I will arise and see him."

Passing through the cloister—which was full of the

hum of boys, like busy bees, learning their tasks—and ascending a flight of steps to the "*dorture*," the Abbot followed the infirmarer to a pleasant and airy cell, full of the morning sunlight, which streamed through the panes of thin membrane—such as frequently took the place of glass.

There on a couch lay extended the form of the victim of the prowess of Brian Fitz-Count, his giant limbs composed beneath the coverlet, his face seamed with many a wrinkle and furrow, and marked with deep lines of care, his eyes restless and wandering.

"Thou hast craved to speak with me, my son," said Abbot Alured.

"Alone," was the reply, in a deep hoarse voice.

"My brother, leave us till I touch the bell," said the Abbot, pointing to a small handbell which stood on the table.

The infirmarer departed.

"And now, my son, what hast thou to tell me? First, who art thou? and whence?"

"I am in sanctuary here, and none can drag me hence; is it not so?"

"It is, my son, unless thou hast committed such crime as sacrilege, which God forbid."

"Such crime can none lay to my charge. Tell me, father, dost thou think it wrong for a man to slay those who have deprived him of his loved ones, of all that made life worth living?"

"'Vengeance is Mine,' saith God."

"Well, I took mine into my own hand, and now my task is ended. I am assured that I am a cripple, never to strike a fair blow again."

"The more time for repentance, the better for thy soul. Thou hast not yet told me thy name and home?"

"I tell it thee in confidence, for thou wilt not betray me to mine enemy."

"Not unless justice should demand it."

"Well, I will tell thee my tale first. I was a husband and a father, and a happy one, living in a home on the downs. In consequence of some paltry dispute about black-mail or feudal dues, Brian Fitz-Count sent men who burnt my house in my absence, and my wife and children perished in the flames."

"All!"

"Yes, I found not one alive, so I took to the life of a hunted wolf, rending and destroying, and slew many foreigners, for I am Wulfnoth of Compton; now I have told thee all."

"God's mercy is infinite, thy provocation was indeed great. I judge thee not, poor man. I never had wife or child, but I can guess how they feel who have had and lost them. My brother, thine has been a sad life, thy misery perhaps justified, at least, excused thy life as a leader of outlaws; I, who am a man in whose veins flows the blood of both races, can feel for thee, and pardon thy errors."

"Errors! to avenge her and them."

"The Saviour forgave His murderers, and left us an example that we should follow His steps. Listen, my brother, thou must live for repentance, and to learn submission to God's will; tell thy secret to no man, lest thy foe seek thee even here, and trouble our poor house."

"But I hoped to have seen him bite the dust."

"And God has denied thee the boon; he is a man of strife and blood, and no well-wisher to Holy Church; he seldom hears a Mass, never is shriven, at least, so I have been told in confidence, for in this neighbourhood men speak with bated breath of Brian Fitz-Count, at least within sight of the tall tower of his keep. We will leave him to God. He is a most unhappy man; his children are lepers."

"No, at least not *one*."

"So I have heard; they are in the great Leper House at Byfield, poor boys; my cousin is the Chaplain there."

"And now, father, I will tell thee more. Thou knowest I have been delirious, yet my senses have been awake to other scenes than these. Methought my dear wife came to me in my delirium, came to my bedside, sat in that seat, bathed my fevered brow, nay, it was no dream, her blest spirit was allowed to resume the semblance of throbbing flesh, and there she sat, where thou sittest now."

The Abbot of course saw in this only a phase of delirium, but he said nought; it was at least better than visions of imps and goblins.

"Alas, dear one," continued he, as in a soliloquy, "hadst thou lived, I had not made this life one savage hunting scene, caring only to rush in, knock down, and drag out the prey, and now I am unfit to be where thou art, and may never meet thee again."

"My brother," said the sympathising Alured, "thou believest her to be in Paradise?"

"I do, indeed; I know they are there."

"And thou wouldst fain meet them?"

"I would."

"Repent then, confess, thou shall be loosed from thy sins; and since thou art unfitted for the active walks of life, take upon thee the vows of religion."

"May I? what order would admit me?"

"We will; and thus strive to restore thee to thy dear ones again."

"And Brian Fitz-Count will escape?"

"Leave him to God."

"Well, I will; doubtless he will die and be damned, and we shall never see him; Heaven would not be Heaven if he were there."

The Abbot sighed.

"Ah, brother, thou hast much yet to learn ere thou becomest a true follower of Him, Who at the moment of His supremest agony prayed for His murderers."

But the patient could bear no more, hot tears were streaming down his cheeks.

"Brother, peace be with thee, from the Lord of peace, all good Saints aid thee; say nought of this to any one but me and thou wilt be safe."

He touched the bell, the infirmarer came in.

"God hath touched his heart, he will join our order; as soon as possible he shall take the vows of a novice and assume our garb, then neither Brian Fitz-Count nor any other potentate, not the king himself, can drag him forth."

The last words were uttered in a sort of soliloquy, the infirmarer, for whom they were not meant, did not catch them.

. . . . .

And so the days sped on towards the Feast of All Saints, darkening days and long nights too, often reddened by the light of distant conflagrations, for that terrible period of civil strife—nay, of worse than civil strife—was approaching, when, instead of there being only two parties in the land, each castle was to become its own centre of strife—declaring war upon all its neighbours; when men should fear to till the land for others to reap; when every man's hand should be against every man; when men should fill their strongholds with human devils, and torture for torture sake, when there was no longer wealth to exact; when men should say that God and His Saints were asleep—to such foul misery and distress did the usurpation of Stephen bring the land.

But those days were only beginning, as yet the tidings reached Dorchester slowly that the Empress was the guest of her mother-in-law, the Queen-Dowager, the widow of Henry the First, at Arundel Castle, in Sussex, under the protection of only a hundred and forty horsemen; then, that Robert, Earl of Gloucester, leaving his sister in comparative safety, had proceeded through the hostile country to Bristol with only twelve horsemen, until he was joined midway on his journey by Brian Fitz-Count and his troop from Wallingford Castle; next, that Henry, Bishop of Winchester, and brother of the king, had declared for her, and brought her in triumph to Bristol. Lastly, that she had been conducted by her old friend, Milo, Sheriff of Gloucester, in triumph to that city, and there received the allegiance of the citizens.

Meanwhile, the storm of fire and sword had begun; wicked men took advantage at once of the divided state of the realm, and the eclipse of the royal authority.

They heard at Dorchester that Robert Fitz-Hubert, a savage baron, or rather barbarian, had clandestinely entered the city of Malmesbury and burnt it to the ground, so that divers of the wretched inhabitants perished in the flames, of which the barbarian boasted as though he had obtained a great triumph, declaring himself on the side of the Empress Queen; and, further, that King Stephen, hearing of the deed, had come after him, put him to flight, and retaken Malmesbury Castle.

So affairs progressed up to the end of October.

It was All Saints' Day, and they held high service at Dorchester Abbey; the Chant of William of Fescamp was introduced, without any of the dire consequences which followed it at Glastonbury.

It was a day never to be forgotten by our reclaimed outlaw, Wulfnoth of Compton, he was that day admitted to the novitiate, and received the tonsure; dire had been the conflict in his mind; again and again the old Adam waxed strong within him, and he longed to take advantage, like others, of the political disturbances, in the hope of avenging his own personal wrongs; then the sweet teachings of the Gospel softened his heart, and again and again his dear ones seemed in his dreams to visit him, and bid him prepare for that haven of peace into which they had entered.

"God hath done all things well," the sweet visitants of his dreams seemed to say; "let the past be the past, and let not its black shadow darken the glorious future—the parting was terrible, the meeting shall be the sweeter."

The ceremony was over, Wulfnoth of Compton had become the Novice Alphege of Dorchester, for, in accordance with custom, he had changed his name on taking the vows.

After the long ceremony was over, he sat long in the church undisturbed, a sensation of sweet peace came upon him, of rest at last found, the throbbing heart seemed quiet, the stormy passions stilled.

And now, too, he no longer needed the protection of carnal weapons, he was safe in the immunities of the church, none could drag him from the cloister—he belonged to God.

What a refuge the monastic life afforded then! Without it men would have been divided between beasts of burden and beasts of prey.

And when at last he took possession of his cell, through the narrow window he could see Synodune rising over the Thames; it was a glorious day, the last kiss of summer, when the "winter wind was as yet suspended, although the fading foliage hung resigned."

Peace ineffable filled his mind.

The hills of Synodune for one moment caught his gaze, they had been familiar landmarks in his days of war, rapine, and vengeance, the past rose to his mind, but he longed not after it now.

But was the old Adam dead or only slumbering? We shall see.

CHAPTER XI

OSRIC'S FIRST RIDE

AMIDST a scene of great excitement, the party of Brian Fitz-Count left Wallingford Castle, a hundred men, all armed to the teeth, being chosen to accompany him, while at least five hundred were left behind, capable of bearing arms, charged with the defence of the Castle, with orders, that at least two hundred of their number should repair to a rendezvous, when the progress of events should require their presence, and enable the Baron to fix the place of meeting by means of a messenger.

The day was—as it will be remembered—the second of October, in the year 1139; the season was late, that is, summer was loth to depart, and the weather was warm and balmy. The wild cheers of their companions, who envied them their lot, contrasted with the sombre faces of the townsfolk, foreboding evil in this new departure.

By the Baron's side rode Milo of Gloucester, and they engaged in deep conversation.

Our young friend Osric was committed to the care of the senior page Alain, who anticipated much sportive pleasure in catechising and instructing his young companion —such a novice in the art of war.

And it may be added in equitation, for we need not say old Sexwulf kept no horses, and Osric had much ado to ride, not gracefully, but so as to avoid the jeers and laughter of his companions.

The young reader, who remembers his own first essay in horsemanship, will appreciate poor Osric's difficulty, and will easily picture the suppressed, hardly suppressed, laughter of Alain, at each uneasy jolt. However, Osric was a youth of good sense, and instead of turning red, or seeming annoyed, laughed heartily too at himself. His spirits were light, and he soon shook off the depression of the morning under the influence of the fresh air and smiling landscape, for the tears of youth are happily—like an April shower—soon followed by sunshine.

They rode across Cholsey common, then a wide meadowed space, stretching from Wallingford to the foot of the downs; they left the newly-*restored* or rather *rebuilt* Church of St. Mary's of Cholsey on their right, around which, at that time, clustered nearly all the houses of the village, mainly built upon the rising ground to the north of the church, avoiding the swampy common.[1]

Farther on to the left, across the clear and sparkling brook, they saw the burnt and blackened ruins of the former monastery, founded by Ethelred "the unready," in atonement for the murder of his half-brother, Edward the Martyr, and burnt in the same terrible inroad; one more mile brought them to the source of the Cholsey brook, which bubbled up from the earth amidst a thicket of trees at the foot of a spur of the downs.

Here they all stopped to drink, for the spring was famous, and had reputed medicinal properties, and, in sooth, the water was pleasant to the taste of man and beast.

A little beyond was a moated grange belonging to the Abbot of Reading, a pleasant summer residence in peaceful times; but the days were coming when men should avoid lonely country habitations; there were a few invalid monks there, they came forth and gazed upon the party, then

---

[1] It was a cruciform structure, a huge tower on the intersection of the arms of the cross, the present chancel was not then in existence, a smaller sanctuary of Norman architecture supplied its place. The old church had been destroyed with the village in that Danish invasion of which we have told in the tale of *Alfgar the Dane*, which took place in 1006, and the place had lain waste till the manor was given to Reading Abbey, under whose fostering influence it had risen from its ashes.

shook their tonsured heads as the burgesses of Wallingford had done.

Another mile, and they began to ascend the downs, where, according to tradition, the battle of Æscendune had been fought, in the year of grace, 871. Arriving at the summit, they looked back at the view: Wallingford, the town and churches, dominated by the high tower of the keep, was still in full view, and, beyond, the wavy line of the Chilterns stretched into the misty distance, as described in the preface to our tale.

But most interesting to Osric was the maze of woodland which filled the country about Aston (East-tun) and Blewbery (Blidberia), for there lay the hut of his grandfather; and the tears rose to the affectionate lad's eyes at the thought of the old man's future loneliness, with none but poor old Judith to console him for the loss of his boy.

Before them rose Lowbury Hill—dominated then by a watch-tower—which they ascended and stood on the highest summit of the eastern division of the Berkshire downs; before them on the south rose the mountainous range of Highclere, and a thin line of smoke still ascended from the bale-fire on the highest point.

Here a horseman was seen approaching, and when he came near enough, a knight, armed *cap-a-pie*, was disclosed.

"Friend or foe?" said Alain to his companion.

"If a foe, I pity him."

"See, the Baron rides forth alone to meet him!"

They met about a furlong from the party; entered into long and amicable conference, and soon returned to the group on the hill; the order brought news which changed their course, they turned to the west, and instead of riding for Sussex, followed the track of the Icknield Street for Devizes and the west.

This brought them across the scene of the midnight encounter, and Alain's quick eyes soon detected the traces of the combat.

"Look, there has been a fight here—see how the ground

is trampled, and here is a broken sword—ah! the ground is soaked with blood—there has been a gallant tussle here—would I had seen it."

Osric was not yet so enthusiastic in the love of strife.

Alain's exclamations brought several of the riders around him; and they scrutinised the ground closely, and they speculated on the subject.

The Baron smiled grimly, and thought—

"What has become of the corpse?" for he doubted not he had fed fat his ancient grudge, and slain his foe.

"Look in yon thicket for the body," he cried.

They looked, but as our readers anticipate, found nought.

The Baron wondered, and said a few confidential words to his friend Milo, which none around heard.

Shortly afterwards their route led them by Cwichelm's Hlawe, described before; the Baron halted his party; and then summoning Osric to attend him, rode into the thicket.

The reputed witch stood at the door of her cell.

"So thou art on thy way to battle; the dogs of war are unslipped."

"Even so, but dost thou know this boy?"

"Old Sexwulf's grandson, down in the woods; so thou hast got him, ha! ha! he is in good hands, ha! ha!"

"What means thy laughter, like the noise of an old croaking crow?"

"Because thou hast caught him, and the decrees of fate are about to be accomplished."

"Retire, Osric, and join the rest."

"Now, mother, tell me what thou dost mean?"

"'That thy conjunction with this youth bodes thee and thine little good—the stars have told me that much."

"Why, what harm can he do *me*, a mere boy?"

"The free people of old taught their children to sing, 'Tremble, tyrants; we shall grow up.'"

"If he proved false, a blow would rid me of so frail an encumbrance"

"Which thou mightest hesitate to strike."

"Tell me why; I thought he might be my stolen child, but the lips of old Sexwulf speak truth, and he swears the lad is his grandson."

"It is a wise grandfather who knows his own grandson."

"Thou knowest many things; the boy is so like my poor——" he hesitated, and suppressed a name; "that, hard as my heart is, he has softened it: his voice, his manner, his gestures, tell me——"

"I cannot as yet."

"Dost thou know?"

"Only that old Sexwulf would not wilfully deceive."

"And is that all thou hast to say?"

"No, wait, keep the boy near thee, thou shalt know in time; thy men are calling for thee—hark thee, Sir Brian, the men of Donnington are out."

"That for them," and the Baron snapped his fingers.

When he rejoined his troop, he found them in a state of great excitement, which was explained when they pointed to moving objects some two or three miles away on the downs; the quick eye of the Baron immediately saw that it was a troop which equalled his own in numbers.

"The witch spoke the truth," he said; and eager as a war-horse sniffing the fray afar, he gave the word to ride towards the distant party, which rapidly rose and became distinct to the sight.

"I see their pennons, they are the men of Donnington, and their lord is for King Stephen; now, my men, to redden our bright swords. Osric, thou art new to all this—Alain, thou art young—stay behind on that mound, and join us when we have done our work."

Poor Alain looked grievously hurt.

"My lord!"

"Well?"

"Do let me share the fight!"

"Thou wilt be killed."

"I will take my chance."

"And Osric?"

"I am not afraid, my lord," said Osric.

"But thou canst hardly ride, nor knowest not yet the use of lance and sword; here, old Raoul, stay with this lad."

"My lord!"

"And thou, too; well, boy, wilt thou pledge me thy word not (he lowered his voice) to attempt to escape?"

He marked a slight hesitation.

"Remember thy grandfather."

"My lord, I will do as thou biddest—stay where thou shalt bid me, or ride with thee."

"Stay on the crest of yonder hill."

All this time they had been riding forward, and now the enemy was within hearing.

Both parties paused.

Brian rode forward.

A knight on the other side did the same.

"For God and the Empress," said the former.

"For God and the King," cried the latter.

Instantly the two charged, and their followers waited to see the result: the lance of the King's man broke; that of Sir Brian held firm, and coming full on the breast, unhorsed the other, who fell heavily prone, on his head, like one who, as old Homer hath it, "seeketh oysters in the fishy sea."

The others waited no longer, but eager on either side to share their leader's fortunes, charged too. Oh, the awful shock as spear met spear; oh, the crash, the noise, the wild shouts, the splintering of lances, then the ringing of swords upon armour; the horses caught the enthusiasm of the moment and bit each other, and struck out with their fore-legs: it was grand, at least so they said in that iron age.

But it was soon decided—fortune kept steadfast to her first inclinations—the troops fared as their leaders had fared—and those who were left alive of the Donnington men were soon riding southward for bare life.

Brian ordered the trumpeter to recall his men from the pursuit.

"Let them go—I have their leader—he at least shall pay ransom; they have been good company, and we feel sorry to see them go."

The poor leader, Sir Hubert of Donnington, the eldest son of the lord of that ilk, was lifted, half-stunned, upon a horse behind another rider, while Brian remembered Osric.

What had been the feelings of the latter?

Did the reader ever meet that story in St. Augustine's Confessions, of a young Christian taken against his will to see the bloody sports of the amphitheatre. His companions dragged him thither, he said they might have his body, but he shut his eyes and stopped his ears until a louder shout than usual pierced through the auricular protection —one moment of curiosity, he opened his eyes, he saw the victor thrust the trident into the palpitating body of the vanquished, the demon of blood-thirstiness seized him, he shouted too, and afterwards sought those cruel scenes from choice, until the grace of God stopped him.

So now with our Osric.

He felt no desire at first to join the *mêlée*, indeed, he knew how helpless he was; but as he gazed a strange, wild longing came over him, he felt inclined, nay, could hardly restrain himself from rushing in; but his promise to stay on the hill prevailed over him: perhaps it was hereditary inclination.

But after all was over, he saw Alain wiping his bloody sword as he laughed with savage glee.

"Look, Osric, I killed one—see the blood."

Instead of being shocked, as a good boy should have been, Osric envied him, and determined to spend all the time he possibly could in mastering the art of jousting and fencing.

They now rode on, leaving twenty of their own dead

on the plain, and forty of the enemy; but, as Napoleon afterwards said—"You cannot make an omelette without breaking eggs."

And now, alas, the eggs were human lives—men made in the image of God—too little accounted of in those days.

They now passed Letcombe Castle,—a huge circular camp with trench and vallum, capable of containing an army; it was of the old British times, and the mediæval warriors grimly surveyed this relic of primæval war. Below there lay the town of Wantage,—then strongly walled around,—the birthplace of Alfred. Three more miles brought them to the Blowing Stone, above Kingston Lisle, another relic of hoar antiquity; and Alain, who had been there before, amused Osric by producing that deep hollow roar, which in earlier days had served to alarm the neighbourhood, as he blew into the cavity.

Now the ridgeway bore straight to the highest summit of the whole range,—the White Horse Hill,—and here they all dismounted, and tethering their horses, prepared to refresh man and beast. Poor Osric was terribly sore and stiff, and could not even walk gracefully; he was still able to join Alain in his laughter, but with less grace than at first.

But we must cut this chapter short; suffice it to say, that after a brief halt they resumed their route; camped that night under the shelter of a clump of trees on the downs, and the next day, at Devizes, effected a junction with the troops of Earl Robert of Gloucester, who, having left his sister safe in Arundel Castle, was on his way to secure Bristol, attended by only twelve horsemen.

CHAPTER XII

THE HERMITAGE

FOR many days Evroult and Richard, the sons—unhappy, leprous sons—of Brian Fitz-Count, bore their sad lot with apparent patience in the lazar-house of Byfield; but their minds were determined, come weal or woe, they would endeavour to escape.

"Where there is a will," says an old proverb, "there is a way,"—the chance Evroult had spoken of soon came.

It was the hour of evening recreation, and in the spacious grounds attached to the lazar-house, the lepers were walking listlessly around the well-trodden paths, in all stages of leprous deformity; it was curious to note how differently it affected different people; some walked downcast, their eyes on the ground, studiously concealing their ghastly wounds; some in a state of semi-idiotcy—no uncommon result—"moped and mowed"; some, in hopeless despair, sighed and groaned; and one cried "Lost, lost," as he wrung his hands.

There were keepers here and there amongst them, too often lepers themselves. The Chaplain, too, was there, endeavouring to administer peripatetic consolation first to one, then to another.

"Well, Richard, well, Evroult, my boys, how are you to-day?"

"As well as we ever shall be here."

"I want to get out of this place."

"And I."

"Oh will you not get us out? Can you not speak to

the governor? see, we are *nearly* well." Then Richard looked at his hand, where two fingers were missing, and sobbed aloud.

"It is no use, my dear boys, to dash yourselves against the bars of your cage, like poor silly birds; I fear the time of release will never come, till death brings it either for you or me—see, I share your lot."

"But you have had your day in the world, and come here of your own accord; we are only boys, oh, perhaps with threescore and ten years here before us, as you say in the Psalms."

"Nay, few here attain the age the Psalmist gives as the ordinary limit of human life in his day, and, indeed, few outside in these days."[1]

"Well, we should have been out of it all, had you not interfered."

"And where?"

Echo answered "Where?"—the boys were silent.

The Chaplain saw that in their present mood he could do no good—he turned elsewhere.

Nothing but an intense desire to alleviate suffering had brought him to Byfield lazar-house. The Christianity of that age was sternly practical, if superstitious; and with all its superstition it exercised a far more beneficent influence on society than fifty Salvation Armies could have done; it led men to remember Christ in all forms of loathsome and cruel suffering, and to seek Him in the suffering members of His mystical body; if it led to self-chosen austerities, it also had its heights of heroic self-immolation for the good of others.

Such a self-immolation was certainly our Chaplain's. He walked amongst these unfortunates as a ministering angel; where he could do good he did it, where consolation

---

[1] Too true. Bad sanitary arrangements causing constant plague and fever, ignorance of medicine, frequent famines, the constant casualties of war, had brought men to think fifty years a ripe old age in the twelfth century.

found acceptance he gave it, and many a despairing spirit he soothed with the hope of the sunny land of Paradise.

And how he preached to them of Him Who sanctified suffering and made it the path to glory; how he told them how He should some day change their vile leprous bodies that He might make them like His own most glorious Body, until the many, abandoning all hope here, looked forward simply for that glorious consummation of body and soul in bliss eternal.

> "Oh! how glorious and resplendent
> Shall this body some day be;
> Full of vigour, full of pleasure,
> Full of health, and strong and free:
> When renewed in Christ's own image,
> Which shall last eternally."

But all this was lost on Evroult and Richard. The inherited instincts of fierce generations of proud and ruthless ancestors were in them—as surely as the little tigerling, brought up as a kitten, begins eventually to bite and tear, so did these poor boys long for sword and lance—for the life of the wild huntsman or the wilder robber baron.

Instincts worthy of condemnation, yet not without their redeeming points; such were all our ancestors once, whether Angle, Saxon, Jute, or Northman; and the fusion has made the Englishman what he is.

. . . . .

The bell began to ring for Vespers; there was quite a quarter of an hour ere they went into chapel.

It was a dark autumnal evening, the sun had just gone down suddenly into a huge bank of dark clouds, and gloom had come upon the earth, as the two boys slipped into the bushes, which bordered their path, unseen.

The time seemed ages until the bell ceased and they knew that all their companions were in chapel, and that they must immediately be missed from their places.

Prompt to the moment, Evroult cried "*Now*, Richard," and ran to the wall; he had woven a rope from his bedclothes, and concealed it about his person; he had wrenched a bar from his window, and twisted it into a huge hook; he now threw it over the summit of the lofty wall, and it bit—held.

Up the wall the boys swarmed, at the very moment when the Chaplain noticed their missing forms in their seats in chapel, and the keepers, too, who counted their numbers as they went in, found "two short," and went to search the grounds.

To search—but not to find. The boys were over the wall, and running for the woods.

Oh, how dark and dismal the woods seemed in the gloom. But happily there was a full moon to come that night, as the boys knew, and they felt also that the darkness shielded them from immediate pursuit.

Onward they plunged—through thicket and brake, through firm ground and swamp, hardly knowing which way they were going, until they came upon a brook, and sat down on its bank in utter weariness.

"Oh, Evroult, how shall we find our way? And we have had no supper; I am getting hungry already," cried the younger boy.

"Do you not know that all these brooks run to the Cherwell, and the Cherwell into the Thames? We will keep down the brook till we come to the river, and then to the river till we come to Oxnaford."

"Listen, there is the bay of a hound! Oh, Evroult, he will tear us in pieces! It is that savage mastiff of theirs, 'Tear-'em.' The keepers are after us. Oh, what shall we do?"

"Be men—like our father," said the sterner Evroult.

"But we have no weapons."

"I have my fist. If he comes at me I will thrust it down his foul throat, or grasp his windpipe, and strangle him."

"Evroult, I have heard that they cannot track us in water. Let us walk down the brook."

"Oh, there is a fire!"

"No, it is the moon rising over the trees; that is the

light she sends before her. You are right—now for the brook. Ah! it feels clear and pebbly, no mud to stick in. Come, Richard! let us start. No, stay, I remember that if the brute finds blood he will go no farther. Here is my knife," and the desperate boy produced a little pocket-knife.

"What are you going to do?"

"Drop a little blood. There is a big blue vein in my arm."

And the reckless lad opened a vein in his arm, which bled freely.

"Let me do the same," cried the other.

"No; this is enough." And he scattered the blood all about, then looked out for some "dock-leaf," and bound it over the wound with part of the cord which had helped them over the wall.

"Now, that will do. Let us hurry down the brook, Richard, before they come in sight."

Such determination had its reward; they left all pursuit behind them, and heard no more of the hound.

Tired out at last, they espied with joy an old barn by the brook side, turned in, found soft hay, and, reckless of all consequences, slept till the sun was high in the heavens.

Then they awoke, and lo! a gruff man was standing over them.

"Who are you, boys?"

"The sons of the Lord of Wallingford."

"How came you here?"

"Lost in the woods."

"But Wallingford is far away to the south."

"We are on our road home; can you give us some food?"

"If you will come to my house, you shall have what I can give you. Why! what is the matter with that hand, that cheek? Good heavens, ye are lepers; keep off!"

The poor boys stood rooted to the spot with shame.

"And ye have defiled my hay—no one will dare touch it. I have a great mind to shut you both in, and burn you and the hay together."

"That you shall not," said the fierce Evroult, and

dashed through the open door, almost upsetting the man, who was so afraid of touching the lepers that he could offer no effective resistance, and the two got off.

"That was a narrow escape, but how shall we get food?"

A few miles down the brook they began to feel very faint.

"See, there is a farm; let us ask for some milk and bread."

"Richard, you are not marked as I am, you go first."

A poor sort of farm in the woods—farmhouse, ricks, stables, barns, of rude construction. A woman was milking the cows in a hovel with open door.

"Please give us some milk," said Richard, standing in the doorway; "we are very hungry and thirsty."

"Drink from the bowl. How came you in the woods?"

"Lost."

"And there is another—your brother, is he?—round the door. Drink and pass it to him."

They both drank freely, Evroult turning away the bad cheek.

As Richard gave back the bowl, the woman espied his hands.

"Mother of mercy! why, where are your fingers? you are a leper, out! out! John, turn out the dogs."

"Nay! nay! we will go; only throw us a piece of bread."

"Why are you not shut up? Good Saints!"

"Please do not be hard upon us—give us some bread."

"Will you promise to go away?"

"Yes, if you will give us some bread."

"Keep off, then;" and the good woman, a little softened, gave them some oaten cakes, just as her husband appeared in the distance coming in from the fields.

"Now off, before any harm come of it; go back to Byfield lazar-house."

"It was so dreadful; we have run away."

"Poor boys, so young too; but off, or my good man may set the dogs at you."

And they departed, much refreshed.

"Oh Evroult, how every one abhors us!"

"It is very hard to bear."

At midday, still following the brook, they were saluted with a stern "Stand, and deliver!"

A fellow in forester's garb, with bow and arrow so adjusted that he could send the shaft in a moment through any body, opposed their passage.

"We are only poor boys."

"Whither bound?"

"For Wallingford."

"Why, that is three days' journey hence; come with me."

He led them into an open glade; there was a large fire over which a cauldron hung, emitting a most savoury stew as it bubbled, and stretched around the fire were some thirty men, evidently outlaws of the Robin Hood type.

"What are these boys?"

"Wanderers in the woods, who say they want to go to Wallingford."

"Whose sons are ye?"

"Of Brian Fitz-Count, Lord of Wallingford."

"By all the Saints! then my rede is to hang them for their father's sake, and have no more of the brood. Have you any brothers? Good heavens! they are lepers."

"Send an arrow through each."

"For shame, Ulf, the hand of God hath touched them; but depart."

"Give us some food."

"Not unless you promise to go back to the lazar-house, from which we see you have escaped."

Poor boys, even hungry as they were, they would not promise.

"Put some bread on that stump," said the leader, "and let them take it; come not near: now off!"

It was the last food the poor boys got for many hours, for every one abhorred their presence and drove them off with sticks and stones, until, wearied out, Richard sank fainting on the ground on the eventide of that weary day.

Evroult was at the end of his resources, and at last felt beaten; tears were already trickling down his manly young face.

An aged man bent over them.

"Why do you weep, my son? what is the matter with your companion?"

It was an old man who spoke, in long coarse robe, and a rope around his waist. Evroult recognised the hermit.

"We are lepers," said he despairingly.

The old man bent down and kissed their sores.

"I see Christ in you; come to my humble cell—there you shall have food, fire, and shelter."

He helped them to ascend the rocky side of the valley, until they came to a natural cave half concealed by herbage—an artificial front had been built of stone, with door and window; a spring of water bubbled down the rock, to find its destination in the brook below. Far over the forest they could see a river, red in the light of the setting sun, and the buildings of a town of some size in the dim distance. The river, although they knew it not, was the Cherwell, the town, Banbury.

He led them and seated them by a fire, gave them food, then, after he had heard their tale—

"My dear children," he said, "if you dread the lazar-house so much, ye may stay with me while ye will; go not 'forth again into the cruel, cruel world, poor wounded lambs."

And the good man put them to bed upon moss and leaves.

CHAPTER XIII

OSRIC AT HOME

It is not our intention to follow Osric's career closely during the early period of his pagehood under the fostering care of Brian Fitz-Count and the influence of Alain, but we shall briefly dwell in this chapter upon the great change which was taking place in his life and character.

When we first met him, he was simple to a fault, but he had the sterling virtues of truthfulness and obedience, purity and unselfishness, sedulously cultivated in a congenial soil by his grandfather, one of Nature's noblemen, although not ranked amongst the Norman *noblesse*.

But it was the virtue which had never yet met real temptation. Courageous and brave he was also, but still up to the date of the adventure with the deer, he had never struck a blow in anger, or harmed a fellow-creature, save the beasts of the chase whom he slew for food, not for sport.

Then came the great change in his life: the gentle, affectionate lad was thrown into the utterly worldly and impure atmosphere of a Norman castle—into a new world; thoughts and emotions were aroused to which he had been hitherto a perfect stranger, and, strange to say, he felt unsuspected traits in his own character, and desires in his own unformed mind answering to them.

For instance, he who had never raised a hand in angry strife, felt the homicidal impulse rush upon him during the skirmish we described in a previous chapter. He longed to take part in the frays, to be where blows were going;

thenceforward he gave himself up with ardour to the study of war; he spent all his spare time in acquiring the arts of fence and the management of weapons; and Brian smiled grimly as he declared that Osric would soon be a match for Alain.

But it was long before the Baron allowed him to take part in actual bloodshed, and then only under circumstances which did not involve needless risk, or aught more than the ordinary chances of mortal combat, mitigated by whatsoever aid his elders could afford; for Brian loved the boy with a strange attachment; the one soft point in his armour of proof was his love for Osric—not a selfish love, but a parental one, as if God had committed the boy to his charge in the place of those he had lost.

Yet he did not believe Osric was his long-lost son: no, that child was dead and gone,—the statements of the old man were too explicit to allow of further doubt.

Osric was present when that brutal noble, Robert Fitz-Hubert, stormed Malmesbury; there he beheld for the first time the horrors of a *sack;* there he saw the wretched inhabitants flying out of their burning homes to fall upon the swords of the barbarous soldiery. At the time he felt that terrible thirst so like that of a wild beast,—which in some modern sieges, such as Badajos, has turned even Englishmen into wild and merciless savages,—and then when it was over, he felt sick and loathed himself.

He was fond of Alain, who returned the preference, yet Alain was a bad companion, for he was an adept in the vices of his day—not unlike our modern ones altogether, yet developed in a different soil, and of ranker growth.

Therefore Osric soon had many secrets he could not confide to his grandfather, whom he was permitted to see from time to time,—a great concession on the part of the Lord of Wallingford, who craved all the boy's love for himself.

"Thou art changed, my dear Osric," said his grandfather on one of these occasions, a fine Sunday morn when Osric had leave of absence.

They were on their way through the tangled wood to the old Saxon Church of Aston Upthorpe, in which King Alfred was said to have heard Mass.[1]

> "The woods were God's first temples, ere man raised
> The architrave."

The very fountains babbled in His honour Who made them to laugh and sing, the birds sang their matin songs in His praise—this happy woodland was exempted from all those horrors of war which already devastated the rest of England, for it was safe under the protection of Brian, to whom, wiser than Wulfnoth of Compton, it paid tribute; and at this juncture Maude and her party were supreme, for it was during Stephen's captivity at Bristol.

"Thou art changed, my dear Osric."

"How, my grandsire?"

"Thy face is the same, yet not the same, even as Adam's face was the same, yet not the same, after he learned the secret of evil, which drove him from Paradise."

"And I too have been driven from Paradise: my Eden was here."

"Wouldst thou return if thou couldst; if Brian consented to release thee." And the old man looked the youth full in the face.

Osric was transparently truthful.

"No, grandfather," he said, and then blushed.

"Ah, thou art young and lovest adventure and the gilded panoply of war: what wonder! such was thy father, Wulfnoth of Compton, of whom thou art the sole surviving child."

"Tell me, grandfather, is he dead—is my poor father dead?"

"That is a secret which may not be committed even to thee; were he alive, he would curse thee, did he know thou wert fighting under Brian's banner."

"It was to save thy life."

"I know it, my child, and would be the last to blame

---

[1] It still stands, one of the oldest of our old village churches.

thee, yet I am glad thy father knows it not. He has never inquired concerning thee."

"Then he is alive?"

"Did I say he was? I meant not to do so—seek not to know—knowledge is sometimes dangerous."

"Well, if he is alive," said Osric, a little piqued, "he does not care half so much for me as does my Lord of Wallingford. *He* would have asked about me."

"He treats thee well then."

"As if he loved me."

"It is strange—passing strange; as soon should I expect a wolf to fondle a kid."

"I am not a kid, at least not now."

"What then, dear boy? a wolf?"

"More like one, I think, than a kid."

"And thou hast looked on bloodshed with unflinching eye and not shuddered?"

"I shuddered just at first; but I have got used to it: you have often said war is lawful."

"Yes, for one's country, as when Alfred fought against the Danes or Harold at Senlac. So it was noble to die as died my father,—your own ancestor, Thurkill of Kingestun; so, had I been old enough to have gone with him, should I have died."

"And you took part in the skirmishes which followed Senlac?"

"I fought under the hero Hereward."

"And did *you* shudder to look upon war?"

"Only as a youth naturally does the first time he sees the blood of man poured forth like water—it is not for that I would reproach thee, only *we* fought for liberty; and it is better to die than to live a life of slavery,—happier far were they who fell around our noble Harold on the hill of Senlac, than they who survived to see the desolation and misery, the chains and slavery which awaited the land; but, my child, what are you fighting for? surely one tyrant is no better than another, Maude or Stephen, what does it matter?"

"Save, grandfather, that Maude is the descendant of our old English kings—her great-grandfather was the Ironside of whose valiant deeds I have often heard you boast."

"True, my son, and therefore of the *two*, I wish her success; but she also is the grandchild of the Conqueror, who was the scourge of God to this poor country."

"In that case God sent him."

"Deliver my soul from the ungodly, which is a sword of Thine," quoted the pious old man, well versed in certain translations from the Psalms.

"My grandfather, I fought against it as long as I could, as thou knowest; I would have died, and did brave the torture, rather than consent to become a page of the Lord of Wallingford; and when I did so become to save *thy* life, I felt bound in honour to be faithful, and so to the best of my power I have been."

"And now thou lovest the yoke, and wouldst not return?"

Again the youth coloured.

"Grandfather, I cannot help it—excitement, adventure, the glory of victory, the joy even of combat, has that attraction for me of which our bards have sung, in the old songs of the English Chronicles which you taught me around the hearth."

"The lion's cub is a lion still; let him but taste blood, and the true nature comes out."

"Better be a lion than a deer—better eat than be eaten, grandfather."

"I know not," said the old man pensively, "but, my child, never draw thy sword to oppress thy poor countrymen, unless thou wouldst have thy father curse thee."

"He is not dead then?"

"I said not so."

"Why not tell me whether my father lives?"

"Because in thy present position, which thou canst not escape, the knowledge would be dangerous to thee."

"How came my father to leave me in thy care? how

did my mother die? why am I the only one left of my kin?"

"All this I am bound not to tell thee, my child; try and forget it all until thou art of full age."

"And then?"

"Perchance even *then* it were better to let the dead bury their dead."

Osric sighed.

"Why am I the child of mystery? why have I not a surname like my compeers? they mock me now and then, and I have had two or three sharp fights in consequence; at last the Baron found it out, for he saw the marks upon my face, and he spoke so sternly to them that they ceased to gibe."

"My dear boy, commit it all to thy Heavenly Father; thou dost not forget thy prayers?"

"Not when I am in the Castle chapel."

"And not at other times?"

"It is impossible. I sleep amidst other pages. I just cross myself when I think of it, and say a Pater and an Ave."

"And how often dost thou go to Mass?"

"When we are not out on an expedition, each Sunday."

"Does the Baron go to church with you?"

"Yes, but he does not believe much in it."

"I feared not: and thy companions?"

"They often laugh and jest during Matins or Mass."

"And you?"

"I try not to join them, because it would grieve you."

"There should be a higher motive."

"I know it."

"And with regard to other trials and temptations, are your companions good lads?"

Osric laughed aloud.

"No, grandfather, anything but that."

"And you?"

"I go to the good priest of St. Mary's to Confession, and that wipes it off."

"Nay, my child, not without penitence, and penitence is shown by ceasing to sin."

Now they had arrived at the rustic church of East-town, or Aston, on the slope of the old Roman camp, which uprose above the forest. Many woodsmen and rustics of the humble village were there. It was a simple service: rude village psalmody; primitive vestments and ritual, quite unlike the gorgeous scenes then witnessed in cathedral or abbey church, in that age of display. Osmund of Sarum had not made his influence felt much here, although the church was in the diocese he once ruled. All was of the old Anglo-Saxon type, as when Alfred was alive, and England free. There was not a Norman there to criticise; they shunned the churches to which the rustics resorted, and where the homilies were in the English tongue, which they would not trouble to learn.

Poor Osric! his whole character and disposition may be plainly enough traced in the conversation given above. The reader must not condemn the grandfather, old Sexwulf, for his reticence concerning the mystery of Osric's birth. When Wulfnoth of Compton brought the babe to his door, it was with strict injunctions not to disclose the secret till he gave permission. The old grandfather did not understand the reasons why so much mystery was made of the matter, but he felt bound to obey the prohibition.

Hence all that Osric knew was that he was the last survivor of his family, and that all besides him had perished in the wars, save a father of whom little was known, except that he manifested no interest whatsoever in his son.

Perhaps the reader can already solve the riddle; we have given hints enough. Only he must remember that neither Brian nor Sexwulf had his advantages.

The service of the village church sounded sweetly in the ears of Osric that day. He was affected by the associations which cling about the churches where we once knelt by a father or mother's side; and Osric felt like a child again as he knelt by his grandfather—it might be for the last time, for the possibility of sudden death on the battle-field, of entering a deadly fray never to emerge alive, of succumbing beneath the sword or lance of some stronger or more fortunate adversary, was ever present to the mind; yet Osric did not fear death on the battle-field. There was, and is, an unaccountable glamour about it: men who would not enter a "pest-house" for the world, would volunteer for a "forlorn hope."

But it is quite certain that on that day all the religious impulses Osric had ever felt, were revived, and that he vowed again and again to be a true knight, *sans peur et sans reproche*, fearing nought but God, and afraid only of sin and shame, as the vow of chivalry imported, if knight he was ever allowed to become.

Ite missa est[1]—it was over, and they left the rustic church. Outside the neighbours clustered and chatted as they do nowadays. They congratulated Sexwulf on his handsome grandson, and flattered the boy as they commented on his changed appearance, but there always seemed something they left unsaid.

Neither was their talk cheerful; it turned chiefly upon wars and rumours of wars. They had been spared, but there were dismal tales of the country around—of murder and arson, of fire and sword, of worse scenes yet behind, and doom to come.

They hoped to gather in *that* harvest, whether another would be theirs to reap was very doubtful. And so at last they separated, and through some golden fields of corn, for it was nearly harvest time, Sexwulf and his grandson wended their way to their forest home. It was a day long remembered, for it was the very last of a long series of peaceful Sundays in the forest. Osric felt unusually happy that afternoon, as he returned home with his grandfather, full of the strength of new resolutions with which we are told the way to a place, unmentionable

---

[1] *Ite missa est, i.e.* the concluding words of the Mass.

to ears polite, is paved ; and his manner to his grandfather was so sweet and affectionate, that the dear old man was delighted with his boy.

The evening was spent at home, for there was no Vesper service at the little chapel—amidst the declining shadows of the trees, the solemn silence of the forest, the sweet murmuring of the brook. The old man slept in the shade, seated upon a mossy bank. Osric slept too, with his head pillowed upon his grandfather's lap; while in wakeful moments the aged hands played with his graceful locks. Old Judith span in the doorway and watched the lad.

"He is as bonny as he is brave, and as brave as he is bonny, the dear lad," she said.

Then came the shadows of night. The old man brought forth his dilapidated harp, and the three sang the evening hymn to its accompaniment—

"Te lucis ante terminum,"

and repeated the psalm *Qui habitat;* then with a short prayer, not unlike our "Lighten our darkness," indeed its prototype, they retired to sleep, while the wind sighed a requiem about them through the arches of the forest, and dewy odours stole through the crevices of the hut—

"The torrent's smoothness ere it dash below."

CHAPTER XIV

THE HERMITAGE

NOTHING is more incomprehensible to the Christians of the nineteenth century than the lives of the hermits, and the general verdict passed upon them is, that they were useless, idle men, who fled from the world to avoid its work, or else were possessed with an unreasoning superstition which turned them into mere fanatics.

But this verdict is one-sided and unjust, and founded upon ignorance of the world of crime and violence from which these men fled,—a world which seemed so utterly abandoned to cruelty and lust that men despaired of its reformation; a world wherein men had no choice between a life of strife and bloodshed, and the absolute renunciation of society; a world wherein there was no way of escape but to flee to the deserts and mountains, or enter the monastic life, for those, who, as ancient Romans, might have committed suicide, but as Christians, felt they *must* live, till God in His mercy called them hence.

And so while the majority of those who sought God embraced what is commonly called, *par excellence*, the religious life, others sought Him in solitude and silence; wherein, however, they were followed by that universal reverence which men, taught by the legends of the Church, bestowed on the pious anchorite.

Poverty, celibacy, self-annihilation, were their watchwords; and in contemplation of death, judgment, Hell, and Heaven, these lonely hours were passed.

Such a man was Meinhold, with whom the youthful

sons of Brian Fitz-Count had found refuge. From childhood upwards he had loathed the sin he saw everywhere around him, and thence he sought the monastic life; but as ill-hap would have it, found a monastery in which the monks were forgetful of their vows, and slaves of sin, somewhat after the fashion of those described in Longfellow's "Golden Legend," for such there were, although, we believe, they were but exceptions to the general rule—

"Corruptio optimi est pessima."

The corruption of that which is very good is commonly the worst of all corruption: if monks did not rise above the world, they fell beneath it. Meinhold sternly rebuked them; and, in consequence, when one day it was his turn to celebrate the Eucharist, they poisoned the wine he should have used. By chance he was prevented from saying the Mass that day, and a poor young friar who took his place fell down dead on the steps of the altar. Meinhold shook off the dust of his feet and left them, and they in revenge said a Mass for the Dead on his behalf, with the idea that it would hasten his demise; for if not religious they were superstitious.

Then he determined that he would have nought more to do with his fellow-men, and sought God's first temples, the forests. In the summer time he wandered in its glades, reciting his Breviary, until he found out a place where he might lay his head.

A range of limestone hills had been cleft in the course of ages by a stream, which had at length scooped out a valley, like unto the "chines" in the Isle of Wight, and now rushed brawling into the river below, adown the vale it had made. In the rock, on one side of the vale, existed a large cave, formed by the agency of water, in the first place, but now high and dry. It had not only one, but several apartments; cavern opened out of cavern, and so dark and devious were their windings, that men feared to penetrate them.

Hither, for the love of God, came Meinhold. He had found the place he desired—a shelter from the storms of Heaven. In the outer cave he placed a rude table and seat, which he made for himself; and in an inner cavern he made a bed of flags and leaves.

In the corner of the cell he placed his crucifix. Wandering in the woods he found the skeleton of some poor hapless wayfarer, long since denuded of its flesh. He placed the skull beneath the crucifix as a *memento mori*, not without breathing a prayer for the poor soul to whom it had once belonged.

Here he read his Breviary, which, let the reader remember, was mainly taken from the Word of God, psalms and lessons forming three-fourths of the contents of the book, arranged, as in our Prayer Book, for the Christian year. It was his sole possession,—a bequest of a deceased friend, worth its weight in gold in the book market, but far more valuable in Meinhold's eyes.

Here, then, he passed a blameless if monotonous existence, to which but one objection could be made—it was a *selfish* life. Even if the selfishness were of a high order, man was not sent into the world simply to save, each one, his own soul. The life of the Chaplain at Byfield lazar-house showed how men could abjure self far more truly than in a hermitage.

Sometimes thoughts of this kind passed through the mind of our hermit and drove him distracted, until his cry became,

"Lord, what wilt Thou have me to do?"

And while he thus sought to know God's Will, the two poor fugitives, Evroult and Richard, came into his way.

Poor wounded lambs! no fear had he of their terrible malady. The Lord had sent them to him, and the hermit felt his prayers were answered. Wearied out and tired by their long day's journey, the poor boys passively accepted his hospitality; and they ate of his simple fare, and slept on his bed of leaves as if it had been a couch of down; nor did they awake till the sun was high in the heavens.

The hermit had been up since sunrise. He had long since said his Matins and Lauds from his well-thumbed book; and then kindling a fire in a sort of natural hearth beneath a hole in the rock, which opened to the upper air, he roasted some oatmeal cakes, and went out to gather blackberries and nuts, as a sort of dessert after meat, for the boys. It was all he had to offer.

At last they awoke.

"Where are we, Evroult?"

It was some moments before they realised where they were—not an uncommon thing when one awakes in the morning in a strange place.

Soon, however, they bethought themselves of the circumstances under which they stood, and rising from their couch, arranged their apparel, passed their fingers through their hair in lieu of comb, rubbed their sleepy eyes, and came into the outer cave, where the hermit crouched before the fire acting the part of cook.

He heard them, and stood up.

"*Pax vobiscum*, my children, ye look better this morning; here is your breakfast, come and eat it, and then we will talk."

"Have you no meat?" Evroult was going to say, but the natural instinct of a gentleman checked him. They had fed well at the lazar-house, but better oaten cakes and liberty.

"Oh what nice nuts," said Richard; "and blackberries, too."

The hermit's eyes sparkled as he noted the sweet smile which accompanied the words. The face of the younger boy was untouched by the leprosy. They satisfied their hunger, and then began to talk.

"Father, how long may we stay here?"

"As long as you like—God has sent you hither."

"But we want to get to Wallingford Castle."

"No! no! brother: let us stay here," said the younger and milder boy; "think how every one hates us; that terrible day yesterday—oh, it was a terrible day! they treated us as if we had been mad dogs or worse."

"Yes, we will stay, father, at least for a while, if you will let us; we are not a poor man's sons—not English, but Normans; our father is——"

"Never mind, my child—gentle or simple is all one to God, and all one here. Did your father then send you to the lazar-house?"

"Yes, three years agone."

"And has he ever sought you since?"

"No, he has never been to see us—he has forgotten us; we were there for life; we knew and felt it, and only a week ago strove to drown ourselves in the deep pond."

"That was very wrong—no one may put down the burden of the flesh, till God give him leave."

"Do you think you can cure us?"

"Life and death, sickness and health, are all in God's hands. I will try."

Their poor wan faces lit up with joy.

"And this hole in my cheek?"

"But my poor fingers, two are gone; you cannot give them me back," and Richard burst into tears.

"Come, my child, you must not cry—God loves you and will never leave nor forsake you. Every cloud has its bright side; what if you have little part in the wicked world?"

"But I *love* the world," said Evroult.

"Love the world! Do you really love fighting and bloodshed, fire and sword? for they are the chief things to be found therein just now."

"Yes I do; my father is a warrior, and so would I be," said the unblushing Evroult.

"And thou, Richard?"

"I hardly know," said he of the meeker spirit and milder mood.

"Come, ye children, and hearken unto me, and I will teach you the fear of the Lord."

"Slaves fear."

"Ah, but it is not the fear of a *slave*, but a *son* of which I speak—that fear which is the beginning of wisdom; and which, indeed, every true knight should possess if he fulfil the vows of chivalry. But I will not say more now. Wander in the woods if you like, just around the cave, or down in the valley; gather nuts or blackberries, but go not far, for fear ye meet men who may ill-treat you."

Then the hermit went forth, and threw the crumbs out of his cave; the birds came in flocks. Evroult caught up a stone.

"Nay, my child, they are *my* birds; we hurt nothing here. See! come, pet! birdie!" and a large blackbird nestled on his shoulder, and picked at a crust which the hermit took in his hand.

"They all love me, as they love all who are kind to them. Birds and beasts are alike welcome here; some wolves came in the winter, but they did me no harm."

"I should have shot them, if I had had a bow."

"Nay, my child, you must not slay my friends."

"But may we not kill rabbits or birds to eat?"

"No flesh is eaten here; we sacrifice no life of living thing to sustain our own wretched selves."

"No meat! not of any kind! not even on feast-days!"

"My boy, you will be better without it—it nourishes all sorts of bad passions, pride, cruelty, impurity, all are born of the flesh; and *see*, it is not needed. I am well and strong and never ill."

"But I should soon be," said Evroult.

"Nay, I like cakes, nuts, and blackberries better," said Richard.

"Quite right, my son; now go and play in the valley beneath, until noonday, when you may take your noon meat."

They lay in the shade of a tree. It was one of the last

days of summer, and all seemed pleasant—the murmur of the brook and the like.

"I can never bear this long," said Evroult.

"I think it very pleasant," said Richard; "do not ask me to go away."

Evroult made no reply.

"It is no use, brother," said Richard, "*no* use; we can never be knights and warriors unless we recover of our leprosy; and so the good God has given us a home and a kind friend, and it is far better than the lazar-house."

"But our father?"

"He has forsaken us, cast us off. We should never get out with his permission. No! be content, let us stay here—yesterday frightened me—we should never reach Wallingford alive."

And so Evroult gave way, and tried his best to be content—tried to learn of Meinhold, tried to do without meat, to love birds and beasts, instead of shooting them, tried to learn his catechism; yes, there was always a form of catechetical instruction for the young, taught generally *viva voce*, and the good hermit gave much time to the boys and found delight therein.

Richard consented to learn to read and write; Evroult disdained it, and would not learn.

So the year passed on; autumn deepened into winter. There was plenty of fuel about, and the boys suffered little from cold; they hung up skins and coverings over the entrances to the caves, and kept the draught out.

There was a mystery about those inner caves; the hermit would never let them enter beyond the two or three outer ones—those dark and dismal openings were, he assured them, untenanted; but their windings were such that the boys might easily lose their way therein, and never get out again—he thought there were precipitous gulfs into which they might fall.

But sometimes at night, when all things were still, the strangest sounds came from the caves, like the sobbings of living things, the plaintive sigh, the hollow groan: and the boys heard and shuddered.

"It is only the wind in the hollows of the earth," said Meinhold.

"How does it get in?" asked the boys.

"There are doubtless many crevices which we know not."

"I thought there were ghosts there."

"Nay, my child. It is only the wind: sleep in peace."

But as the winter storms grew frequent, these deep sighs and hollow groans seemed to increase, and the boys lay and shuddered, while sometimes even the hermit was fain to cross himself, and say a prayer for any poor souls who might be in unrest.

The winter was long and cold, but spring came at last. The change of air had worked wonders in the general health of the boys, but the leprosy had not gone: no, it could not really be said that there was any change for the better.

Only the poor boys were far happier than at Byfield; they entered into the ideas and ways of the hermit more and more. Evroult at last consented to learn to read, and found time pass more rapidly in consequence.

But he could not do one thing—he could not subdue those occasional bursts of passion which seemed to be rooted in the very depths of his nature. When things crossed him he often showed his fierce disposition, and terrified his brother; who, although brave enough,—how could one of such a breed be a coward,—stood in awe of the hermit, and saw things with the new light the Gospel afforded more and more each day.

One day the old hermit read to them the passage wherein it is written, "If a man smite you on one cheek, turn to him the other." Evroult could not restrain his dissent.

"If I did that I should be a coward, and my father, for one, would despise me. If *that* is the Gospel, I shall never be a real Christian, nor are there many about."

"I would, my son, that you had grace, to think differently. These be counsels of perfection, given by our Lord Himself to His disciples."

"I could not turn the other cheek to my enemy to save my life."

"Then let him smite you on the *same* one."

"I could not do that either," said Evroult more sharply.

"If you cannot, at least do not return evil for evil."

"I should if I had the power."

"My child, it is the devil in you which makes you say that."

Evroult turned red with passion, and Richard began to cry.

"Nay, my child, do not cry; that is useless. Pray for him," said the hermit.

Another time Evroult craved flesh.

"No, my son," said Meinhold, "when a man fills himself with flesh, straightway the great vices bubble out. I remember a monk who one Lent went secretly and bought some venison from a wicked gamekeeper, and put it in his wallet; when lo! as he was returning home, the dogs, smelling the flesh, fell upon him, and tore him up as well as the meat."

"Why is it wrong to eat meat? The Chaplain at Byfield told me that the Bible said it was lawful at proper times, and this is not Lent."

"It is always Lent here,—in a hermit's cell,—and it is a duty to be contented with one's food. I knew a monk who grumbled at his fare and said he would as soon eat toads; and lo! the just God did not disappoint him of his desire. For a month and more his cell was filled with toads. They got into his soup, they jumped upon his plate, they filled his bed, until I think he would have died, had not all the brethren united in prayer that he might be free from the scourge."

Evroult laughed merrily at this, and forgot his craving. In short, the old man was so loving and kind, and so transparently sincere, that he could not be angry long.

Another fault Evroult had was vanity. Once he was admiring himself in the mirror of a stream, for he really was, but for the leprosy, a handsome lad. "Ah, my child," said Meinhold, "thou art like a house which has a gay front, but the thieves have got in by the back door."

"Nay," said poor Evroult, putting his hand to his hollowed cheek, "they have broken through the front window."

"Ah, what of that; the house shall be set in order by and by, if thou art a good lad."

He meant in Heaven. But Evroult only sighed. Heaven seemed to him far off: his longings were of the earth.

And Richard : well, that supernatural influence we call "grace" had found him in very deed. He grew less and less discontented with his lot ; murmured no more about the lost fingers; scarcely noticed the fact that the others were going; but drank in all the hermit's talk about the life beyond, with the growing conviction that there alone should he regain even the perfection of the body. One effect of his touching resignation was this, that the hermit conceived so much love towards him, that he had to pray daily against idolatry, as he fancied the affection for an earthly object must needs be, and so restrained it that there was little fear of his spoiling the boy.

The hermit, who, as we have seen, was a priest, had hitherto been restrained by the canons from saying Mass alone, and had sought some rustic church for Communion. Of course he could not take the young lepers there, so he celebrated the Holy Mysteries in a third cave, fitted up as best it might be for a chapel, and the boys assisted. One would think Nature had designed this third cave for a chapel. There was a natural recess for the altar; there were fantastic pillars like those in a cathedral, only more irregular, supporting the roof, which was lofty; and stalactites, graceful as the pendants in an ice-cavern, hung from above.

They never saw other human beings, save now and then some grief-stricken soul came for spiritual advice and assistance, always given without their dwelling, with the stream between the hermit and the seeker. For leprosy was known to be in the cave, and it was commonly reported that Meinhold had paid the natural penalty of his self-devotion.

It was too true.

One day Evroult saw him looking at a red burning spot on his palm.

He recognised it and burst into tears.

"Father, you have given yourself for us: I wish the dogs had torn me before I came here."

"Christ gave Himself for me," said Meinhold quietly.

"Did you not know it, Evroult? I knew it long ago," said Richard quietly. It seemed natural to him that one who loved the Good Shepherd should give his life for the sheep. But the sweet smile with which he looked into the hermit's face was quite as touching as Evroult's tears.

The hermit was quite indifferent to the fact.

"As well this as any other way," he said; yet the affection of the boys was pleasant to him.

They lacked not for food. The people of the neighbouring farms, some distance across the forest, sent presents of milk and eggs and fruit from time to time, and of other necessaries. They had once been boldly offered: now they were set down on the other side of the stream and left.

Occasionally hunters—the neighbouring barons—broke the silence with hound and horn. They generally avoided the hermit's glen—conspicuously devoted to the peace of God; but once a poor flying stag, pursued by the hounds, came tearing down the vale. Evroult glistened with animation: he would have rushed on in the train of the huntsmen, but the hermit restrained him.

"They would bid their dogs tear you," he said, "when

they saw you were a leper." Then he continued, "Ah, my child, it is a sad sight: sin brought all this into the world,—God's creatures delighting to rend each other; so will the fiends hunt the souls of the wicked after death, until they drive them into the lake of fire."

"Ah, here comes the poor deer," said Richard, who had caught the hermit's love of all that moved. "See, he has turned: open the door, father."

The deer actually scaled the plateau, wild with terror,—its eyes glaring, the sweat bedewing its limbs; and it rushed through the opened door of the cave.

"Close the door—the dogs will be here."

The dogs came in truth, and raved about the closed door until the huntsmen came up, when the hermit emerged upon a ledge above.

"Where is our deer? hast thou seen it, father?"

"It has taken sanctuary."

They looked at each other.

"Nay, father, sanctuary is not for such creatures: drive it forth."

"God forbid! the shadow of the Cross protects it. Call off your dogs and go your way."

"Let us force the door," said a rough sportsman.

"Accursed be he who does so; his light shall be extinguished in darkness," said the hermit.

"Come, there are more deer than one;" and the knight called off his dogs with great difficulty.

"Thou hast done well: so shall it be for thy good in time of need, Sir Knight."

"I would sooner fight the deadliest fight I have ever fought than violate that sanctuary," said the latter; "a curse would be sure to follow."

When the hunters had at last taken themselves away, dogs and all, and the discontented whines and howls of the hounds and the crack of the huntsman's whip had ceased to disturb the silence of the dell, the hermit and the boys went in to look at the deer: he had thrown himself down, or fallen, panting, in the boys' bed of leaves, and turned piteous yet confiding eyes on them, large and lustrous, which seemed to implore pity, and to say, "I know you will not let them hurt me."

The better instinct of Evroult was touched.

"Well, my son," said the hermit, "dost thou still crave for flesh? Shall we kill him and roast some venison collops?"

"No," said Evroult, with energy.

"Ah, I thought so, thou art learning compassion: 'Blessed are the merciful, for they shall obtain mercy.'"

"Brother," said Richard, "let us try and get that blessing."

Evroult pressed his hand.

And when it was dark and all was quiet, they let the deer go. The poor beast, as if it had reason, almost refused to depart, and licked their hands as if it knew its protectors, as doubtless it did.

But we must close this chapter, having begun the sketch of a life which continued uneventfully for two full years.

Here ends the first part of our tale. We must leave the boys with the good hermit; Osric learning the usages of war, and other things, under the fostering care of Brian Fitz-Count; Wulfnoth as a novice at Dorchester; and so allow a period to pass ere our scattered threads reunite.

CHAPTER XV[1]

THE ESCAPE FROM OXFORD CASTLE

Two years had passed away, and it was the last week of Advent, in the year of our Lord 1141.

The whole land lay under a covering of deep snow, the frost was keen and intense, the streams were ice-bound when they could be seen, for generally snow had drifted

---

[1] The historical course of events during these two years may be briefly summed up. The English at first embraced the cause of Maude with alacrity, because of her descent from their ancient monarchs, and so did most of the barons. A dire civil war followed, in which multitudes of freebooters from abroad, under the name of "free lances," took part in either side. Hereford, Gloucester, Bristol, Oxford, Wallingford—all became centres of Maude's power; and at last, at the great battle of Lincoln—the only great battle during the miserable chaos of strife—Stephen became her prisoner.

Then she had nearly gained the crown: Henry, Bishop of Winchester, Papal legate and brother of Stephen, joined her cause, and received her as Queen at Winchester. The wife of King Stephen begged her husband's liberty on her knees, promising that he should depart from the kingdom and become a monk. But Maude was hard-hearted, and spurned her from her presence, rejecting, to her own great detriment, the prayer of the suppliant; and not only did she do this, but she also refused the petition of Henry of Winchester, that the foreign possessions of Stephen might pass to his son Eustace. In consequence, the Bishop abandoned her cause, and Maude found that she had dashed the cup of fortune from her hand by her harsh conduct, which at last became past bearing. She refused the Londoners the confirmation of their ancient charters, because they had submitted to the rule of Stephen; whereupon they rose, *en masse*, against her, and drove her from the city. She hastened to Winchester, but the Bishop followed, and drove her thence; and in the flight Robert, Earl of Gloucester was captured. He was exchanged for Stephen, both leaders were at liberty and the detestable strife began, *de novo*.

Then Maude took up her abode at Oxford, where Stephen came and besieged her, as related in the text.

and filled their channels; only the ice on the Thames, wind-swept, could be discerned.

Through the dense woods of Newenham, which overhung the river, about three miles above the Abbey Town (Abingdon), at the close of the brief winter's day, a youth might have been seen making his way (it was not made for him) through the dense undergrowth towards the bed of the stream.

He was one of Dame Nature's most favoured striplings,— tall and straight as an arrow, with a bright smile and sunny face, wherein large blue eyes glistened under dark eyebrows; his hair was dark, his features shapely, his face, however, sunburnt and weather-beaten, although he only numbered eighteen years.

Happily unseen, for in those days the probability was that every stranger was a foe to be avoided, and for such foes our young friend was not unprepared; it is true, he wore a simple woollen tunic, bound round by a girdle, but underneath was a coat of the finest chain-armour, proof against shafts, and in his hand he had a boar-spear, while a short sword was suspended in its sheath, from his belt.

Fool indeed would one have been, whether gentle or simple, to traverse that district, or indeed any other district of "Merrie" England, unarmed in the year 1141, and our Osric was not such a simple one.

He has "aged" since we last saw him. He is quite the young warrior now. The sweet simplicity, begotten of youth and seclusion, is no longer there, yet there is nought to awaken distrust. He is not yet a knight, but he is the favourite squire of Brian Fitz-Count—that terrible lord, and has been the favourite ever since Alain passed over to the immediate service of the Empress Queen.

We will not describe him further—his actions shall speak for him; and if he be degenerate, tell of his degencracy.

As he descended the hill towards the stream, a startling interruption occurred; a loud snarl, and a wolf—yes, there were wolves in England then—snapped at him: he had trodden on her lair.

Quick as thought the boar-spear was poised, and the animal slank away, rejecting the appeal to battle. For why? She knew there were plenty of corpses about unburied for her to eat, and if they were not quite so sweet as Osric's fair young flesh, they would be obtained without danger. Such was doubtless wolfish philosophy.

He passed on, not giving a second thought to an adventure which would fill the mind of a modern youth for hours—but he was hardened to adventures, and *blasé* of them. So he took them as a matter of course and as the ordinary incidents of life: it was a time of carnage, when the "survival of the fittest" was being worked out amongst our ancestors.

"Ah, here is the river at last," he said to himself, "and now I know my way: the ice will bear me safely enough, and I shall have an easier road; although I must be careful, for did I get in, I could hardly swim in this mail-shirt."

So he stopped, and taking a pair of rude skates from his wallet, bound them to his iron-clad shoes, and skated up stream—through a desolate country.

Anon the grim old castle of the Harcourts frowned down upon him from the height where their modern mansion now stands. The sentinels saw him and sent an arrow after him, but it was vain defiance—the river was beyond arrow shot, and they only sent one, because it was the usual playful habit of the day to shoot at strangers, young or old. Every man's hand was against every man.

They did not think the dimly discerned stranger, scudding up stream, worth pursuit, especially as it was getting dark, and the snow drifts were dangerous. So they let him go, not exactly with a benediction.

And soon he was opposite the village of Sandford, or rather where the village should have been; but it was burnt to the very ground—not a house or hovel was standing; not a dog barked, for there were no dogs left to bark;

nor was any living creature to be seen. Soon Iffley, another scene of desolation, was in sight; but here there were people. The old Norman Church, the same the voyager still sees, and stops to examine, was standing, and was indeed the only edifice to be seen: all else was blackened ruin, or would have been did not the snow mercifully cover it.

Here our young friend left the river, and taking off his rude skates, ascended the bank to the church by a well-trodden path, and pushed open the west door.

He gazed upon a scene to which this age happily affords no parallel. The church was full, but not of worshippers; two or three fires blazed upon the stone pavement, and the smoke, eddying upwards, made its exit through holes purposely broken in the roof for that end; around each fire sat or squatted groups of men, women, and children—hollow-eyed, famine-pinched, plague-stricken, or the like. There was hardly a face amongst them which distress had not deprived of any beauty it might once have possessed. Many a household was there—father, mother, sons and daughters, from the stripling to the babe. The altar and sanctuary were alone respected: a screen then divided them from the nave, and the gate was jealously locked, opened only each day when the parish priest, who lived in the old tower above, still faithful to his duty, went in at dawn, and said Mass; while the poor wretched creatures forgot their misery for a while, and worshipped.

Osric passed, unquestioned, through the groups,—the church was a sanctuary to all,—and at last he reached the chancel gate. A youth of his own age leant against it.

"Osric."

"Alain."

They left the church together, and sought a solitary place on the brink of the hill above.

Where the modern tourist often surveys the city from the ridge of Rose Hill, our friends gazed. The city, great even then, lay within its protecting rivers and its new walls, dominated by the huge keep of the castle of Robert d'Oyley which the reader still may see from the line, as he nears the city.

But what a different scene it looked down upon. The moon illumined its gray walls, and the fires of the besiegers shone with a lurid glare about the city and within its streets, while the white, ghostly country environed it around.

"Thou hast kept thy tryst, Osric."

"And thou thine, Alain; but thine was the hardest. How didst thou get out? by the way we agreed upon before I left Oxford?"

"It was a hard matter. The castle is beleaguered, the usurper is there, and that treacherous priest, his brother, says a sort of black Mass every day in the camp: the city is all their own, and only the castle holds out."

"And how is our lady?"

"Poor Domina,[1] as she signs herself. Ah, well, she shall not starve while there is a fragment of food in the neighbourhood, but, Oh, Osric! hunger is hard to bear; fortunate wert thou to be chosen to accompany our lord in that desperate sally a month agone which took you all safely to Wallingford. But what news dost thou bring?"

"That the great Earl of Gloucester and Henry Plantagenet have landed in England, and will await the Empress at Wallingford if she can escape from Oxford."

"I can get out myself, as thou seest, and have been able to keep our tryst, but the Empress—how can we risk her life so precious to us all? Osric, she must descend by *ropes*, and to-day my hands were so frozen by the cold that I almost let go, and should have fallen full fifty feet had I done so; but for a woman—even if, like 'Domina,' she be more than woman—it will be parlous difficult."

"It must be tried, for no more reinforcements have appeared: we are wofully disappointed."

"And so are we: day by day we have hoped to see

---

[1] Maude did not venture to call herself Queen, but signed her deeds Domina or Lady of England.

your pennons advancing over the frozen snow to our rescue. Alas! it was nought we saw, save bulrushes and sedges. Then day by day we hear the trumpets blow, and the usurper summons us to surrender, without terms, to his discretion."

"We will see him perish first," said Osric. "Hear our plans. If thou canst persuade the lady to descend from the tower, and cross the stream at the midnight after tomorrow, we will have a troop on the outskirts of Bagley wood, to escort the precious freight to Wallingford, in spite of all her foes, or we will die in her defence."

"It is well spoken; and I think I may safely say that it shall be attempted."

"And the Baron advises that ye all wear white woollen tunics like mine, as less likely to be distinguished in the snow, and withal warm."

"We have many such tunics in the castle. At midnight to-morrow the risk will be run, you may depend upon it. See, the Domina has entrusted me with her signet, that you may see that I am a sort of plenipotentiary."

"And now farewell. Canst thou find thy way through the darkness to Wallingford? Oxford is near at hand."

"Nay, I shall rest in the church to-night, and depart at dawn: I should lose my way in the snow."

"After Mass, I suppose," said Alain sarcastically.

"Yes," said Osric, blushing. He was getting ashamed of the relics of his religious observances; "but Mass and meat, you know, hinder no man. I shall be at Wallingford ere noon, and the horse will start about the dusk of the evening. God speed thee." And they parted.

The Castle of Oxford was one of the great strongholds of the Midlands. Its walls and bastions enclosed a large area, whereon stood the Church of St. George. On one side was the Mound, thrown up in far earlier days than those of which we write, by Ethelflæda, sister of Alfred, and near it the huge tower of Robert d'Oyley, which still survives, a stern and silent witness of the unquiet past.

In an upper chamber of that tower was the present apartment of the warlike lady, alike the descendant of Alfred and the Conqueror, and the unlike daughter of the sainted Queen Margaret of Scotland. And there she sat, at the time when Osric met Alain at Iffley Church, impatiently awaiting the return of her favourite squire, for such was Alain, whose youthful comeliness and gallant bearing had won her heart.

"He tarries long: he cometh not," she said. "Tell me, my Edith, how long has he been gone?"

"Scarce three hours, madam, and he has many dangers to encounter. Perchance he may never return."

"Now the Saints confound thy boding tongue."

"Madam!"

"Why, forsooth, should he be unfortunate? so active, so brave, so sharp of wit."

"I only meant that he is mortal."

"So are we all—but dost thou, therefore, expect to die to-day?"

"Father Herluin says we all should live as if we did, madam."

"You will wear my life out. Well, yes, a convent will be the best place for thee."

"Nay, madam."

"Hold thy peace, if thou canst say nought but 'nay,'" said the irascible Domina.

Her temper, her irritability and impatience, had alienated many from her cause. Perchance it would have alienated Alain like the rest, only he was a favourite, and she was seldom sharp with him.

How like her father she was in her bearing! even in her undress, for she wore only a thick woollen robe, stained, by the art of the dyers, in colours as various as those of the robe Jacob made for Joseph. Sometimes it flew open, and displayed an inner vesture of rich texture, bound round with a golden zone or girdle; and around her head, confining her luxuriant hair, was a circlet of like precious metal, which did duty for a diadem.

Little of her sainted mother was there in the Empress Queen; far more of her stern grandfather, the Conqueror.

The chamber, of irregular dimensions, was lighted by narrow loopholes. There was a hearth and a chimney, and a brazier of wood and charcoal burned brightly. Even then the air was cold, for it was many degrees below the freezing point, not that they as yet knew how to measure the temperature.

She sat and glowered at the grate, as the light departed, and the winter night set in, dark and gloomy. More than once she approached the windows, or loopholes, and looked upon the ruined city in the chill and intermittent moonlight.

It was nearly *all* in ruins. Here and there a church tower rose intact; here and there a lordly dwelling; but fire and sword had swept it. Neither party regarded the sufferings of the poor. Sometimes the besiegers made a fire in sport, and warmed themselves by the blaze of a burgher's dwelling, nor recked how far it spread. Sometimes, as we have said, the besieged made a sally, and set fire to the buildings which sheltered their foes. Whichever prevailed, the citizens suffered; but little recked their oppressors.

From her elevated chamber Maude could see the watchfires of the foe in a wide circle around, but she was accustomed to the sight, tired of it, in fact, and her one desire was to escape to Wallingford, a far more commodious and stronger castle.

In Frideswide, of which she could discern the towers, which as yet had escaped the conflagration, were the headquarters of her rival, who was living there at ease on the fat of the land, such fat as was left, at the expense of the monastic community. And while she gazed, she clenched her dainty fist, and shook it at the unheeding Stephen, while she muttered unwomanly imprecations.

And while she was thus engaged, they brought up her supper. It consisted of a stew of bones, which had already been well stripped of their flesh at "the noon-meat."

"We are reduced to bones, and shall soon be nought but bones ourselves; but our gallant defenders, I fear, fare worse. Here, Edith, Hilda, bring your spoons and take your share."

And with small wooden spoons they dipped into the royal dish.

A step on the stairs and the chamberlain knocked, and at her bidding entered. "Lady, the gallant page has returned: how he entered I know not."

"He is unharmed?"

"Scatheless, by the favour of God and St. Martin."

"Let him enter at once."

And Alain appeared.

"My gallant squire, how hast thou fared? I feared for thee."

"They keep bad watch. A rope lowered me to the stream: I crossed, and seeking covered ways, gat me to Iffley, and in like fashion returned. I bear good news, lady! Thy gallant brother of Gloucester, and the Prince, thy son, have landed in England, and will meet thee at Wallingford."

"Thank God!" said Maude. "My Henry, my royal boy, I shall see thee again. With such hope to cheer a mother's heart, I can dare anything. Well hast thou earned our thanks, my Alain, my gallant squire."

"The Lord of Wallingford will send a troop of horse to scout on the road between Abingdon and Oxford to-morrow night, the Eve of St. Thomas."

"We will meet them if it be possible—if it be in human power."

"The river is free—all other roads are blocked."

"But hast thou considered the difficulties of descent?"

"They are great, lady: it was easy for me to descend by the rope, but for thee, alas, that my queen should need such expedients!"

"It is better than starvation. We are reduced to the bones, as thou seest; but thou art hungry and faint. Let me order a basin of this *savoury* stew for thee; it is all we have to offer."

"What is good enough for my Empress and Queen, is good enough for her faithful servants; but I may not eat in thy presence."

"Nay, scruple not; famine effaces distinctions."

Thus encouraged, Alain did not allow his scruples to interfere further with his appetite, and partook heartily of the stew of bones, in which, forsooth, the water and meal were in undue proportion to the meat.

The meal despatched, the Empress sent Alain to summon the Earl of Oxford, Robert d'Oyley, to her presence. He was informed of the arrival of the Earl and the Prince, and the plan of escape was discussed.

All the ordinary avenues of the castle were watched so closely that extraordinary expedients were necessary, and the only feasible mode of escape appeared to be the difficult road which Alain had used successfully, both in leaving and returning to the beleaguered fortress.

A branch of the Isis washed the walls of the tower. It was frozen hard. To descend by ropes upon it in the darkness, and cross to the opposite side of the stream, appeared the only mode of egress.

But for a lady—the Lady of England—was it possible? was it not utterly unworthy of her dignity?

She put this objection aside like a cobweb.

"Canst thou hold out the castle much longer?"

"At the most, another week; our provisions are nearly exhausted. This was our last meal of flesh, of which I see the bones before me," replied the Lord of Oxford.

"Then if I remain, thou must still surrender?"

"Surrender is *inevitable*, lady."

"Then sooner would I infringe my dignity by dangling from a rope, than become the prisoner of the foul usurper Stephen, and the laughing-stock of his traitorous barons."

"Sir Ingelric of Huntercombe, and two other knights, besides thy gallant page, volunteer to accompany thee, lady."

THE ESCAPE FROM OXFORD CASTLE 127

"And for thyself?"

"I must remain to the last, and share the fortunes of my vassals. Without me, they would find scant mercy from the usurpers."

"Then, to-morrow night, ere the moon rise, the attempt shall be made."

And the conference broke up.

It was a night of wildering snow, dark and gloomy. The soft, dry, powdery material found its way in at each crevice, and the wind made the tapestry, which hung on the walls of the presence chamber of the "Lady Maude," oscillate to and fro with each blast.

Robert d'Oyley was alone in deep consultation with his royal mistress.

"Then if I can escape, thou wilt surrender?"

"Nought else is to be done; we are starving."

"They will burn the castle."

"There is little to burn, and I hardly think they will attempt that: it will be useful to them, when in their hands."

"It is near the midnight hour: the attempt must be made. Now summon young Alain and my faithful knights."

They entered at the summons, each clothed in fine mail, with a white tunic above it. The Empress bid adieu to her handmaidens, who had clad her in a thick white cloak to match: they wept and wailed, but she gently chid them—

"We have suffered worse things: the coffin and hearse in which we left Devizes was more ghastly; and God will give an end to these troubles also: fear not, we are prepared to go through with it."

A small door was opened in the thickness of the wall; it led to the roof, over a lower portion of the buildings beneath the shadow of the tower; and the knights, with Alain and their lady, stood on the snow-covered summit.

Not long did they hesitate. The river beneath was frozen hard; it lay silent and still in its ice-bound sepulchre. The darkness was penetrated by the light of the watch-fires in all directions: they surrounded the town on all sides, save the one they had not thought it necessary to guard against. There was a fire and doubtless a watch over the bridge, which stood near the actual site of the present Folly Bridge. There was a watch across Hythe Bridge; there was another on the ruins of the castle mill, which Earl Algar had held, under the Domesday survey; another at the principal entrance of the castle, which led from the city. But the extreme cold of the night had driven the majority of the besiegers to seek shelter in the half-ruined churches, which, long attuned to the sweet melody of bells and psalmody, had now become the bivouacs of profane soldiers.

The Countess Edith, the wife of Robert d'Oyley, now appeared, shivering in the keen air, and took an affectionate leave of the Empress, while her teeth chattered the while. A true woman, she shared her husband's fortunes for weal or woe, and had endured the horrors of the siege. Ropes were brought—Alain glided down one to the ice, and held it firm. Another rope was passed beneath the armpits of the Lady Maude. She grasped another in her gloved hand, to steady her descent.

"Farewell, true and trusty friend," she said to Robert of Oxford; "had all been as faithful as thou, I had never been brought to this pass; if they hurt thy head, they shall pay with a life for every hair it contains."

Then she stepped over the battlements.

For one moment she gave a womanly shudder at the sight of the blackness below; then yielding herself to the care of her trusty knights and shutting her eyes, she was lowered safely to the surface of the frozen stream, while young Alain steadied the rope below. At last her feet touched the ice.

"Am I on the ground?"

"On the ice, Domina."

One after another the three knights followed her, and they descended the stream until it joined the main river at a farm called "The Wick," which formerly belonged to one Ermenold, a citizen of Oxford, immortalised in the abbey records of Abingdon for his munificence to that community.

Now they had crossed the main channel in safety, not far below the present railway bridge, and landing, struck out boldly for the outskirts of Bagley, where the promised escort was to have met them. But in the darkness and the snow, they lost their direction, and came at last over the frozen fields to Kennington, where they indistinctly saw two or three lights through the fast-falling snow, but dared not approach them, fearing foes.

Vainly they strove to recover the track. The country was all alike—all buried beneath one ghastly winding-sheet. The snow still fell; the air was calm and keen; the breath froze on the mufflers of the lady. Onward they trudged, for to hesitate was death; once or twice that ghastly inclination to lie down and sleep was felt.

"If I could only lie down for one half hour!" said Maude.

"You would never wake again, lady," said Bertram of Wallingford; "we *must* move on."

"Nay, I must sleep."

"For thy son's sake," whispered Alain; and she persevered.

"Ah! here is the river; take care."

They had nearly fallen into a diversion of the stream at Sandford; but they followed the course of the river, until they reached Radley, and then they heard the distant bell of the famous abbey ringing for Matins, which were said in the small hours of the night.

Here they found some kind of track made by the passage of cattle, which had been driven towards the town, and followed it until they saw the lights of the abbey dimly through the gloom.

Spent, exhausted with their toil, they entered the precincts of the monastery, on the bed of the stream which, diverging from the main course a mile above the town, turned the abbey mills and formed one of its boundaries. Thus they avoided detention at the gateway of the town, for they ascended from the stream within the monastery "pleasaunce."

The grand church loomed out of the darkness; its windows were dimly lighted. The Matins of St. Thomas were being sung, and the solemn strains reached the ears of the weary travellers outside. The outer door of the nave was unfastened, for the benefit of the laity, who cared more for devotion than their beds, like the mother of the famous St. Edmund, Archbishop of Canterbury, a century later, who used to attend these Matins nightly.

Our present party entered from a different motive. It was a welcome shelter, and they sank upon an oaken bench within the door, while the solemn sound of the Gregorian psalmody rolled on in the choir. Alain meanwhile hastened to the hospitium to seek aid for the royal guest; which he was told he would find in a hostel outside the gates, for although they allowed female attendance at worship, they could not entertain women; it was contrary to their rule —royal although the guest might be.

CHAPTER XVI

AFTER THE ESCAPE

MEANWHILE Brian Fitz-Count himself, with Osric by his side and a dozen horsemen, rode to and fro on the road to Oxford, which passed through the forest of Bagley; for to halt in the cold was impossible, and to kindle a fire might attract the attention of foes, as well as of friends. How they bore that weary night may not be told, but they were more accustomed to such exposure than we are in these days.

Again and again did Brian question Osric concerning the interview with Alain, but of course to no further purpose; and they might have remained till daylight had not they taken a shepherd, who was out to look after his sheep, and brought him before the Count, pale and trembling, for it was often death to the rustics to be seized by the armed bands.

"Hast thou seen any travellers this night?"

"I have, my lord, but they were not of this earth."

"What then, fool?"

"They were the ghosts of the slain, five of them, all in white, coming up from the river, where the fight was a month agone."

"And what didst thou do?"

"Hid myself."

"Where were they going?"

"Towards Abingdon."

"Men or women?"

"One was muffled up like a lady; the others were like men, but all in white."

"My lord," interrupted Osric, "I bore thy recommendation that they should wear white garments, the better to escape observation in the snow, and Alain promised me that such precaution should be taken: no doubt the shepherd has seen them."

"Which way were the ghosts going, shepherd?"

"They were standing together, when all at once the boom of the abbey bell came through the air from Abingdon, and then they made towards the town, to seek their graves, for there many of the slain were buried."

"*Requiescant in pace*," said Osric.

"Peace, Osric; do not you know that if you pray for a living man or woman as if they were dead, you hasten their demise?" said Brian sarcastically. "Let the old fool go, and we will wend our weary way to the abbey. They give sanctuary to either party."

The snow ceased to fall about this time, and a long line of vivid red appeared low down in the east: the snow caught the tinge of the coming day, and was reddened like blood.

"One would think there had been a mighty battle there, my squire."

"It reminds me of the field of Armageddon, of which I heard the Chaplain talk. I wonder whether it will come soon."

"Dost thou believe in all those priestly pratings?"

"My grandfather taught me to do so."

"And the rough life of a castle has not yet made thee forget his homilies?"

"No," sighed Osric.

The sigh touched the hardened man.

"If he has faith, why should I destroy it?" Then he added as if almost against his will—

"Keep thy faith; I would I shared it."

The fortifications of the town, the castle on the Oxford road, the gateway hard by, came in sight at the next turn of the road, but Brian avoided them, and sought a gate lower down which admitted to the abbey precincts, where he was not so likely to be asked inconvenient questions.

He bade one of his men ring the bell.

The porter looked forth.

"What manner of men are ye?"

"Travellers lost in the snow come to seek the hospitality prescribed by the rule of St. Benedict."

"Enter," and the portal yawned: no names were asked, no political distinctions recognised.

They stood in the outer quadrangle of the hoar abbey, the stronghold of Christianity in Wessex for five centuries past; and well had it performed its task, and well had it deserved of England. Founded so long ago that its origin was even then lost in conflicting traditions, surviving wave after wave of war, burnt by the Danes, remodelled by the Normans—yet this hoary island of prayer stood in the stream of time unchanged in all its main features, and, as men thought, destined to stand till the archangel's trump sounded the knell of time.

> "They built in marble, built as they
> Who thought these stones should see the day
> When Christ should come ; and that these walls
> Should stand o'er them when judgment calls."

Alas, poor monks, and alas for the country which lost the most glorious of her architectural riches, the most august of her fanes, through the greed of one generation!

"Have any other travellers sought shelter here during the night?"

"Five—a lady and four knights."

"Where be they?"

"The lady is lodged in a house without the eastern gate; the others are in the guest-house, where thou mayst join them."

Have my readers ever seen the outer quadrangle of Magdalene College? It is not unlike the square of buildings in which the Baron and his followers now stood. On three sides the monastic buildings, with cloisters looking upon a green sward, wherein a frozen fountain was surmounted by a cross; on the other, the noble church, of which almost all trace is lost.

In the hospitium or guest-house Brian found Sir Ingelric of Huntercombe, with Alain and the other attendants upon the lady's flight. They met with joy, and seated before a bright fire which burned upon the hearth, learned the story of each other's adventures on that gruesome night, which, however, had ended well. Osric had gone in charge of the horses to some stables outside the gates, which opened upon the market-place, but he now returned, and Alain greeted him warmly.

Soon the *déjeûner* or breakfast was served, of which the chief feature was good warm soup, very acceptable after the night they had passed through. Scarcely was it over when the bells rang for the High Mass of St. Thomas's Day.

"Yes, we must all go," said Brian, "out of compliment to our hosts, if for no better reason."

They entered the church, of which the nave and transepts were open to the general public, while the choir, as large as that of a cathedral church, was reserved for the monks alone. The service was grand and solemn: it began with a procession, during which holy water was sprinkled over the congregation, while the monks sang—

"Asperges me hyssopo et mundabor,
Lava me, et super nivem dealbabor."

Then followed the chanted Mass at the High Altar. There were gleaming lights, gorgeous vestments, clouds of incense. All the symbolism of an age when the worship of the English people was richer in ceremonial than that of Continental nations was there. It impressed the minds of rude warriors who could neither read nor write with the sense of a mysterious world, other than their own—of dread realities and awful powers beyond the reach of mortal warfare. If it appealed rather to the imagination than the reason, yet it may be thought, it thereby reached its mark the more surely. The Church was still the salt of the earth, which preserved the whole mass from utter corruption, and in a world of violence and wrong, pointed to a land of peace and joy beyond this transitory scene.

So felt Osric, and his eyes filled with tears as emotions he could hardly analyse stirred his inmost soul.

And Brian—well, he was as a man who views his natural face in a glass, and going away, forgets what manner of man he was.

After Mass the Empress Maude greeted her dear friend and faithful follower Brian Fitz-Count with no stinted welcome. She almost fell upon his shoulder, proud woman though she was, and wept, when assured she should soon see her son, Prince Henry, at Wallingford, for she was but a woman after all.

She insisted upon an interview with the Abbot, from which Brian would fain have dissuaded her, but she took the bit in her teeth.

After a while that dignitary came, and bowed gracefully, but not low.

"Dost thou know, lord Abbot, whom thou hast entertained?"

"Perchance an Angel unawares: all mortals are equal within the Church's gate."

"Thy true Queen, who will not forget thy hospitality."

"Nor would King Stephen, did he know that we had shown it, lady. I reverence thy lofty birth, and wish thee well for the sake of thy father, who was a great benefactor to this poor house: further I cannot say; we know nought of earthly politics here—our citizenship is above."

She did not appreciate his doctrines, but turned to Brian.

"Have we any gold to leave as a benefaction in return for this hospitality; it will purchase a Mass, which, doubtless, we need in these slippery times, when it is difficult always to walk straight."

Brian drew forth his purse.

"Lady, it needs not," said the Abbot; "thou art welcome, so are all the unfortunate, rich or poor, who suffer in these cruel wars, to which may God soon give an end."

"Lay the blame, lord Abbot, on the usurper then, and pray for his overthrow; but for him I should have ruled as my father did, with justice and equity. If thou wishest for peace, pray for our speedy restoration to our rightful throne. Farewell."

So the Empress and her train departed, and crossing the river at Culham, made for the distant hills of Synodune, across a country where the snow had obliterated nearly all the roads, and even covered the hedges and fences. So that they were forced to travel very slowly, and at times came to a "standstill."

However, they surmounted all difficulties; and travelling along the crest of the hills, where the wind had prevented the accumulation of much snow, they reached Wallingford in safety, amidst the loudest of loud rejoicings, where they were welcomed by Maude d'Oyley, Lady of Wallingford—the sister of the Lord of Oxford and wife of Brian.

How shall we relate the festivities of that night? it seems like telling an old tale: how the tables groaned with the weight of the feast, as in the old ballad of Imogene; how the minstrels and singers followed after, and none recked of the multitude of captives who already crowded the dismal dungeons beneath. Some prisoners taken in fair fight, some with less justice prisoners held to ransom, their sole crime being wealth; others from default of tribute paid to Brian, be it from ill-will or only from want of means.

But of these poor creatures the gay feasters above thought not. The contrast between the awful vaults and cells below, and the gay and lighted chambers above, was cruel, but they above recked as little as the giddy children who play in a churchyard think of the dead beneath their feet.

"My lady," said Brian, "we shall keep our Christmas yet more merrily, for on the Eve we hope to welcome thy right trusty brother of Gloucester and thy gallant son."

The mother's eyes sparkled.

"My good and trusty subject," she said, "how thou dost place me under obligations beyond my power to repay?"

"Nay, my queen, all I have is thine, for thy own and thy royal father's sake, who was to me a father indeed."

The festivities were not prolonged to a very late hour; nature must have its way, and the previous night had been a most trying one, as our readers are well aware. That night was a night of deep repose.

On the following day came the news that Oxford Castle had surrendered, and that Robert d'Oyley, lord thereof, was prisoner to Stephen; it was at first supposed that the king would follow his rival to Wallingford, but he preferred keeping his Christmas in the castle he had taken. Wallingford was a hard nut to crack.

It was Christmas Eve, and the Empress stood by the side of the lord of the castle, on the watch-towers; the two squires, Alain and Osric, waited reverently behind.

The scenery around has already been described in our opening chapter. The veil of winter was over it, but the sun shone brightly, and its beams glittered on the ice of the river and the snow-clad country beyond: one only change there was—the forts on the Crowmarsh side of the stream, erected in a close of the parish of Crowmarsh—then and now called Barbican; they were so strong as to be deemed impregnable, and were now held against Brian by the redoubtable Ranulph, Earl of Chester. The garrisons of the two fortresses, so near each other, preyed in turn on the country around, and fought wherever they met—to keep their hands in; but they were now keeping "The Truce of God," in honour of Christmas.

"It is a lovely day. May it be the harbinger of better

fortune," said Maude. "When do you think they will arrive?"

"They slept at Reading Abbey last night, so there is little doubt they will be here very soon."

"If they started early they might be in sight now: ah, God and St. Mary be praised! there they be. Is not that their troop along the road?"

A band, with streamlets gay and pennons fair, was indeed approaching the gates of the town from the south, by the road which led from Reading, along the southern bank of the Thames.

"To horse! to horse!" said the Empress; "let us fly to meet them."

"Nay, my liege, they will be here anon—almost before our horses could be caparisoned to appear in fit state before the citizens of my town." The fact was, Brian had a soldier's dislike of a scene, and would fain get the meeting over within the walls.

And the royal mother contented herself with standing on the steps of the great hall to receive her gallant son, Henry Plantagenet, the future King of England, destined to restore peace to the troubled land, but whose sun was to set in such dark clouds, owing to his quarrel with the Church, and the cruel misbehaviour of his faithless wife and rebellious sons.

But we must not anticipate. The gallant boy was at hand, and his mother clasped him to the maternal breast: "so greatly comforted," said the chronicler, "that she forgot all the troubles and mortifications she had endured, for the joy she had of his presence." Then she turned to her right trusty brother, and wept on his neck.

The following day was the birthday of the "Prince of Peace," and these children of war kept it in right honour. They attended Mass at the Church of St. Mary's in the town in great state, and afterwards banqueted in the Castle hall with multitudes of guests. Meanwhile Ranulph, Earl of Chester, had returned home to keep the feast; but his representatives kept it right well, and the two parties actually sent presents to each other, and wished mutual good cheer.

The feast was over, and the maskers dropped their masks, and turned to the business of life in right earnest—that was war, only war. The Empress Maude, with her son, under the care of her brother, shortly left Wallingford for Bristol, where the young prince remained for four years, under the care of his uncle, who had brought him up.

But all around the flames of war broke out anew, and universal bloodshed returned. It was a mere gory chaos: no great battles, no decisive blows; only castle against castle, all through the land, as at Wallingford and Crowmarsh. Each baron delved the soil for his dungeons, and raised his stern towers to heaven. All was pillage and plunder; men fought wherever they met; every man's hand was against every man; peaceful villages were burnt daily; lone huts, isolated farms, were no safer; merchants scarcely dared to travel, shops to expose their wares; men refused to till the fields for others to reap; and they said that God and His Saints were fast asleep. The land was filled with death; corpses rotted by the sides of the roads; women and children took sanctuary in the churches and churchyards, to which they removed their valuables. But the bands of brigands and murderers, who, like vultures, scented the quarry afar, and crowded from all parts of the Continent into England—unhappy England—as to a prey delivered over into their hands, did not always respect sanctuary. Famine followed; men had nought to eat; it was even said that they ate the bodies of the dead like cannibals. Let us hope this ghastly detail is untrue, but we do not feel *sure* it is; the pangs of hunger are so dreadful to bear.

Then came pestilence in the train of famine, and claimed its share of victims. And so the weary years went on— twelve long years of misery and woe.

Summer had come—hot and dry. There had been no rain for a month. It was the beginning of July, in the year 1142. Fighting was going on in England in general; at Wilton, near Salisbury, in particular. The king was there: he had turned the nunnery of that place into a castle, driving out the holy sisters, and all the flock of the wounded and poor to whom, with earnest piety, they were ministering. The king put up bulwark and battlement, and thought he had done well, when on the 1st of July came Robert of Gloucester from Bristol, and sat down before the place to destroy it.

The king and his brother—the Papal legate, the fighting Bishop of Winchester, the turncoat—were both there, and after a desperate defence, were forced to escape by a secret passage, and fly by night. Their faithful seneschal, William Martel, Lord of Shirburne, and a great enemy and local rival of Brian, remained behind to protract the defence, and engage the attention of the besiegers until his king had had time to get far enough away with his affectionate brother Henry; and his self-devotion was not in vain, but he paid for it by the loss of his own liberty. He was taken prisoner after a valiant struggle, and sent to Wallingford, to be under the custody of Brian Fitz-Count, his enemy and rival.

CHAPTER XVII

LIFE AT WALLINGFORD CASTLE

IN sketching the life of a mediæval castle, we have dwelt too much upon the brighter side of the picture. There was a darker one, contrasting with the outward pomp and circumstance as the dungeons with the gay halls above.

What then was the interior of those dark towers, which we contemplate only in their ruined state? Too often, the surrounding peasants looked at them with affright: the story of Blue-Beard is not a mere tale, it is rather a veritable tradition: what was the lord to his vassals, whom his own wife regarded with such great fear? We know one of the brood by the civil process issued against him—Gilles de Retz—the torturer of children. It has been said that the "Front de Boeuf" of Sir Walter Scott is but a poor creature, a feeble specimen of what mediæval barons could be. A more terrible portrait has been given in recent days by Erckmann-Chatrian, in their story, *The Forest House.*

And such, we regret to say, by degrees did Brian Fitz-Count become. Few men can stand the test of absolute power, and the power of a mediæval lord was almost absolute in his own domain.

And the outbreak of civil war, by loosening the bonds of society, gave him the power of doing this, so that it was soon said that Wallingford Castle was little better than a den of brigands.

The very construction of these old castles, so far as one can see them, tells us far more than books can: men-at-arms, pages, valets, all were shut in for the night, sleeping in common in those vaulted apartments. The day summoned them to the watch-towers and battlements, where they resembled the eagle or hawk, soaring aloft in hope of seeing their natural prey.

Nor was it often long before some convoy of merchandise passing along the high road, some well appointed travellers or the like, tempted them forth on their swift horses, lance in hand, to cry like the modern robber, "Your money or your life," or in sober truth, to drag their prisoners to their dungeons, and hold them to ransom, in default of which they amused themselves by torturing them.

Such inmates of the castles were only happy when they got out upon their adventures—and as in the old fable of "The Frogs and the Boys,"—what was sport to them was death to their neighbours.

It was eventide, the work of the day was over, and Brian was taking counsel with Malebouche, who had risen by degrees to high command amongst the troopers, although unknighted. Osric was present, and sat in an embrasure of the window.

"A good day's work, Malebouche," said Brian; "that convoy of merchandise going from Reading to Abingdon was a good prize—our halls will be the better for their gauds, new hangings of tapestry, silks, and the like; but as we are deficient in women to admire them, I would sooner have had their value in gold."

"There is this bag of rose nobles, which we took from the body of the chief merchant."

"Well, it will serve as an example to others, who travel by by-roads to avoid paying me tribute, and rob me of my dues. Merchants from Reading have tried to get to Abingdon by that road over Cholsey Hill before."

"They will hardly try again if they hear of this."

"At least these will not—you have been too prompt with them; did any escape?"

"I think not; my fellows lanced them as they fled, which was the fate of all, as we were well mounted, save a lad who stumbled and fell, and they hung him in sport for the sake of variety. They laughed till the tears stood in their eyes at his quaint grimaces."[1]

Brian did not seem to heed this pleasant story. Osric moved uneasily in his seat, but strove to repress feelings which, after all, were less troublesome than of yore; all at once he spied a sight which drove merchants and all from his mind.

"My lord, here is Alain."

"Where?"

"Just dismounting in the courtyard."

"Call to him to come up at once; he will have news from Wilton."

Osric leant out of the narrow window, which in summer was always open.

"Alain! Alain!" he cried, "come up hither, my lord is impatient for your tidings."

Alain waved back a friendly greeting and hurried up the stairs.

"Joy, my Lord, joy; thine enemy is in thy hands."

"Which one, my squire? I have too many enemies to remember all."

"William Martel, Lord of Shirburne."

"Ah, now we shall get Shirburne!" cried Osric.

"Silence, boys!" roared Brian; "now tell me all: where he was taken, and what has become of him."

"He was taken by Earl Robert at Wilton, and will be here in an hour; you may see him from the battlements now. The good Earl has sent him to you to keep in durance, and sent me to command the escort: I only left them on the downs—they are descending the hills even now; I galloped forward to 'bring the good news.'"

---

[1] Rien de plus gai que nos vieux contes—ils n'ont que trois plaisanteries—le desespoir du mari, les cris du battu, la grimace du pendu : au troisieme la gaiete est au comble, on se tient les cotés.—*Michelet.*

"By our Lady, I am indeed happy. Alain, here is a purse of rose nobles for thee; poor as I am, thy news are all too good. Send the gaolers to me; have a good dark dungeon prepared; we must humble his spirits."

"We are getting too full below, my lord."

"Orders are given for another set to be dug out at once, the architect only left me to-day; it is to be called Cloere Brien—or Brian's Close, and the first guest shall be William Martel; there shall he rot till he deliver up Shirburne and all its lands to me in perpetuity. The Castle of Shirburne is one of the keys of the Chilterns."

"Now, my lord, they are in sight—look!

And from the windows they saw a troop of horse approaching Wallingford, over Cholsey Common.

"Let us don our robes of state to meet them," said Brian; and he threw on a mantle over his undress; then he descended, followed by his two pages, and paced the battlements, till the trumpets were blown which announced the arrival of the cortege.

Brian showed no womanly curiosity to feast his eyes with the sight of a captive he was known to hate, but repaired to the steps of the great hall, and stood there, Alain on one side, Osric on the other; and soon the leading folk in the castle collected about them.

The troop of horse trotted over the three drawbridges, and drew rein in front of the Baron; then wheeling to right and left, disclosed their prisoner.

"I salute thee, William Martel, Lord of Shirburne; my poor castle is too much honoured by thy presence."

"Faith, thou mayst well say so," said the equally proud and fierce captive. "I take it thou hast had few prisoners before higher in rank than the wretched Jews you torture for their gold; but I trust you know how to treat a noble."

"That indeed we do, especially one like thyself; not that we are overawed by thy grandeur; the castle which has entertained thy rightful sovereign may be quite good enough for thee. Companions thou shalt have, if but the toad and adder; light enough to make darkness visible, until such time as thy ransom be paid, or thou submit to thy true Queen."

"To Henry's unworthy child—never. Name thy ransom."

"The Castle of Shirburne and all things pertaining thereto."

"Never shall it be thine."

"Then here shalt thou rot. Tustain, prepare a chamber—one of the dungeons in the north tower, until a more suitable one be builded. And meanwhile it may please thee to learn that we purpose a ride to look at your Shirburne folk, and see the lands which shall be ours; this very night we may light a bonfire or two to amuse them."

And they led the captive away.

Now lest this should be thought a gross exaggeration, it may as well be said that the ungovernable savagery of this contest, the violent animosities engendered, did lead the nobility so called, the very chief of the land, to forget their chivalry, and treat their foes, not after the fashion of the Black Prince and his captive, the King of France, but in the brutal fashion we have described.

And probably Brian would have fared just as badly at William Martel's hands, had their positions been reversed.

"Trumpeter, blow the signal to horse; let the Brabanters prepare to ride, and the Black Troopers of Ardennes—the last comers. We will ride to-night, Alain. Art thou too wearied to go with us?"

"Nay, my lord, ready and willing."

"And Osric—it will refresh thee; we start in half an hour—give the horses corn."

In half an hour they all rode over a new bridge of boats lower down the stream, and close under the ordnance of the castle,[1] for the forts at Crowmarsh commanded the lower Bridge of Stone. They were full three hundred in number—very miscellaneous in composition. There was a new troop of a hundred Brabanters; another of so-called Free

[1] *i.e.* Mangonels, arbalasts, and the like.

Companions, numbering nearly the same. Scarce a hundred were Englishmen, in any sense of the word, neither Anglo-Norman nor Anglo-Saxon—foreigners with no more disposition to pity the unfortunate natives than the buccaneers of later date had to pity the Spaniards, or even the shark to pity the shrinking flesh he snaps at.

Just before reaching Bensington, which paid tribute to both sides, and was exempt from fire and sword from either Wallingford or Crowmarsh, a troop from the latter place came in sight.

Trumpets were blown on both sides, stragglers recalled into line, and the two bodies of horsemen charged each other with all the glee of two bodies of football players in modern times, and with little more thought or care.

But the Wallingford men were strongest, and after a brief struggle the Crowmarsh troopers were forced to fly. They were not pursued: Brian had other business in hand; it was a mere friendly charge.

Only struggling on the ground were some fifty men and horses, wounded or dying, and not a few dead.

Brian looked after Osric with anxiety.

The youth's bright face was flushed with delight and animation. He was returning a reddened sword to the scabbard; he had brought down his man, cleaving him to the chine, himself unhurt.

Brian smiled grimly.

"Now for Alain," he said; "ah, there he is pursuing these Crowmarsh fellows. We have no time to waste—sound the recall, now onward, for the Chilterns."

Alain rejoined them.

"Thou art wasting time."

"My foe fled; Osric has beaten me to-day."

"Plenty of opportunity for redressing the wrong—now onward."

They passed through Bensington. The gates—for every large village had its walls and gates as a matter of necessity —opened and shut for them in grim silence; they did no harm there. They passed by the wood afterwards called "Rumbold's Copse," and then got into the territory of Shirburne, for so far as Britwell did William Martel exact tribute, and offer such protection as he was able.

From this period all was havoc and destruction—all one grim scene of fire and carnage. They fired every rick, every barn, every house; they slew everything they met.

And Osric was as bad as the rest—we do not wonder at Alain.

Then they reached Watlington, "the wattled town," situated in a hollow of the hills. Its gates were secured, and it was surrounded by a ditch, a mound, and the old British defence of wattles, or stakes pointed outwards.

Here they paused.

"It is too strong to be taken by assault," said the Baron. "Osric, go to the gate with just half a dozen, who have English tongues in their heads, and ask for shelter and hospitality."

Osric, to his credit, hesitated.

Brian reddened—he could not bear the lad he loved to take a more moral tone than himself.

"Must I send Alain?"

Osric went, and feigning to be belated, asked admittance, but he did not act it well.

"Who are you? whence do ye come? what mean the fires we see?"

"Alain, go and help him; he cannot tell a fair lie," said Brian.

Alain arriving, made answer, "The men of Wallingford are out—we are flying from Britwell for our lives—haste or they will overtake us—we are only a score."

The poor fools opened, and were knocked on the head at once for their pains.

The whole band now galloped up and rushed in.

"Fire every house. After you have plundered them all, if you find mayor and burgesses, take them for ransom; slay the rest."

The scene which followed was shocking; but in this wretched reign it might be witnessed again and again all over England. But many things shocked Osric afterwards when he had time to think.

Enough of this. We have only told what we have told because it is essential to the plot of our story, that the scenes should be understood which caused so powerful a reaction in Osric—*afterwards*.

Laden with spoil, with shout and song, the marauders returned from their raid. Along the road which leads from Watlington to the south, with the range of the Chilterns looking down from the east, and the high land which runs from Rumbold's Copse to Brightwell Salome on the west, they drove their cattle and carried their plunder; whilst they recounted their murderous exploits, and made night hideous with the defiant bray of trumpets and their discordant songs.

And so in the fire and excitement of the moment the sufferings of the poor natives were easily forgotten, or served to the more violent and cruel as zest to their enjoyment.

Was it so with our Osric? Could the grandson of Sexwulf, the heir of a line of true Englishmen, so forget the lessons of his boyhood? Alas, my reader, such possibilities lurk in our fallen nature!

> "Ah, when shall come the time
> When war shall be no more?
> When lust, oppression, crime,
> Shall flee Thy Face before?"

We must wait until the advent of the Prince of Peace.

They got back to Wallingford at last. The gates were opened, there was a scene of howling excitement, and then they feasted and drank until the small hours of the night; after which they went to bed, three or four in one small chamber, and upon couches of the hardest—in recesses of the wall, or sometimes placed, like the berths of a ship, one over the other—the robbers slept.

For in what respect were they better than modern highwaymen or pirates?

Osric and Alain lay in the same chamber.

"How hast thou enjoyed the day, Osric?"

"Capitally, but I am worn out."

"You will not sleep so soundly even now as the fellow you brought down so deftly in that first skirmish. You have got your hand in at last."

Osric smiled with gratified vanity—he was young and craved such glory.

"Good-night, Alain." He could hardly articulate the words from fatigue, and Alain had had even a harder day.

They slept almost as soundly as the dead they had left behind them; no spectres haunted them and disturbed their repose; conscience was hardened, scarred as with a hot iron, but her time was yet to come for Osric.

CHAPTER XVIII

BROTHER ALPHEGE

FROM the abode of strife and turmoil to the home of peace, from the house of the world to the house of religion, from the Castle of Wallingford to the Abbey of Dorchester, do we gladly conduct our readers, satiated, we doubt not, with scenes of warfare.

What wonder, when the world was given up to such scenes, that men and women, conscious of higher aspirations, should fly to the seclusion of the monastic life, afar from

"Unloving souls with deeds of ill,
And words of angry strife."

And what a blessing for that particular age that there were such refuges, thickly scattered throughout the land—veritable cities of refuge. It was not the primary idea of these orders that they should be benevolent institutions, justifying their existence by the service rendered to the commonwealth. The primary idea was the service of God, and the salvation of the particular souls, who fled from a world lying in wickedness and the shadow of death, to take sweet counsel together, and walk in the House of God as friends.

Later on came a *nobler* conception of man's duty to man; and thence sprang the active orders, such as the Friars or Sisters of Mercy, as distinguished from the cloistered or contemplative orders.

Of course, in the buildings of such a society, the Church was the principal object—as the ruins of Tintern or Glastonbury show, overshadowing all the other buildings, dwarfing them into insignificance. Upon this object all the resources of mediæval art were expended. The lofty columns, the mysterious lights and shadows of a Gothic fane, the sculptures, the statues, the shrines, the rich vestments, the painted glass—far beyond aught we can produce, the solemn music,—all this they lavished on the Church as the house of prayer—

> "It is the house of prayer,
> Wherein Thy servants meet;
> And Thou, O God, art there,
> Thy hallowed flock to greet."

Here they met seven times daily, to recite their offices, as also at the midnight office, when only the professed brethren were present. In these active times men may consider so much time spent in church a great waste of time, but we cannot judge other generations by our own ideas. A very sharp line was then drawn between the Church and the world, and they who chose the former possessed a far greater love for Divine worship than we see around us now, coupled with a most steadfast belief in its efficacy. "Blessed are They who dwell in Thy house; they will be alway praising Thee," was the language of their hearts.

Here men who had become the subjects of intense grief—from whom death, perhaps, had removed their earthly solace—the partners of their sorrow or joy—found refuge when the sun of this world was set. Here, also, studious men, afar from the clamour and din of arms, preserved for us the wisdom of the ancients. Here the arts and sciences lived on, when nought save war filled the minds of men outside. Well has it been said, that for the learning of the nineteenth century to revile the monastic system is for the oak to revile the acorn from which it sprang.

But most of all, when the shadow of a great horror of himself and his past fell upon a man, how blessed to have such an institution as a mediæval monastery wherein to hide the stricken head, and to learn submission to the Divine Will.

Such a home had Wulfnoth found at Dorchester Abbey. The year of his novitiate had passed, and he had won the favour of his monastic superiors. We do not say he had always been as humble as a novice should, or that he never, like Lot's wife, looked back again to Sodom, but the good had triumphed, and the day came for his election as a brother.

Every day after the Chapter Mass which followed Terce, the daily "Chapter" was held, wherein all matters of discipline were settled, correction, if needed, administered, novices or brethren admitted by common consent, and all other weighty business transacted. Here they met four centuries later, when they affixed their reluctant seal to their own dissolution, to avoid worse consequences.

It was here that, after the ordinary business was over, the novice Alphege, the once sanguinary Wulfnoth, rose with a calm and composed exterior, but with a beating heart, to crave admission into the order by taking the life vows.

The Abbot signed to him to speak.

"I, Wulfnoth the novice, crave admission to the full privileges and prayers of the order, by taking the vows for life, as a brother professed."

There was silence for a space.

Then the Abbot spoke—

"Hast thou duly considered the solemn step? Canst thou leave the world behind thee—its friendships and its enmities? and hast thou considered what hard and stern things we endure?"

"I have, Father Abbot."

"And the yet harder and sterner discipline which awaits the transgressor?"

"None of these things move me: I am prepared to bear yet harsher and sterner things, if so be I may save my soul."

"The Lord Jesus Christ so perform in you what for His love's sake you promise, that you may have His grace and life eternal."

"Amen," said all present.

The rule of the order was then read aloud.

"Here," said the Abbot, "is the law under which thou desirest to serve: if thou canst observe it, enter; but if thou canst not, freely depart."

"I will observe it, God being my helper."

"Doth any brother know any just cause or impediment why Alphege the novice should not be admitted to our brotherhood?"

None was alleged.

"Do you all admit him to a share in your sacrifices and prayers?"

The hands were solemnly raised.

"It is enough: prepare with prayer and fasting for the holy rite," said the Abbot.

For there was of course a solemn form of admission into the order yet to be gone through in the Church, which we have not space to detail.

It was not necessary that a monk should take Holy Orders, yet it was commonly done; and dismissing the subject in a few words, we will simply say that Wulfnoth took deacon's orders after he had taken the life vows, and later on was ordained priest by Bishop Alexander of Lincoln, aforesaid.

His lot in life was now fixed: no longer was he in any danger from the Lord of Wallingford; nor could he execute vengeance with sword and woe for the household stricken so sorely by that baron's hands at Compton on the downs. It was over—he left it all to Him Who once said, "Vengeance is Mine, I will repay." Nor mindful of his own sins, did he pray for such vengeance. He *left it*, and strove to pray for Brian.

One bright day at the close of July the Abbot called him to ride with him, for the order was not strictly a cloistered one, nor could it indeed be; they had their landed estates, their tenantry, their farms to look after. The offices were numerous, of necessity, and it was the policy of the order to give each monk, if possible, some special duty or office. Almost all they ate or drank was produced at home. The corn grew on their own land; they had their own mill; the brethren brewed, baked, or superintended lay brothers who did so. Other brethren were tailors, shoemakers for the community; others gardeners; others, as we have seen, scribes and illuminators; others kept the accounts—no small task.[1] In short, none led the idle life commonly assigned in popular estimation.

They rode forth then, the Abbot Alured and Alphege, the new brother. First into the town without the gates, far larger then than now, it was partly surrounded by walls, partly protected by the Rivers Isis and Tame; but within the space was a crowd of inhabitants dwelling in houses, or rather huts; dwelling even in tents, like modern gypsies, crowding the space within the walls, with good reason, for no man's life was safe in the country, and here was sanctuary! Even Brian Fitz-Count would respect Dorchester Abbey: even if some marauding baron assailed the town, there was still the abbey church, or even the precincts for temporary shelter.

But food was scarce, and here lay the difficulty. The abbey revenues were insufficient, for many of the farms had been burnt in the nightly raids, and rents were ill-paid. Everything was scarce: many a hapless mother, many a new-born babe, died from sheer want of the things necessary to save; the strong lived through it, the weak sank under it: there may have been those who found comfort, and said it was "the survival of the fittest."

Day by day was the dole given forth at the abbey gates; day by day the hospitium was very crowded. The hospitaller was at his wits' end. And the old infirmarer happening to die just then, folk said, "It was the worry."

---

[1] Many monastic rolls of accounts remain, and their minuteness is even startling.

"Who is sufficient for these things?" said Abbot Alured to his companion, as they rode through the throng and emerged upon the road leading to the hamlet of Brudecott (Burcot) and Cliffton (Clifton Hampden).

Their dress was a white cassock under a black cloak, with a hood covering the head and neck and reaching to the shoulders, having under it breeches, vest, white stockings and shoes; a black cornered cap, not unlike the college cap of modern days, completed the attire.

"Tell me, brother," said the Abbot, "what is thy especial vocation? what office wouldst thou most desire to hold amongst us?"

"I am little capable of discharging any weighty burden: thou knowest I have been a man of war."

"And he who once gave wounds should now learn to heal them. Our brother the infirmarer has lately departed this life, full of good works—would not that be the office for thee?"

"I think I could discharge it better than I could most others."

"It is well, then it shall be thine; it will be onerous just now. Ah me, when will these wars be over?"

"Methinks there was a great fire amongst the Chilterns last night—a thick cloud of smoke lingers there yet."

"It is surely Watlington—yes it is Watlington; they have burned it. What can have chanced? it is under the protection of Shirburne."

"I marvel we have had none of the people here, to seek hospitality and aid."

They arrived now at Brudecott, a hamlet on the Thames. One Nicholas de Brudecott had held a mansion here, one knight's fee of the Bishop of Lincoln; but the house had been burnt by midnight marauders. The place was desolate: on the fields untilled a few poor people lived in huts, protected by their poverty.

They rode on to Cliffton, where the Abbot held three "virgates" of land, with all the farm buildings and utensils for their cultivation; the latter had escaped devastation, perhaps from the fact it was church property, although even that was not always respected in those days.

Upon the rock over the river stood the rustic church. Wulfnoth had often served it as deacon, attending the priestly monk who said Mass each Sunday there, for Dorchester took the tithes and did the duty.

Here they crossed the river by a shallow ford where the bridge now stands, and rode through Witeham (Wittenham), where the Abbot had business connected with the monastery. The same desertion of the place impressed itself upon their minds. Scarcely a living being was seen; only a few old people, unable to bring themselves to forsake their homes, lingered about half-ruined cottages. The parish priest yet lived in the tower of the church, unwilling to forsake his flock, although half the village was in ruins, and nearly all the able-bodied had taken refuge in the towns.

They were on the point of crossing the ford beneath Synodune Hill, situated near the junction of Tame and Isis, when the Abbot suddenly conceived the desire of ascending the hills and viewing the scene of last night's conflagration from thence. They did so, and from the summit of the eastern hill, within the entrenchment which still exists, and has existed there from early British times, marked the cloud of black smoke which arose from the ruins of Watlington.

"What can have happened to the town—it is well defended with palisades and trench?"

Just then a powerful horseman, evidently a knight at the least, attended by two squires, rode over the entrance of the vallum, and ascended to the summit of the hill. He saluted the Abbot with a cold salute, and then entered into conversation with his squires.

"It is burning even yet, Osric; dost thou mark the black smoke?"

"Thatch smoulders a long time, my lord," replied the squire addressed.

The Abbot Alured happened to look round at Wulfnoth; he was quivering with some suppressed emotion like an aspen leaf, and his hand involuntarily sought the place where the hilt of his sword should have been had he possessed one.

"What ails thee, brother?" he said.

"It is the destroyer of my home and family, Brian Fitz-Count," and Wulfnoth drew the cowl over his head.

The Abbot rode down the hill; he felt as if he were on the edge of a volcano, and putting his hand on his companion's rein, forced him to accompany him.

It was strange that Wulfnoth did not also recognise his own *son*.

CHAPTER XIX

IN THE LOWEST DEPTHS

THE morning watch looked forth from the summit of the lofty keep, which rose above Wallingford Castle, to spy the dawning day. From that elevation of two hundred feet he saw the light of the summer dawn break forth over the Chiltern Hills in long streaks of azure, and amber light flecked with purple and scarlet. The stream below caught the rays, and assumed the congenial hue of blood; the sleepy town began to awake beyond the castle precincts; light wreaths of smoke to ascend from roof after roof— we can hardly say of those days chimney after chimney; the men of the castle began to move, for there was no idleness under Brian's rule; boats arrived by the stream bearing stores from the dependent villages above and below, or even down from Oxford and up from Reading, for the river was a great highway in those days.

Ah, how like the distant view was to that we now behold from the lessened height of the ruined keep! The everlasting hills were the same; the river flowed in the same channel: and yet how unlike, for the cultivated fields of the present day were mainly wood and marsh; dense forests of bush clothed the Chilterns; Cholsey Common, naked and bare, stretched on to the base of the downs; but on the west were the vast forests which had filled the vale of White Horse in earlier times, and now were but slightly broken into clearings, and diversified with hamlets.

But still more unlike, the men who began to wake into life!

The gaolers were busy with the light breakfasts of their prisoners, or attending to their cells, which they were forced sometimes to clean out, to prevent a pestilence; the soldiers were busy attending to their horses, and scouring their arms; the cooks were busy providing for so many mouths; the butler was busy with his wines; the armourers and blacksmiths with mail and weapons; the treasurer was busy with his accounts, counting the value of last night's raid and assigning his share of prize-money to each raider, for all had their share, each according to rank, and so "moss-trooping" was highly popular.

Even the Chaplain, as he returned from his hastily said Mass, which few attended—only, indeed, the Lady of the Castle, Maude d'Oyley, and her handmaidens—received his "bonus" as a bribe to Heaven, and pocketed it without reflecting that it was the price of blood. He was the laziest individual in the castle. Few there confessed their sins, and fewer still troubled him in any other spiritual capacity. Still Brian kept him for the sake of "being in form," as moderns say, and had purposely sought out an accommodating conscience.

In the terrace, which looked over the glacis towards the Thames, of which the remains with one window *in situ* may still be seen, was the bower of Maude d'Oyley, wife of Brian Fitz-Count and sister of the Lord of Oxford Castle, as we have before observed. It was called otherwise "the solar chamber;" perhaps because it was best fitted with windows for the admission of the sunlight, the openings in the walls being generally rather loopholes than windows.

The passion for great reception-rooms was as strong in mediæval days as in our own, and the family apartments suffered for it,—being generally small and low,—while the banqueting-hall was lofty and spacious, and the Gothic windows, which looked into the inner quadrangle, were of ample proportions. But the "ladye's bower" on the second floor consisted of, first an ante-chamber, where a handmaiden always waited within hearing of the little silver hand-bell; then a bower or boudoir; then the bedroom proper. All these rooms were hung with rich tapestry, worked by the lady and her handmaidens. For in those days, when books were scarce, and few could read, the work of the needle and the loom was the sole alleviation of many a solitary hour.

The windows looked over the river, and were of horn, not very transparent, only translucent; the outer world could but be dimly discerned in daylight.

There was a hearth at one end of the bower, and "dog-irons" upon it for the reception of the logs, of which fires were chiefly composed, for there was as yet no coal in use.

There were two "curule" chairs, that is, chairs in the form of St. Andrew's Cross, with cushions between the upper limbs, and no backs; there were one or two very small round tables for the reception of trifles, and "leaf-tables" between the windows. No one ever sat on these "curule" chairs save those of exalted rank: three-legged stools were good enough for ladies in waiting, and the like.

The hangings, which concealed the bare walls, were very beautiful. On one set was represented Lazarus and Dives; Father Abraham appeared very much in the style of a mediæval noble, and on his knee, many sizes smaller, sat Lazarus. In uncomfortable proximity to their seats was a great yawning chasm, and smoke looking very substantial, as represented in wool-work, arose thence, while some batlike creatures, supposed to be fiends, sported here and there. On the other side lay Dives in the midst of rosy flames of crimson wool, and his tongue, which was stretched out for the drop of water, was of such a size, that one wondered how it ever could have found space in the mouth. But for all this, the lesson taught by the picture was not a bad one for the chambers of barons, if they would but heed it; it is to be feared it was little heeded just then in Wallingford Castle.

There was no carpet on the floor, only rushes, from the

marshes. The Countess sat on her "curule" chair in front of the blazing fire. Three maidens upon three-legged stools around her were engaged on embroidery. They were all of high rank, entrusted to her guardianship, for she liked to surround herself with blooming youth. *She* was old,—her face was wrinkled, her eyes were dull,—but she had a sweet smile, and was quite an engaging old lady, although, of course, with the reserve which became, or was supposed to become, her high rank.

A timid knock at the door, and another maiden entered.

"Jeannette, thou art late this evening."

"I was detained in Dame Ursula's room; she needed my help, lady."

"Wherefore?"

"To attend to the wounded of last night's raid."

"Ah, yes, we have heard but few particulars, and would fain learn more. Send and see whether either of the young squires Osric or Alain can come and give us the details."

And shortly Osric entered, dressed in his handsomest tunic—the garb of peace, and properly washed and combed for the presence of ladies.

He bowed reverently to the great dame, of whom he stood in more awe than of her stern husband: he was of that awkward age when lads are always shy before ladies.

But her kind manner cheered him.

"So thou didst ride last night, Osric?"

"I did, my lady."

"Come, tell us all about it."

"We started, as thou knowest, soon after the arrival of the prisoner William Martel, to harry his lands."

"We all saw you start; and I hear the Crowmarsh people saw you too."

"And assailed us at Bensington."

"And now tell me, my Osric, didst thou not slay one of Lord Ranulph's people?"

M

"I did, by my good fortune, and his ill-luck."

"And so thou shouldst receive the meed of valour from the fair. Come, what sayest thou, ladies?"

"He should indeed; he is marvellous young to be so brave."

"We are short of means to reward our brave knights and squires, but take this ring;" and she gave one containing a valuable gem; "and we only grieve it is not of more worth."

So Osric, encouraged, continued his tale; and those fair ladies—and fair they were—laughed merrily at his narration of the burning of Watlington, and would have him spare no details.

"Thou hast done well, my Osric. Come, thou wilt be a knight; thou dost not now pine for the forest?"

"Not now; I have grown to love adventures."

"And it is so exciting to ride by night, as thou didst last winter with the Empress Queen."

"But I love the summer nights, with their sweet freshness, best."

"Thou dost not remember thy boyhood with regret now, and wish it back again?"

"Not now." And Osric made his bow and departed.

"There is a mystery about that youth; he is not English, as my lord thinks; there is not an atom of it about him," said the Countess, and fell into a fit of musing.

From the halls of pleasure let us turn to the dungeons beneath; but first a digression.

Even mediæval barons were forced to keep their accounts, or to employ, more commonly, a "scrivener" or accountant for that purpose; and all this morning Brian was closeted with his man of business, looking over musty rolls and parchments, from which extract after extract was read, bearing little other impression on the mind of the poor perplexed Baron than that he was grievously behind in his finances. So he despatched the scrivener to negotiate a further advance—loan he called it—from the mayor, while he summoned Osric, who was quick at figures, to his presence.

"There is scarcely enough money to pay the Brabanters, and they will mutiny if kept short: that raid last night was a god-send," said Brian to himself.

Osric arrived. The Baron felt lighter of heart when the youth he loved was with him. It was another case of Saul and David. And furthermore, the likeness was not a superficial one. Often did Osric touch the harp, and sing the lays of love and war to his patron, for so much had he learned of his grandsire.

They talked of the previous evening's adventures, and Brian was delighted to draw Osric out, and to hear him express sentiments so entirely at variance with his antecedents, as he did under the Baron's deft questions.

So they continued talking until the scrivener returned, and then the Baron asked impatiently—

"Well, man! and what does the mayor say?"

"That their resources are exhausted, and that you are very much in their debt already."

The reader need not marvel at this bold answer. Brian dared not use violence to his own burghers; it would have been killing the goose who laid the golden eggs. In our men of commerce began the first germs of English liberty. Men would sometimes yield to all other kinds of violence, but the freemen of the towns, even amidst the wild barons of Germany, held their own; and so did the burgesses of Wallingford: they had their charter signed and sealed by Brian, and ratified by Henry the First.

"The greedy caitiffs," he said; "well, we must go and see the dungeons. Osric, come with me."

Osric had seldom been permitted to do this before. He had only once or twice been "down below." Perhaps Brian had feared to shock him, and now thought him seasoned, as indeed he seemed to be the night before, and in his talk that day.

And here let me advise my gentler readers, who hate to read of violence and cruelty, to skip the rest of this chapter, which may be read by stronger-minded readers as essential to a complete picture of life at Wallingford Castle. What men once had to bear, we may bear to read.

They went first to the dungeon in the north tower, where William, Lord of Shirburne, was confined. Tustain the gaoler and two satellites attended, and opened the door of the cell. It was a cold, bare room : a box stuffed with leaves and straw, with a coverlet and pillow for a bed ; a rough bench ; a rude table—that was all.

The prisoner could not enjoy the scenery; his only light was from a grated window above, of too small dimensions to allow a man to pass through, even were the bars removed.

"How dost thou like my hospitality, William of Shirburne ? "

"I suppose it is as good as I should have shown thee."

"Doubtless : we know each other. Now, what wilt thou pay for thy ransom ? "

" A thousand marks."

Brian laughed grimly.

"Thou ratest thyself at the price of an old Jew."

" What dost thou ask ? "

"Ten thousand marks, or the Castle of Shirburne and its domains."

"Never ! thou villain—robber ! "

"Thou wilt change thy mind : thou mayst despatch a messenger for the money, who shall have free conduct to come and go ; and mark me, if thou dost not pay within a week, thou shalt be manacled and removed to the dungeons below, to herd with my defaulting debtors, and a week after to a lower depth still."

Then he turned as if to depart, but paused and said, " It is a pity this window is so high in the wall, otherwise thou mightst have seen a fine blaze last night about Shirburne and its domains."

He laughed exultantly.

"Do thy worst, thou son of perdition; my turn may yet come," replied Martel.

And the Baron departed, accompanied still by Osric.

"Osric," said he, "thou hast often asked to visit the lower dungeons: thou mayst have thy wish, and see how we house our guests there; and also in a different capacity renew thine acquaintance with the torture-chambers: thou shalt be the notary."

"My lord, thou dost recall cruel memories."

"Nay, it was for love of thee. I have no son, and my bowels yearned for one; it was gentle violence for thine own good. I know not how it was, but I could not even then have done more than frighten thee. Thou wilt see I can hurt others without wincing. Say, wouldst thou fear to see what torture is like? it may fall to thy duty to inflict it some day, and in these times one must get hardened either to inflict or endure."

"I may as well learn all I have to learn; but I love it not. I do not object to fighting; but in cold blood——"

"Well, here is the door which descends to the lower realms."

They descended through a yawning portal to the dungeons. The steps were of gray stone: they went down some twenty or thirty, and then entered a corridor—dark and gloomy—from which opened many doors on either side.

Dark, but not silent. Many a sigh, many a groan, came from behind those doors, but neither Brian nor his squire heeded them.

"Which shall I open first?" said Tustain.

"The cell of Nathan, the Abingdon Jew."

The door was a huge block of stone, turning upon a pivot. It disclosed a small recess, about six feet by four, paved with stone, upon which lay some foul and damp litter. A man was crouched upon this, with a long, matted beard, looking the picture of helpless misery.

"Well, Nathan, hast been my guest long enough? Will not change of air do thee good?"

"I have no more money to give thee."

"Then I must bid the tormentor visit thee again. Thy race is accursed, and I cannot offer a better burnt-offering to Heaven than a Jew."

"Mercy, Baron! I have borne so much already."

"Mercy is to be bought: the price is a thousand marks of gold."

"I have not a hundred."

"Osric," said Brian; and gave his squire instructions to fetch the tormentor.

"We will spare thee the grate yet awhile; but I have another plan in view. Coupe-gorge, canst thou draw teeth?"

"Yes," said the tormentor, grinning, who had come at Osric's bidding.

"Then bring me a tooth from the mouth of this Nathan every day until his ransom arrive. Nathan, thou mayst write home—a letter for each tooth." And with a merry laugh they passed on to the other dungeons.

There was one who shared his cell with toads and adders, introduced for his discomfort; another round whose neck and throat a hideous thing called a *sachentage* was fastened. It was thus made: it was fastened to a beam, and had a sharp iron to go round a man's neck and throat, so that he might nowise sit or lie or sleep, but he bore all the iron.

In short, the castle was full of prisoners, and they were subjected to daily tortures to make them disclose their supposed hidden treasures, or pay the desired ransom. Here were many hapless Jews, always the first objects of cruelty in the Middle Ages; here many usurers, paying interest more heavy than they had ever charged others; here also many of the noblest and purest mixed up with some of the vilest upon earth.

Well might the townspeople complain that they were startled in their sleep by the cries and shrieks which came from the grim towers.

And the Baron, followed by Osric, went from dungeon to dungeon; in some cases obtaining promises of ransom to be paid, in others hearing of treasures, real or imaginary, buried in certain places, which he bid Osric note, that search might be made.

"Woe to them who fool me," he said.

Then they came to a dungeon in which was a chest, sharp and narrow, in which one poor tormented wight lay in company with sharp flints; as the light of the torch they bore flashed upon him, his eyes, red and lurid, gleamed through the open iron framework of the lid which fastened him down.

"This man was the second in command of a band of English outlaws, who made much spoil at Norman expense. Now I slew his chief in fair combat on the downs, and this man succeeded him, and waged war for a long time, until I took him; and here he is. How now, Herwald, dost want to get out of thy chest?"

A deep groan was the only reply.

"Then disclose to me the hidden treasures of thy band."

"We have none."

"Persevere then in that lie, and die in thy misery."

Osric felt very sick. He had not the nerves of his chief, and now he felt as if he were helping the torture of his own countrymen; and, moreover, there was a yet deeper feeling. Recollections were brought to his mind in that loathsome dungeon which, although indistinct and confused, yet had some connection with his own early life. What had his father been? The grandfather had carefully hidden all those facts, known to the reader, from Osric, but old Judith had dropped obscure hints.

He longed to get out of this accursed depth into the light of day, yet felt ashamed of his own weakness. He heard the misery of these dens turned into a joke by Alain and others every day. He had brought prisoners into the castle himself—for the hideous receptacles—and been complimented on his prowess and success; yet humanity was not quite extinguished in his breast, and he felt sick of the scenes.

But he had not done. They came to the torture-chamber, where recalcitrant prisoners, who would not own their wealth, were hanged up by the feet and smoked with foul smoke: some were hanged up by the thumbs, others by the head, and burning rings were put on their feet. The torturers put knotted strings about men's heads, and writhed them till they went into the brain. In short, the horrid paraphernalia of cruelty was entered into that day with the utmost zest, and all for gold, accursed gold—at least, that was the first object; but we fear at last the mere love of cruelty was half the incitement to such doings.

And all this time Brian sat as judge, and directed the torturers with eye or hand; and Osric had to take notes of the things the poor wretches said in their delirium.

At last it was over, and they ascended to the upper day.

"How dost thou like it, Osric?" said Alain, whom they met on the ramparts.

Osric shook his head.

"It is nothing when you are used to it; I used to feel squeamish at first."

"I never shall like it," whispered Osric.

The whisper was so earnest that Alain looked at him in surprise; Osric only answered by something like a sigh. The Baron heard him not.

"Thou hast done well for a beginner," said Brian; "how dost thou like the torture chamber?"

"I was there in another capacity once."

"And thou hast not forgot it. But we must remember these *canaille* are only made for such uses—only to disgorge their wealth for their betters, or to furnish sport."

"How should we like it ourselves?"

"You might as well object to eating venison, and say how should we like it if we were the deer?"

"But does not God look upon all alike?"

They were on the castle green. Upon the sward some ants had raised a little hill.

"Look at these ants," said Brian; "I believe they have a sort of kingdom amongst themselves—some are priests, some masters, some slaves, one is king, and the like: to themselves they seem very important. Now I will place my foot upon the hill, and ruin their republic. Just so are the gods to us, if there be gods. They care as little about men as I about the ants; our joys, our griefs, our good deeds, our bad deeds, are alike to them. I was in deep affliction once about my poor leprous boys. I prayed with all my might; I gave alms; I had Masses said—all in vain. Now I go my own way, and you see I do not altogether fail of success, although I buy it with the tears and blood of other men."

This seemed startling, nay, terrible to Osric.

"Yet, Osric, I can love, and I can reward fidelity; be true to me, and I will be truer to you than God was to me—that is, if there be a God, which I doubt."

Osric shuddered; and well he might at this impious defiance.

Then this strange man was seized with a remorse, which showed that after all there was yet some good left in him.

"Nay, pardon me, my Osric; I wish not to shake thy faith; if it make thee happy, keep it. Mine are perchance the ravings of disappointment and despair. There are times when I think the most wretched of my captives happier than I. Nay, *keep* thy faith if thou canst."

CHAPTER XX

MEINHOLD AND HIS PUPILS

WE are loth to leave our readers too long in the den of tyranny: we pant for free air; for the woods, even if we share them with hermits and lepers—anything rather than the towers of Wallingford under Brian Fitz-Count, his troopers and free lances.

So we will fly to the hermitage where his innocent sons have found refuge for two years past, under the fostering care of Meinhold the hermit, and see how they fare.

First of all, they had not been reclaimed to Byfield. It is true they had been traced, and Meinhold had been "interviewed"; but so earnestly had both he and the boys pleaded that they might be allowed to remain where they were, that assent was willingly given, even Father Ambrose feeling that it was for the best; only an assurance was required that they would not stray from the neighbourhood of the cell, and it was readily given.

Of course their father was informed, and he made no opposition,—the poor boys were dead to him and the world. Leprosy was incurable: if they were happy—"let them be."

So they enjoyed the sweet, simple life of the forest. They found playmates in every bird and beast; they learned to read at last; they joined the hermit in the recitation of two at least of the "hours" each day—*Lauds* and *Vespers*, the morning and evening offerings of praise. They learned to sing, and chanted *Benedictus* and *Magnificat*, as well as the hymns *Ecce nunc umbræ* and *Lucis Creator optime*.

"We sing very badly, do we not?"

"Not worse than the brethren of St. Bernard."

"Tell us about them."

"They settled in a wild forest,—about a dozen in number. They could not sing their offices, for they lacked an ear for music; but they said God should at least be honoured by the *Magnificat* in song; so they did their best, although it is said they frightened the very birds away.

"Now one day a wandering boy, the son of a minstrel, came that way and craved hospitality. He joined them at Vespers, and when they came to the *Magnificat*, he took up the strain and sang it so sweetly that the birds all came back and listened, entranced; and the old monks were silent lest they should spoil so sweet a chant with their croaking and nasal tones.

"That evening an Angel flew straight from Heaven and came to the prior.

"'My lady hath sent me to learn why *Magnificat* was not sung to-night?'

"'It was sung indeed—so beautifully.'

"'Nay, it ascended no farther than human ken; the singer was only thinking of his own sweet voice.'

"Then they sent that boy away; and, doubtless, he found his consolation amongst troubadours and trouveres. So you see, my children, the heart is everything—not the voice."

"Yet I should not like to sing so badly as to frighten the birds away," said Richard.

So the months passed away; and meanwhile the leprosy made its insidious progress. The red spot on the hermit's hand deepened and widened until the centre became white as snow; and so it formed a ghastly ring, which began to ulcerate in the centre, the ulcer eating deep into the flesh.

Richard's arm was now wholly infected, and the elbow-joint began to get useless. Evroult's disease extended to the neighbouring regions of the face, and disfigured the poor lad terribly.

Such were the stages of this terrible disease; but there was little pain attending it—only a sense of uneasiness, sometimes feverish heats or sudden chills, resembling in their nature those which attend marsh or jungle fevers, ague, and the like. Happily these symptoms were not constant.

And through these stages the unfortunate boys we have introduced to our readers were slowly passing; but the transitions were so gradual that the patient became almost hardened to them. Richard was so patient; he had no longer a left hand, but he never complained.

"It is the road, dear child, God has chosen for us, and His Name is 'Love,'" said the hermit. "Every step of the way has been foreordained by Him Who tasted the bitter cup for us; and when we have gained the shore of eternity we shall see that infinite wisdom ordered it all for the best."

"Is it really so? Can it be for the best?" said Evroult.

"Listen, my son: this is God's Word; let me read it to you." And from his Breviary he read this extract from that wondrous Epistle to the Romans—

"'For we know that all things work together for good to them that love God, who are the called according to His purpose.'"

"Now God has called you out of this wicked world: you might have spent turbid, restless lives of fighting and bloodshed, chasing the phantom called 'glory,' and then have died and gone where all hope is left behind. Is it not better?"

"Yes, *it is*," said Richard; "*it is*, Evroult, is it not—better as it is?"

"Nay, Richard, but had I been well, I had been a knight like my father. Oh, what have we not lost!"

"An awful doom at the end perhaps," said Meinhold. "Let me tell you what I saw with mine own eyes. A rich baron died near here who had won great renown in the wars, in which, nevertheless, he had been as merciless as barons too often are. Well, he left great gifts to the Church, and money for many Masses for his soul: so he was buried with great pomp—brought to be buried, I mean, in the priory church he had founded.

"Now when we came to the solemn portion of the service, when the words are said which convey the last absolution and benediction of the Church, the corpse sat upright in the bier and said, in an awful tone, 'By the justice of God, I am condemned to Hell.' The prior could not proceed; the body was left lying on the bier; and at last it was decided so to leave it till the next day, and then resume the service.

"But the second day, when the same words were repeated, the corpse rose again and said, 'By the justice of God, I am condemned to Hell.'

"We waited till the third day, determined if the interruption occurred again to abandon the design of burying the deceased baron in the church he had founded. A great crowd assembled around, but only the monks dared to enter the church where the body lay. A third time we came to the same words in the office, and we who were in the choir saw the body rise in the winding-sheet, the dull eyes glisten into life, and heard the awful words for the third time, 'By the justice of God, I am condemned to Hell.'

"After a long pause, during which we all knelt, horror-struck, the prior bade us take the body from the church, and bade his friends lay it in unconsecrated ground, away from the church he had founded. So you see a man of blood cannot always bribe Heaven with gifts."

"It is no use then to found churches and monasteries; I have heard my father say the same," said Evroult.

"Yet in any case it is better than to build castles to become dens of cruelty—to torture captives and spread terror through a neighbourhood."

"It is pleasant to be the lord of such a castle," said

the incorrigible Evroult, "and to be the master of all around."

"And, alas, my boy, if it end in like manner with you as with the baron whose story I have just related, of what avail will it all be?"

"Yes, brother, we are better as we are; God meant it for our good, and we may thank Him for it," said Richard quite sincerely.

Evroult only sighed as a wolf might were he told how much more nutritious grass is than mutton; inherited instinct, unsubdued as yet by grace, was too strong within him. But let us admire his truthfulness; he would not say what he did not mean. Many in his place would have said "yes" to please his brother and the kind old hermit, but Evroult scorned such meanness.

There is little question that had he escaped this scourge he would have made a worthy successor to Brian Fitz-Count, but—

"His lot forbade, nor circumscribed alone
His growing virtues but his crimes confined,
Forbade to wade through slaughter to a throne,
Or shut the gates of mercy on mankind."

Still, let it be remembered, that in Stephen's days we see only the worst side of the Norman nobility. In less than a century the barons rallied around that man of God, Stephen Langton, and wrested Magna Charta from the tyrant John, the worst of the Plantagenets. Proud by that time of the name "Englishmen," they laid the foundations of our greatness, and jealously guarded our constitutional liberties; and it was not until after the Wars of the Roses, in which so many of the ancient houses perished, that a Norman baron was said to be "as scarce as a wolf," that the Bloodstained House of Tudor was enabled to trample upon English liberty, and to reign as absolute monarchs over a prostrate commonalty.

All through the summer our boys were very happy, in spite of Evroult's occasional longings for the world. They cultivated a garden hard by their cave, and they gathered the roots and fruits of the forest for their frugal repast. They parched the corn; they boiled the milk and eggs which the rustics spontaneously brought; they made the bread and baked the oatcakes. They were quite vegetarians now, save the milk and eggs; and throve upon their simple fare; but it took, as our readers perceive, a long course of vegetable diet to take the fire out of Evroult.

Then came the fall of the leaf, when the trees, like some vain mortals, put on their richest clothing wherein to die; and damps and mists arose around, driving them within the shelter of their cave; then winter with its chilling frosts, keener then than now, and their stream was turned into ice. And had they not, like the ants, laid by in summer, they would have starved sadly in winter.

In the inner cave was a natural chimney, an orifice communicating with the outer air. Fuel was plentiful in the forest, and as they sat around the fire, Meinhold told them stories of the visible and invisible world, more or less, of course, of a supernatural character, like those we have already heard. His was an imaginary world, full of quaint superstitions which were very harmless, for they left the soul even more reliant and dependent upon Divine help; for was not this a world wherein Angels and demons engaged in terrestrial warfare, man's soul the prize? and were not the rites and Sacraments of the Church sent to counteract the spells and snares of the phantom host?

And as they sat around their fire, the wind made wild and awful music in the subterranean caves; sometimes it shrieked, then moaned, as if under the current of earthly origin there was a perpetual wail of souls in pain.

"Father, may not these passages lead down to Purgatory, or even to the abode of the lost?"

"Nay, my child, I think it only the wind;" but he shuddered as he spoke.

"You think *they* lie beneath the earth, Richard?"

"Yes, the heavens above the stars, which are like the

golden nails of its floor; the earth—our scene of conflict beneath; and the depths below for those who fail and reject their salvation," said Meinhold, replying for the younger boy.

"Then the burning mountains of which we have heard are the portals of hell?"

"So it is commonly supposed," said the hermit. The reader will laugh at his simple cosmogony: he had no idea, poor man, that the earth is round.

"Please let me explore these caves," said Evroult.

"Art thou not afraid?" said Meinhold.

"No," said he; "I am never afraid."

"But I fear *for* thee; there are dark chasms and a black gulf within, and I fear, my child, lest they be tenanted by evil spirits, and that the sounds we hear at night be not all idle winds."

"You once said they were winds."

"Yes, but do winds utter blasphemies?"

"Never."

"Of course not. Is it not written, 'O all ye winds of God, bless ye the Lord?' Now as I lay on my bed last night, methought the sounds took articulate form, and they were words of cursing and blasphemy, such as might have come from a lost souL"

A modern would say that the hermit had a sort of nightmare, but in those credulous days the supernatural solution was always accepted.

"And, my son, if there be, as I fear, evil spirits who lurk in the bowels of the earth, and lure men to their destruction, I would not allow thee to rush into danger."

"No, brother, think no more of it," said Richard.

And Evroult promised not to do so, if he could help it.

"There be caves in the African deserts, of which I have heard, where fiends do haunt, and terrify travellers even to death. One there was which was, to look upon, the shadow of a great rock in a weary land, but they who passed a night there—and it was the only resting-place in the desert for many weary miles—went mad, frightened out of their senses by some awful vision which blasted those who gazed."

"But ought Christian men to fear such things?"

"No; neither ought they without a call to endanger themselves: 'He shall give His Angels charge over thee to keep thee in all thy ways.' Now our way does not lie through these dark abodes."

So the caves remained unexplored.

But we must return to Wallingford Castle again, and the active life of the fighting world of King Stephen's days. Suffice it for the present to say, that the lives of the hermit and his two pupils, for such they were, continued to roll on uneventfully for many months—indeed, until the occurrence of totally unexpected events, which we shall narrate in due course.

CHAPTER XXI

A DEATHBED DISCLOSURE

An excessive rainfall during the late summer of this year destroyed the hopes of the harvest,—such hopes as there were, for tillage had been abandoned, save where the protection of some powerful baron gave a fair probability of gathering in the crops. In consequence a dreadful famine succeeded during the winter, aggravated by the intense cold, for a frost set in at the beginning of December and lasted without intermission till February, so that the Thames was again frozen, and the ordinary passage of man and horse was on the ice of the river.

The poor people, says the author of *The Acts of King Stephen,* died in heaps, and so escaped the miseries of this sinful world,—a phrase of more meaning then, in people's ears, than it is now, when life is doubtless better worth living than it could have been then, in King Stephen's days, when horrible and unexampled atrocities disgraced the nation daily, and the misery of the poor was caused by the cruel tyranny of the rich and powerful.

All this time our young friend Osric continued to be the favourite squire of Brian Fitz-Count, and, we grieve to say, became habituated to crime and violence. He no longer shuddered as of yore at the atrocities committed in the dungeons of the castle, or in the constant raids: the conscience soon became blunted, and he felt an ever-increasing delight in strife and bloodshed, the joy of the combat, and in deeds of valour.

Facilis descensus averno, wrote the poet, or, as it has been Englished—

> "The gate of Hell stands open night and day,
> Smooth the descent, and easy is the way;
> But to return and view the upper skies,
> In this the toil, in this the labour lies."

For a long period he had not visited his grandfather—the reader will easily guess why; but he took care that out of Brian's prodigal bounty the daily wants of the old man should be supplied, and he thought all was well there—he did not know that the recipient never made use of Brian's bounty. He had become ashamed of his English ancestry: it needed a thunder-clap to recall him to his better self.

There were few secrets Brian concealed from his favourite squire, now an aspirant for knighthood, and tolerably sure to obtain his wish in a few more months. The deepest dungeons in the castle were known to him, the various sources of revenue, the claims for feudal dues, the tribute paid for protection, the rentals of lands, the purchase of forest rights, and, less creditable, the sums extracted by torture or paid for ransom,—all these were known to Osric, whose keen wits were often called on to assist the Baron's more sluggish intellect in such matters.

Alain was seldom at Wallingford; he had already been knighted by the Empress Maude, and was high in her favour, and in attendance on her person, so Osric lacked his most formidable rival in the Baron's graces.

He could come and go almost when he pleased; he knew the secret exit to the castle, only known to a few chief confidants—two or three at the most, who had been allowed to use it on special necessity.

It led to a landing-place on the bank of the river, and blindfolded prisoners, to be kept in secret, were sometimes introduced to their doleful lodgings through this entrance.

Active in war, a favourite in the bower, possessing a good hand at games, a quick eye for business, Osric soon became a necessity to Brian Fitz-Count: his star was in the ascendant, and men said Brian would adopt him as his son.

Constitutionally fearless, a born lover of combat, a good archer who could kill a bird on the wing, a fair swordsman, skilled in the exercises of chivalry,—what more was needed to make a young man happy in those days?

A quiet conscience? Well, Osric had quieted his: he was fast becoming a convert to Brian's sceptical opinions, which alone could justify his present course of action.

The castle was increasing: the dungeon aforementioned had been built, called Brian's Close,[1] with surmounting towers. The unhappy William Martel was its first inmate, and there he remained until his obstinacy was conquered, and the Castle of Shirburne ceded to Brian, with the large tract of country it governed and the right of way across the Chilterns.

Brian Fitz-Count was now at the height of his glory— the Empress was mistress of half the realm; he was her chief favourite and minister—when events occurred which somewhat disturbed his serene self-complacency, and seemed to infer the existence of a God of justice and vengeance.

It was early one fine day when a messenger from the woods reached the castle, and with some difficulty found access to Osric, bringing the tidings that his grandfather was dying, and would fain see him once more before he died.

"Dying! well, he is very old; we must all die," was Osric's first thought, coupled with a sense of relief, which he tried to disguise from himself, that a troublesome Mentor was about to be removed. Now he might feel like a *Norman*, but he had still a lingering love for the old man, the kind and loving guardian of his early years; so he sought Brian, and craved leave of absence.

[1] "The last trace of a dungeon answering the above description, with huge iron rings fixed in the walls, disappeared about sixty or seventy years ago."—*History of Wallingford* (Hedges).

A DEATHBED DISCLOSURE

"It is awkward," replied the Baron; "I was about to send thee to Shirburne. We have conquered Martel's resolution at last. I threatened that the rack should not longer be withheld, and that we would make him a full foot longer than God created him. Darkness and scant food have tamed him. Had we kept him in his first prison, with light and air, with corn and wine, he would never have given way. After all, endurance is a thing very dependent on the stomach."

"I will return to-morrow, my lord;" and Osric looked pleadingly at him.

"Not later. I cannot go to Shirburne myself, as I am expecting an important messenger from *Queen* Maude (of course *he* called her Queen), and can trust none other but thee."

"It is not likely that any other claim will come between me and thee, my lord; this is passing away, and I shall be wholly thine."

The Baron smiled; his proud heart was touched.

"Go, then, Osric," he said, "and return to-morrow."

And so they parted.

Osric rode rapidly through the woods, up the course of the brook; we described the road in our second chapter. He passed the Moor-towns, left the Roman camp of Blewburton on the left, and was soon in the thick maze of swamp and wood which then occupied the country about Blewbery.

As he drew near the old home, many recollections crowded upon him, and he felt, as he always did there, something more like an Englishman. It was for this very reason he so seldom came "home" to visit his grandfather.

He found his way across the streams: the undergrowth had all been renewed since the fire which the hunters kindled four years agone; the birds were singing sweetly, for it was the happy springtide for them, and they were little affected by the causes which brought misery to less favoured mankind; the foliage was thick, the sweet hawthorn exhaled its perfume, the bushes were bright with

"May." Ah me, how lovely the woods are in spring! how happy even this world might be, had man never sinned

But within the hut were the unequivocal signs of the rupture between man and his Maker—the tokens which have ever existed since by sin came death.

Upon the bed in the inner room lay old Sexwulf, in the last stage of senile decay. He was dying of no distinct disease, only of general breaking-up of the system. Man cannot live for ever; he wears out in time, even if he escape disease.

The features were worn and haggard, the eye was yet bright, the mind powerful to the last.

He saw the delight of his eyes, the darling of his old age, enter, and looked sadly upon him, almost reproachfully. The youth took his passive hand in his warm grasp, and imprinted a kiss upon the wrinkled forehead.

"He has had all he needed—nothing has been wanting for his comfort?" said Osric inquiringly.

"We have been able to keep him alive, but he would not touch your gold, or aught you sent of late."

"Why not?" asked Osric, deeply hurt.

"He said it was the price of blood, wrung, it might be, from the hands of murdered peasants of your own kindred."

Ah! that shaft went home. Osric knew it was *just*. What else was the greater portion of the Baron's hoard derived from, save rapine and violence?

"It was cruel to let him starve."

"He has not starved; we have had other friends, but the famine has been sore in the land."

"Other friends! who?"

"Yes; especially the good monks of Dorchester."

"What do they know of my grandfather?"

Judith pursed up her lips, as much as to say, "That is my secret, and if you had brought the thumb-screws, of which you know the use too well, you should not get it out of me."

"Osric," said a deep, yet feeble voice.

The youth returned to the bedside.

"Osric, I am dying. They say the tongues of dying men speak sooth, and it may be because, as the gates of eternity open before them, the vanities of earth disappear. Now I have a last message to leave for you, a tale to unfold before I die, which cannot fail of its effect upon your heart. It is the secret entrusted to me when you were brought an infant to this hut, which I was forbidden to unfold until you had gained years of discretion. It may be, my dear child, you have not yet gained them—I trow not, from what I hear."

"What harm have mine enemies told of me?"

"*That* thou shalt hear by and by; meanwhile let me unfold my tale, for the sands of life are running out. It was some seventeen years ago this last autumn, that thy father——"

"Who was he—thou hast ever concealed his name?"

"Wulfnoth of Compton."

Osric started.

"Doth he live?"

"He doth."

"Where?"

"He is a monk of Dorchester Abbey. I may tell the secret now; Brian himself could not hurt him there."

"Why should he *wish* to hurt him?"

"Listen, and your ears shall learn the truth. Thy father was my guest in this hut. Seventeen years ago this last autumn he had been hunting all day, and was on the down above, near the mound where Holy Birinus once preached, as the sun set, when he perceived, a few miles away, the flames of a burning house, and knew that it was his own, for he lived in a recess of the downs far from other houses. He hurried towards the scene, sick with fear, but it was miles away, and when he reached the spot he saw a dark band passing along the downs, a short distance off, in the opposite direction. His heart told him they were the incendiaries, but he stopped not for vengeance. Love to his wife and children hurried him on. When he arrived the roof had long since fallen in; a few pitying neighbours stood around, and shook their heads as they saw him, and heard his pitiful cries for his wife and children. Fain would he have thrown himself into the flames, but they restrained him, and told him he had one child yet to live for, accidentally absent at the house of a neighbour.—It was thou, my son."

"But who had burnt the house? Who had slain my poor mother, and my brothers and sisters, if I had any?"

"Brian Fitz-Count, Lord of Wallingford."

"Brian Fitz-Count!" said Osric in horror.

"None other."

Osric stood aghast—confounded.

"Because your father would not pay tribute, maintaining that the land was his own freehold since it had been confirmed to his father, thy paternal grandfather, by the Norman courts, which acknowledged no tenure, no right of possession, dating before the Conquest; but Wigod of Wallingford was thy grandfather's friend, and he had secured to him the possession of the ancestral domains. This Brian denied, and claimed the rent of his vassal, as he deemed thy father. Thy father refused to obey, and appealed to the courts, and Brian's answer was this deed of murder."

Osric listened as one in a dream.

"Oh, my poor father! What did he do?"

"He brought thee here. 'Henceforth,' he said, 'I am about to live the life of a hunted wolf, my sole solace to slay Normans : sooner or later I shall perish by their hands, for Satan is on their side, and helps them, and God and His Saints are asleep; but take care of my child; let him not learn the sad story of his birth till he be of age; nor let him even know his father's name. Only let him be brought up as an Englishman; and if he live to years of discretion, thou mayst tell him all, if I return not to claim him before then.'"

"And he has never returned—never?"

"Never: he became a captain of an outlawed band, haunting the forests and slaying Normans, until, four years ago, he met Brian Fitz-Count alone on these downs, and the two fought to the death."

"And Brian conquered?"

"He did, and left thy father for dead; but the good monks of Dorchester chanced to be passing across the downs from their house at Hermitage, and they found the body, and discovered that there was yet life therein. They took him to Dorchester, and as he was unable to use sword or lance again, he consented to take the vows, and become a novice. He found his vocation, and is now, I am told, happy and useful, fervent in his ministrations amongst the poor and helpless; but he has never yet been here.

"And now, Osric, my son," for the youth sat as one stunned, "what is it that I hear of thee?—that thou art, like a cannibal,[1] preying upon thine own people; that thy hand is foremost in every deed of violence and bloodshed; that thou art a willing slave of the murderer of thy kindred. Boy, I wonder thy mother has not returned from the grave to curse thee!"

"Why—why did you let me become his man?"

The old man felt the justice of the words.

"Why did you not let me die first?"

"Thou forgettest I was not by thee when thou didst consent, or I might have prevented thee by telling thee the truth even at that terrible moment; but when thou wast already pledged to him, I waited for the time when I might tell thee, never thinking thou wouldst become a *willing* slave or join in such deeds of atrocity and crime as thou hast done."

"Oh, what shall I do? what shall I do?"

"Thou canst not return, now thou knowest all."

---

[1] It was a remark of this kind which turned Robert Bruce when fighting against his own people. "See," said an Englishman, as he saw Bruce eating with unwashed and reddened hands, "that Scotchman eating his own blood!"

"Never; but he will seek me here."

"Then thou must fly the country."

"Whither shall I go? are any of my father's band left?"

"Herwald, his successor, fell into the power of Brian, and we know not what was done with him; nor whether he is living or dead."

But Osric knew: he remembered the chest half filled with sharp stones and its living victim.

"One Thorold succeeded, and they still maintain a precarious existence in the forests."

"I will seek them; I will yet be true to my country, and avenge my kindred upon Brian. But oh, grandfather, he has been so good to me! I am his favourite, his confidant; he was about to knight me. Oh, how miserable it all is! Would I had never lived—would I were dead."

"He has been thy worst foe. He has taught thee to slay thine own people, nay, to torture them; he has taught thee—tell me, is it not true?—even to deny thy God."

"It is true, he has; but not intentionally."

"Thou owest him nought."

"Yet I did love him, and would have died sooner than be faithless to him."

"So do sorcerers, as I have been told, love Satan, yet it is happy when they violate that awful faith. Choose, my son, between thy God, thy country, thy slaughtered kindred, and Brian."

"I do choose—I renounce him: he shall never see me again."

"Fly the country then; seek another clime; go on pilgrimage; take the cross; and employ thy valour and skill against the Saracens—the Moslems, the enemies of God."

"I will, God being my helper."

"Thou dost believe then in the God of thy fathers?"

"I think I always did, save when Brian was near. I tried not to believe, happily in vain."

"*He* will forgive thee—*He* is all-merciful. The prodigal son has returned. Now I am weary: let me rest—let me rest."

Osric wandered forth into the woods. Who shall describe his emotions? It was as when S. Remigius said to the heathen Clovis, "Burn that thou hast adored, and adore that thou hast burnt." But the terrible story of the destruction of his kindred, familiar as he was with like scenes, overcame him; yet he could not help blaming his father for his long neglect. Why had he disowned his only surviving son? why had he not trained him up in the ways of the woods, and in hatred of the Normans? why had he left him to the mercies of Brian Fitz-Count?

Then again came the remembrance of that strange partiality, even amounting to fondness, which Brian had ever shown him, and he could but contrast the coldness and indifference of his own father with the fostering care of the awful Lord of Wallingford.

But blood is thicker than water: he could no longer serve the murderer of his kindred—Heaven itself would denounce such an alliance; yet he did not even now wish to wreak vengeance. He could not turn so suddenly: the old man's solution was the right one—he would fly the country and go to the Crusades.

But how to get out of England? it was no easy matter. The chances were twenty to one that he would either meet his death from some roving band or be forcibly compelled to join them.

The solution suddenly presented itself.

He would seek his father, take sanctuary at Dorchester, and claim his aid. Even Brian could not drag him thence; and the monks of all men would and could assist him to join the Crusades.

Strong in this resolution, he returned to the cottage.

"Your grandfather is asleep; you must not disturb him, Osric, my dear boy."

"Very well, my old nurse, I will sleep too; my heart is very heavy."

He lay down on a pile of leaves and rushes in the outer room, and slept a troublous sleep. He had a strange dream, which afterwards became significant. He thought that old Judith came to him and said—

"Boy, go back to Wallingford; '*Brian*,' not 'Wulfnoth,' is the name of thy father."

The sands of old Sexwulf's life were running fast. The last rites of the Church were administered to him by the parish priest of Aston Upthorpe on the day following Osric's arrival. He made no further attempt to enter into the subject of the last interview with his grandson. From time to time he pressed the youth's hands, as if to show that he trusted him now, and that all the past was forgiven; from time to time he looked upon him with eyes in which revived affection beamed. He never seemed able to rest unless Osric was in the room.

Wearied out, Osric threw himself down upon his couch that night for brief repose, but in the still hours of early dawn Judith awoke him.

"Get up—he is passing away."

Osric threw on a garment and entered the chamber. His grandfather was almost gone; he collected his dying strength for a last blessing, murmured with dying lips, upon his beloved boy. Then while they knelt and said the commendatory prayer, he passed away to rejoin those whom he had loved and lost—the wife of his youth, the children of his early manhood—passing from scenes of violence and wrong to the land of peace and love, where all the mysteries of earth are solved.

CHAPTER XXII

THE OUTLAWS

SAD and weary were the hours to Osric which intervened between the death and burial of his grandfather. He gazed upon the dear face, where yet the parting look of love seemed to linger. The sense of desolation overwhelmed him—his earthly prospects were shattered, his dreams of ambition ended; but the dead spake not to console him, and the very heavens seemed as brass; his only consolation that he felt his lapse had been forgiven, that the departed one had died loving and blessing him.

The only true consolation in such hour of distress is that afforded by religion, but poor Osric could feel little of this; he had strayed so far from the gentle precepts which had guarded his boyhood: if he believed in religion, it was as when Satan looked into the gates of Paradise from afar. It was not his. He seemed to have renounced his portion and lot in it, to have sold himself to Satan, in the person of Brian Fitz-Count.

Yet, he could not even now *hate* the Baron, as he ought to have done, according to all regulations laid down for such cases, made and provided, ever since men began to write novels. Let the reader enter into his case impartially. He had never known either paternal or maternal love—the mother, who had perished, was not even a memory; while, on the other hand, the destroyer had adopted him as a son, and been as a father to him, distinguishing him from others by an affection all the more remarkable as coming from a rugged nature, unused to tender emotions. Again, the horror with which we moderns contemplate such a scene as his dead grandfather had described, was far less vivid in one to whom such casualties had been of constant experience, and were regarded as the usual incidents of warfare. Our readers can easily imagine the way in which he would have regarded it before he had fallen under the training of Wallingford Castle.

But it was his own mother, and Brian was her murderer. Ah, if he had but once known the gentle endearment of a fond mother's love, how different would have been his feelings! There would have been no need then to enforce upon him the duty of forsaking the life but yesterday opening so brightly to his eyes, and throwing himself a waif and a stray upon the world of strife.

He walked to and fro in the woods, and thought sometimes of all he was leaving. Sometimes of the terrible fate of her who had borne him. At another moment he felt half inclined to conceal all, and go back to Wallingford, as if nothing had happened; the next he felt he could never again grasp the hand of the destroyer of his kindred.

The hour came for the funeral. The corpse was brought forth on the bier from the hut which had so long sheltered it in life. They used no coffins in those days—it was simply wrapped in the "winding-sheet." He turned back the linen, and gazed upon the still calm face for the last time ere the bearers departed with their burden. Then he burst into a passion of tears, which greatly relieved him: it is they who cannot weep, who suffer most. His grandfather had been father, mother, and all to him, until a very recent period: and the sweet remembrances and associations of boyhood returned for a while.

The solemn burial service of our forefathers was unlike our own—perhaps not so soothing to the mourners, for whom our service seems made; but it bore more immediate reference to the departed: the service was for *them*. The prayers of the Church followed them, as in all ancient liturgies, into that world beyond the grave, as still members of Christ's mystical body, one with us in the "Communion of Saints."

The procession was in those days commonly formed at the house of the deceased, but as Sexwulf's earthly home was far from the Church, the body was met at the lych gate, as in modern times. First went the cross-bearer, then the mourners, then the priest preceding the bier, around which lighted torches were borne.

Psalms were now solemnly chanted, particularly the *De Profundis* and the *Miserere*, and at the close of each the refrain—

"Eternal rest give unto him, O Lord,
And let perpetual light shine upon him."

Then followed the solemn requiem Mass, wherein the great Sacrifice, once offered on Calvary, was pleaded for the deceased. When the last prayer had been said, the corpse was sprinkled with hallowed water, and perfumed with sweet incense, after which it was removed to its last resting place. The grave was also sprinkled with the hallowed water, emblematical of the cleansing power of the "Blood of Sprinkling"; and the body of the ancient thane was committed to the earth, sown in corruption, to be raised in joy unspeakable, and full of glory.

Around the grave were but few mourners. Famine, pestilence, and war had removed from time to time those who had known the old thane in his poverty (for thane he was by birth), but there stood two or three of a different stamp from the care-worn peasants—men clad in jerkins of leather, tall, rugged, resolute-looking fellows. One of these watched Osric closely, and when the last rites were over and the grave-digger commenced his final labour of filling up the grave, he followed the funeral party on their homeward road, as they returned to the desolate home. At last he approached Osric.

"I believe you are Osric, grandson of the true Englishman we have now laid in the earth?'

"I am that unhappy man."

"Thou art the son of a line of patriots. Thy father died fighting against the oppressor, and thou art the sole representative of his family. Canst thou remain longer in the halls of the tyrant?"

"Who art thou?"

"A true Englishman."

"Thorold is thy name, is it not?"

"How didst thou know me?"

"Because my grandfather before he died revealed all to me."

"Then thou wilt cast in thy lot with us?"

"I think not. My father yet lives; you are mistaken in thinking him dead. He is a monk in Dorchester Abbey."

"He is dead at least to the world; Brian's lance and spear slew him, so far as that is concerned."

"But I go to ask his advice. I would fain leave this unhappy land and join the Crusaders."

"And renounce the hope of vengeance upon the slayer of thy kindred?"

"I have eaten of his bread and salt."

"And thou knowest all the secrets of his prison-house. Tell us, hast thou heard of one Herwald, a follower of thy father?"

"I may not tell thee;" and Osric shuddered.

"The Normans have spoilt thee then, in *deed* and in *truth*. Wilt thou not even tell us whether Herwald yet lives?"

"I may not for the present; if my father bid me tell thee, thou shalt know. Leave me for the present; I have just buried my grandfather; let me rest for the day at least."

The outlaw, for such he was, ceased to importune him at this plaintive cry; then like a man who takes a sudden resolution, stepped aside, and Osric passed on. When he reached home he half expected to find a messenger from Wallingford chiding his delay; then he sat a brief while as one who hardly knows what to do, while old Judith brought him a savoury stew, and bade him eat. Several times she looked at him, like one who is burning to tell a secret, then pursed up her lips, as if she were striving to repress a strong inclination to speak.

At length Osric rose up.

"Judith," he said, "I may stay here no longer."

"Thou art going to Dorchester?"

"I am."

"What shall I say when the Lord of Wallingford sends for thee?"

"That I am gone to Dorchester."

"Will that satisfy them?"

"I know not. It must."

"I could tell thee all that thou wilt learn at Dorchester."

"Do so. It may save me the journey."

"I may not. I swore on the Gospels I would not tell the secret to thy"—she paused—"to Wulfnoth."

"What! another secret?"

"Yes; and one thou dost not, canst not, suspect; but, I think, didst thou know it, thou wouldst at once return to Wallingford Castle."

"Tell me—tell me all."

"Wouldst have me forsworn? No; seek thy *father*." She emphasised the word, and then added, "Ask him to let me tell thee the whole truth, if he will not do so himself; then return and learn more than thy dead grandfather has told thee, or could have told thee, for he knew not the truth."

"Judith, I will seek my father, and return at once after I have seen him."

"But the roads are dangerous; beware!'

Osric rose; put on his tunic over a coat of light chain mail; girded his sword to his side; put on a leathern cap, padded inside with steel, for in those days prudent men never travelled unarmed; then he bade Judith farewell, and started for Dorchester, making for the Synodune Hills, beyond which well-known landmarks Dorchester lay, and beneath the hills was a ford across the Thames.

He had not gone far—not half a mile—when he heard a rustling of the branches beyond the brook, and a stern voice cried—

"Stand."

"Who art thou?" he cried.

"Good men and true, and thou art our prisoner."

"If so, come and take me."

"Wilt thou yield thyself unharmed, on the pledge that no harm is intended thee?"

"I will not. I know thee, Thorold: I seek Dorchester and my father."

"Thou wilt hardly reach it or him to-day. Stand, I say, or we must take thee by force."

"No man shall make me go with him against my will," cried Osric, and drew his sword.

Thorold laughed and clapped his hands. Quick as thought five or six men dashed from the covers which had hidden them in all directions. Osric drew his sword, but before he could wield it against a foe who met him face to face, another mastered his arms from behind, and he was a prisoner.

"Do him no harm; he is his father's son. We only constrain him for his good. Bring him along."

They led, or rather bore, him through the woods for a long distance, until they came to a tangled swamp, situated amidst bog and quagmire, wherein any other men save those acquainted with the path might easily have sunk up to the neck, or even lost their lives; but in the centre was a spot of firm ground, and there, beneath the shade of a large tree, was a fire, before which roasted a haunch of venison, and to the right and left were sleeping hutches, of the most primitive construction.

"Canst thou eat?"

"I will not eat with thee."

"Thy father's son should not disdain thy father's friend. Listen; if we have made thee a prisoner, it is to save thee from thyself. The son of a true Englishman should not shed the blood of his countrymen, nor herd with his oppressors. Has not thy grandfather taught thee as much?"

"He has indeed; and no longer will I do so, I promise thee."

"Then wilt thou go a little farther, and help us to deliver thy country?"

"Can it be delivered? What can *you* do?"

"Alas! little; but we do our best and wait better times. Look, my lad, when things are at their worst the tide turns: the darkest hour is just before the dawn. Think of this happy land—happy once—now the sport of robbers and thieves! Think of the hideous dungeons where true Englishmen rot! Think of the multitudes of innocent folk burnt, racked, tortured, starved, driven to herd with the beasts! Think of the horrors of famine! Think of the unburied dead—slain foully, and breeding a pestilence, which oft destroys their murderers! Think, in short, of Wallingford Castle and its lord——"

A deep murmur of assent from the recumbent outlaws stretched on the turf around.

Osric's features twitched; he felt the force of the appeal.

"What do you want of me?"

"Our leader is a miserable captive in the devil's hold you have quitted, and of which you know the secrets."

"What can I do? They were told me in confidence. Can I break my honour?"

"Confidence! honour! If you had promised the Devil's dam to sell your soul, would you feel bound to do so?"

"In short," said another, "we *will* have the secret."

"Nay, Grimbald, patience; he will come right in time. Force is no good with such as he. He must do what is right, because it *is* right; and when he sees it, he will join us heart and soul, or he is not the son of Wulfnoth.'

"He has shown little paternal care for me; yet when you seized me I was about to seek his direction. Why not let me go, and let him decide for me?"

"A truce to folly. We know what Wulfnoth of old would have said, when he was our leader. He gave himself heart and soul to the cause—to avenge thy slaughtered kinsfolk. And now that one whom he trusted and loved well is a prisoner in that hell which you have left, can we think that he would hesitate about your duty? Why then waste time in consulting him? I appeal to your conscience. Where is Herwald?"

Osric was silent.

"By the memory of thy grandfather."

Still silence.

"Of thy murdered mother, expiring in the flames which consumed thy brothers and sisters."

Osric gave a loud cry.

"No more," he said, "no more; I will tell thee: Herwald lives."

"Where?"

"In the lowest dungeon of Wallingford Castle."

"Hast thou seen him?"

"Yes."

"Does he suffer torture?"

"Terribly."

"Of what nature?"

"I hardly dare to tell thee."

"The sachentage?"

"As bad as that; the crucet-chest—the———"

"Stay—wilt thou help us to deliver him?"

"Save my honour."

"Honour! honour! honour!" and they laughed the word to scorn, till the woods caught the echoes, and seemed to repeat it, "Honour! honour!"

"Get that delusion out of thy mind. To fight for one's country, nay, to die for it, that is true honour; to deliver the outcast and poor, to save them from the hands of the ungodly,—it is for this we have brought thee here. Let me tell thee what I have seen, nay, thou hast seen as much, and of the woes of thy bleeding country, bleeding at every pore. If the memory of thy mother stir thee not up, then thou art NIDDERING."

At the sound of this word—this term of utter reproach to an English ear, worse than "coward" a thousand times, suggesting a depth of baseness beyond conception—Osric started.

"And deservest to die," said the outlaw who had just spoken.

Osric's pride took alarm at once; his downcast look changed.

"Slay me, then," he said; "the sooner the better."

"Nay, brother, that is not the way—thou wilt spoil it all; we would win him by *conviction*, not by threats."

"Let me have an hour to think."

"Take some food."

"No."

They left him alone, but he knew he was watched, and could not escape, nor did he wish to; he was yielding to his destiny.

One hour of such mental anguish—the boast of chivalry, the pomp of power, the false glamour, all giving way to the *conviction* that the Englishmen were *right*, and their cause that of truth and justice, nay, of God!

At the end of the hour he rose to his feet and looked around. The men were seated at their repast. He approached them.

"Give me of your food."

They did so. Thorold's eyes sparkled with delight; he saw what it meant.

They waited for him to speak; but he satisfied hunger first, then he drank, and afterwards said calmly—

"Is there any oath of admission to your band?"

"Only to swear to be true to England and Englishmen till death, and to wage war against their oppressors, of whatsoever degree, with all your powers. So help you God."

Osric repeated the oath solemnly and distinctly.

The outlaws shouted with joy.

"And now," he said, "let us talk of Herwald, and I will do all I can to help you to deliver him; but it will be a difficult task. I must take time to consider it."

Meanwhile old Judith sat at home in the lonely hut, as she had done on the occasion recorded in the fourth chapter of our tale. Again she sat by the fire which smoked on the hearth, again she sang quaint snatches of old songs.

"It is a wise son which knows his own sire," she said, and going to a corner of the hut, opened once more her poor old rickety chest, from which she took the packet of musty parchment, containing a ring with a seal, a few articles of infant attire, a little red shoe, a small frock, and a lock of maiden's hair.

"Poor Ethra," she said, "how strange thy fate!" and she kissed the lock of hair again and again. "And now thy boy may inherit his father's honours and titles unchecked, for his supposed grandfather is here no longer to claim him, and his half-brothers are lepers. Wulfnoth never loved him—never. Why, then, should he not give him up to his true father? Vengeance! to be sure, he should not desire this now. A monk, fie! fie! Wulfnoth might seek it; Father Alphege cannot, may not. He will tell Osric the whole truth, or refer him to me; and he may go back with a clear conscience to Wallingford; and I shall have the proofs ready, which the Lord of Wallingford would give all he has to possess. Here they are, stripped from the dead attendants or found on the helpless babe."

Just then she heard steps approaching; she jealously hid her treasures.

A page dismounted from his horse at the door of the hut.

"Is the squire Osric within?"

"Enter."

A youth of fourteen summers, just what Osric had been when he *began*, entered the door, and looked curiously around. "What! was *this* Osric's home—Osric, the Baron's favourite?"

"He has gone to Dorchester Abbey."

"Dorchester Abbey! he was to have returned last night to Wallingford."

"He stayed for the funeral."

The boy looked amazed. What was an old man's funeral compared with Brian's orders?

"And his grandfather, dying, bade him go to Dorchester, whence he will speedily return, and bring, yes, bring with him that shall make full atonement for his offence, if offence it be."

"It had need be something very valuable then. It might cost some of us our heads, did we do the like."

"They will not hurt a hair of his, I am sure. You shall have him with you soon. Ah, yes! very soon."

The boy shook his head, looked once more curiously at the old woman and the hut, and departed, muttering—

"I should be sorry to stand in Osric's shoes; but then he is a favourite;" and young Louis of Trouville, page to Brian for the good of his education, rode down the brook.

"After all, he is no gentleman. Why did my lord choose a page from amongst the peasants?"

Many had asked that question before

CHAPTER XXIII

THE PESTILENCE (AT BYFIELD)

THE time had passed away slowly at the lazar-house at Byfield. Life was tedious there to most people, least of all to the good Chaplain, Father Ambrose; for he loved his poor lepers with a love which could only come direct from Him Who loved us all. He did not feel time lag. Each day had its appointed duties: in holy offices of prayer and praise, or in his labour of love, the days sped on. He felt the strain, it is true, but he bore it. He looked for no holiday here; it could never come. He was cloistered and confined by that general belief in the contagion of leprosy, which was so strong in the world that many would have slain a leper had they met him outside the defined boundaries, or set their mastiffs to tear him in pieces.

One day Father Ambrose was seated in his cell after Terce, when one of the attendants came to him with a serious and anxious face.

"I should be glad for you to come and see Gaspard; he has been very ill all night, and there are some strange symptoms about him."

The Chaplain rose, and followed the "keeper" into the chamber above, where in a small "cubicle," separated by a screen from the other couches, the sick man tossed.

"He is delirious; how long has he been so?"

"Nearly all the night."

"And in a raging fever?—but this blackness; I never saw one so dark before."

It was, alas, too true. The body was fast assuming a

strange dark, yet livid, hue, as if the blood were ink instead of red blood.

"Lift up the left arm," said the Chaplain.

Near the armpits were two or three swellings about the size of a pigeon's egg. The Chaplain saw them and grew serious.

"It is the black fever—the plague!" almost screamed the horrified attendant.

"Keep cool, brother John; nothing is gained by excitement, and all is lost by fear; put your trust in God."

"But I have *touched* him—drawn in his infected breath—I am a dead man."

The Chaplain heeded him not.

"Brother, canst thou speak?" he said to the sick man.

A moan was the only reply.

"Brother, dost thou know that thou art dying?"

A moan again.

"And that the best of us have not lived as we should?"

Another sigh, so dolorous.

"And dost thou believe that God's dear Son died for thee?"

A faint gesture of assent.

"Say thou, brother, 'I put the pitiful Passion of Thy dear Son between me and my sins.'"[1]

"I do, oh God. Sweet Jesus, save me."

And then he relapsed into an unconscious state, in which he continued till he died.

"We must bury him directly, brother John."

The attendant shuddered.

"Yes, we two; we have been in danger, no one else need come. You go and tell the grave-digger to have the grave ready directly, and the moment it is ready we two will bury him."

"Oh God! I am a dead man," said poor brother John.

"Nay, we cannot die till our time come, and if so, the

---

[1] This is an extant form of those ages for the reconciliation of a penitent at the last gasp.

way HE chooses is best. We all owe HIM a death, you know. Fear is the worst thing you can entertain now; it brings on the very thing you dread. Overcome *that*, at all events, if you can."

And the poor frightened fellow went out to do as he was bidden.

Then the brave and good man composed the corpse; placed a crucifix on its breast; drew the bed-clothes round it to serve as a winding-sheet, for they must be buried or burned; said the commendatory prayers; and walked for a time in the fresh air.

He knew his own danger, but he heeded it not. All things, he was persuaded, worked together for good to them that loved God; besides, what had he to live for?— his poor sheep—the lepers? Yes; but God could raise up a better man than he, so in his humility he thought; and if he were—called home——

Did not the thought of that Purgatory, which was in the Creed of his time, come between him and the notion of rest?

Not at all; he was content to leave all that; if his Father thought he needed such correction, he was willing to pass through it; and like a dear son to kiss the rod, as he had done on earth, safe in the hands of his Father.

Neither did his thoughts turn much to the Saints. Of course he believed, as every one did then, that it was right to invoke them—and he had done so that day in the prescribed commendatory prayers for the dying; but, as stars fade away in the presence of the sun, so did all these things fade away before his love for the central sun of his soul—his crucified Lord.

The hours passed away in rapt emotion; he never felt so happy as that afternoon.

Then came the grave-digger.

"The grave is ready."

"Tell brother John to come and help."

"I do not think he is able; he seems unwell himself."

"Then you and I must do it."

"Willingly—where you lead I follow."

"Come up the stairs."

They went to the dormitory; took the sad burden, wrapped in the bed-clothing as it was, and bore it to the grave; the priest said the burial office; the grave-digger filled up the grave; and all was over with poor Gaspard.

But before that sun set the Chaplain was called to brother John, and that same night the poor fellow died of the fever—fear, doubtless, having been a predisposing cause.

The terror began; the facts could not long be concealed. At Evensong that night the Chaplain spoke to them in a short address, so full of vivid faith and Christian hope that those who heard it never forgot it.—"Why should they fear death? They had led a living death, a dying life, these many years. Their exile was over. The Father called them home. They had long done with this wretched world. The Christian's true fatherland was Heaven."

So he spoke rather like an Angel than a man. But they could not all rise to it—how could it be expected? life clings to life. When Newgate was on fire in the great riots, the most anxious to be saved were some condemned criminals left for execution on the morrow.

But for a select few, all fear was gone.

Such men were needed: they had their senses about them; they could help others to the last; they, and they alone, dared to attend the dying, to bury the dead.

Now came the great trial—the confinement. The lepers mutinied against being shut up with death, they longed for liberty, they panted for it; they would not be imprisoned with the plague.

Then began positive fighting. The poor patients had to be restrained by main force, until the Chaplain came, and by his great power over their minds, persuaded them to stay.

Every one was asking, "How came it amongst us?" and the mystery was explained when they were told of a bale of cloth for their tailor consigned to the house from the

Levant, viâ Bristol, and which in all the long tedious voyage had retained the infection ever living in the East.

Day by day fresh victims were carried to the grave. The plague was probably simply a malignant form of typhus, nourished in some human hotbed to the highest perfection. The *bacillus* or germ is, we trust, extinct, but otherwise enough might be bred in a bottle to poison a county, as we have heard stated.

All at once the heaviest blow fell upon them.

Father Ambrose was walking in the grounds, taking rest of mind after intense mental and bodily exertion, when he felt a sudden throb of violent heat, followed by an intense chill and a sickening sensation accompanied by faintness. He took off his cassock—he saw the fatal swelling.

"My summons is come," he said. "Oh, my Father, I thank Thee for calling me home; but these poor sheep whom Thou hast committed to my care, what shall they do?"

Then he walked quietly to his cell and lay down on his bed. He had watched the disease in others; he entertained no hope of recovery. "In a few hours I shall see Him face to face Whom I have loved," said he.

They came and found him. Never was man more patient; but that mediæval idea of intense self-denial was with him to the last. He refused water: they thought him delirious.

"HE would not drink," he said.

They saw his thoughts were on the Cross, and that he was treading the pathway opened by the Crucified One, and they said no more.

He had received the Holy Communion that morning—his last Communion; the usual rites could not be attempted now. Before he relapsed into the last stage, they heard the words in his native tongue—

"Mon Dieu! Mon Dieu! ouvrez moi."

They were his last. The door was open and he had entered. Ah, who shall follow even in imagination, and trace his progress to the gates of day?

> "Go wing thy flight from star to star,
> From world to luminous world, as far
>   As the universe spreads its flaming hall:
> Take all the pleasures of all the spheres,
> And multiply each through endless years,
>   One moment of Heaven is worth them all."

But those left behind in the lazar-house—ah me! deprived of the only man who had gained an empire over their hearts, and could control them—what of them?

They lost *all* control, and broke through all discipline; they overpowered their keepers, who indeed scarcely tried their best to restrain them, sharing the common fear; they broke the gates open; they poured forth and dispersed all through the country, carrying the infection wherever they went.

Still this was not a very wide scope; the woods, the forests, were their chief refuge. And soon the story was told everywhere. It was heard at the lordly towers of Warwick; it was told at the stately pile of Kenilworth; it was proclaimed at Banbury. It startled even those violent men who played with death, to be told that a hundred lepers were loose, carrying the double curse of plague and leprosy wherever they went.

"It must be stamped out," said the stern men of the day: "we must hunt them down and slay them."

So they held a council at Banbury, where all the neighbouring barons—who were generally of one party in that neighbourhood—took counsel.

They decided that proclamation should be everywhere made; that if the lepers returned to the lazar-house at Byfield within three days, all should be forgiven; but otherwise, that the barons should collect their savage hounds, and hunt them down in the forest.

And this was the very forest where we left poor Evroult dying—the forest of the hermitage which these poor lepers were tolerably sure to find out, and to seek shelter.

And here we will leave our poor friends for a while, and return to Wallingford Castle.

CHAPTER XXIV

THE OPENING OF THE PRISON HOUSE

GREAT was the surprise and anger of Brian Fitz-Count that his favourite page should dare to tarry, even to bury his grandfather, much less to fulfil an idle vow, when he had bidden him return at once.

He cared so little for sacred things, whether the true gold of the mint, or the false superstitions of the age, that he could not understand how they should influence other men.

Yet he knew they did exercise a strong power over both the imagination and the will, and sometimes had acknowledged that the world must have a religion, and this was as good as any other.

"Let Osric believe as much or as little as he likes," he said, "only he must remember that Brian Fitz-Count is the deity to be worshipped in Wallingford Castle, and that he allows no other worship to interfere with that due to him."

The next morning Osric reappeared, and at once sought the presence of his lord.

"Thou art more than a day behind?"

"I tarried to bury my grandfather, and to execute a vow in his behalf."

"That is well; but remember, Osric, I permit none here to disobey my orders, either for the sake of the living or the dead. He *is* dead, then?"

"He died the night I arrived."

"May he rest in peace," said Brian carelessly, feeling

glad in his heart that the old man was gone, and that there was no one left to dispute his dominion over the heart of Osric.

"But for my grandfather's vow I had returned last night after the funeral. I have discharged my debt to him, and beg pardon for my delay. I now belong to you."

It was strange, however, the wooden tone in which he spoke, like a schoolboy reciting a lesson.

"And thou shalt find in me a father, if thou always continuest to deserve it — as by obedience thou hast hitherto done—save this lapse, in place of him whom thou hast lost."

"Am I to go to Shirburne?"

"I have sent Malebouche. There are certain matters of business to talk over. I want thee to turn scribe for the rest of the day, and write letters for me. It is a thing I could never accomplish. All I can do is to sign my name, or better still, affix my seal. My pen has been the sword, my book the country around; wherein I write my black characters, as men say."

Yes, he did indeed, and the fame remains till this day.

So all the rest of the day Osric wrote at his lord's dictation. There was some especial correspondence with the leaders of the party, and that night messengers were speeding north, south, east, and west with the missives Osric had penned.

Late in the day, while Osric was walking on the ramparts, a page came after him and bade him hasten to the bower of the Lady Maude. The manner was urgent, and he went at once.

He found the lady in tears, surrounded by her handmaidens, who were standing on each side of her "curule" chair, endeavouring in vain to console her.

The Baron was striding up and down the spacious room, which, as we have said, overlooked the river.

"Read this, Osric," he said, and put a letter into his hands. "I can but half understand it."

Osric read. The letter came from the governor of the lazar-house, and contained a succinct account of the terrible visitation we have recorded in our last chapter.

"But our boys are at the hermitage, dame," said Brian; "they are safe; you need not weep."

Osric read on—how that the lepers had broken loose and taken to the woods. Then came the significant close: "So the neighbouring barons and knights of all degrees are gathering together their dogs, to hunt them in the woods; and I greatly fear lest harm happen to thy sons, who have been, with thy permission, left to the care of the hermit Meinhold, dwelling within the same forest."

It was a terrible thought to the poor mother: the affliction of her boys was the great burden of her life. Yet the customs of the age had required the sacrifice of her. She had been forbidden, perhaps it was kind, to visit them, lest the sight of their state should but increase her woe; but they were never long out of her thoughts.

"Husband! father! thou must go and protect them, or I will go myself."

"Enough, Maude, enough; I will start at once with a troop of a hundred men, and whatever they do in the rest of the forest, methinks I shall enforce respect for the hermit's cave—where we are told they are so happy. Osric, send Osborne to me for orders at once."

"Am I to go, my lord?"

"No; you must remain here, I have special reasons. You will be in attendance on the Lady Maude."

Osric's eyes glistened.

"You will see that certain orders I shall leave are carried out, in reference to the business in which you are employed. If any question your right to command, and refuse obedience, show them this ring. You see how I trust you, my son."

"Would he were our son," sobbed the Lady Maude; "but I have none to comfort me; my poor boys, torn from me—torn from me. Hasten, my lord; it is far to Byfield—very far; you may not be in time."

"I will bring thee the hands and feet of any who have dared to harm them."

That same hour the Baron departed with his troop, and Osric was busy for a while in executing his commission. He occupied his own little chamber in the keep; it was at a great height above the hill on which the lofty tower was raised, and the view of the country was most extensive.

When nightfall came, Osric was here alone, and he did a very singular thing.

He lit a lamp, and placed it in his window; then he took it away in a very undecided fashion; then he replaced it again; then he took it away, and finally replaced it.

"The die is cast," he said.

Two roads lay before him,—it was an awful crisis in his life,—two roads, utterly different, which could only lead to most opposite issues, and the strife was *which* to choose. The way was yet open.

But to enter either he must break his faith. Here lay the sting to his generous heart.

The one road led to honour, to riches, to power, to glory even; and had all which could delight a young warrior's mind, but coupled with the support of foul tyranny, the uprooting of the memory of his kindred and their woes, and the breaking of his newly-pledged faith to the outlaws.

The other road led to a life of obscurity and poverty, perhaps to a death of ignominy, and certainly began with an act of treachery towards one who, however cruel to others, had loved and trusted him, of which the ring he bore was a token and a pledge.

It was when he thought of this that he withdrew the light.

Then came the remembrance of the sufferers in the foul dens below.

"It is the cause of God, and truth, and freedom, and justice, and all that is holy;" and he replaced the light.

Then he knelt; he could pray now—

"Oh God, direct me—help me—show some token of Thine approval this night. Even now I believe in Thee as my grandfather did. Oh save me, and help Thy poor oppressed ones this night; deliver them from darkness and the shadow of death, and break their bonds asunder."

Then he went to attend at the supper of the Lady Maude, where he was received with marked attention. He had of course been trained in all the etiquette exacted from pages and squires, and was expected to make himself agreeable in a hundred ways, to carve the joints with elegance, and to wait upon the ladies.

This part of his duty he had often delighted to execute, but to-night he was "distrait." The poor lady was in so much grief herself at the danger of her sons, whom she had not seen for five years, that she did not notice his abstraction, as she otherwise certainly would have done.

Then it fell ordinarily to the province of the squires and pages to amuse the party,—to sing songs, recite romaunts, play the troubadour, or to join in such games as chess and draughts, lately imported from the East, with the fair ladies of the little court,—when they dined, or rather supped, in private as now. But no songs were sung this night—no tales of valour or chivalry recited; and the party broke up early. Compline was said by the chaplain who was present, for in the bower of so great a lady there must be respect for forms; and then the fair ones went to bed.

Osric was now at liberty.

"Art thou for a composing draught to-night, my squire?" said the chaplain. "I can compound a fair night-cap for an aching head, if thou wilt come to my cell."

"Nay, my calls are urgent now; I have been detained too long by my duties as a squire of dames. I have orders for our worthy gaoler Tustain and his sons."

"Not to put any prisoners on the rack to-night? it is late for that; let the poor things rest till to-morrow."

"It is not to that effect that my orders run."

"They say you did not like that kind of thing at first."

"Neither do I now, but I have perforce got used to it."

"*Bon soir;*" and the chaplain sauntered off to drink mulled sack. It was a shocking thing that the Church, in his person, should set her seal of approbation on such tyranny as that of a Norman hold in Stephen's days.

Osric descended to the foot of the tower, crossed the greensward, and entered the new dungeons of Brian's Close. On the ground-floor were the apartments of Tustain the gaoler, extending over the whole basement of the tower and full of the hateful implements of his office.

There were manacles, gyves, and fetters. There were racks and thumbscrews, scourges, pincers, and other instruments of mediæval cruelty. There were arms of various kinds—swords, axes, lances, bows and arrows, armour for all parts of the body, siege implements, and the like. There were lanterns and torches for the service of the dungeons. There were rows of iron basons, plates, and cups for the food of the prisoners. Lastly, there were many huge keys.

In the midst of all this medley stood a solid oak table, and thereat sat Tustain the gaoler-in-chief—now advanced in years and somewhat impotent on his feet, but with a heart as hard as the nether millstone—with his three sons, all gaolers, like himself, eating their supper. A fairly spread table was before them—very different from the fare they supplied to their prisoners, you may be sure.

"We have locked up for the night, and are taking our ease, Master Osric."

"I grieve to disturb thy ease, but my lord has sent me to thee, Tustain."

"He must be some leagues away at this moment."

"But he has left orders by me; see his ring."

Tustain recognised the token in a moment, and bowed before it.

"Wilt not take some food? Here is a noble haunch of venison, there some good trout, there some wood-pigeons in a pie—fish, flesh, and fowl."

"Nay, I have just supped with our lady."

"Thou art fortunate. I remember when thou wert brought in here with thy grandfather as a prisoner, and saw the torture-chamber for the first time."

"More startling changes have happened, and may yet; but my business—Art tired, my men?"

"We have had little to do to-day—no raid, no convoy of goods to pursue, no fighting, no hunting; it has been dull."

"But there is work afoot *now*, and stern work. You, Richard, must take horse and bear this letter to Shirburne, where you must give it to Malebouche, and wait his orders; you, Tristam, must carry this to Faringdon Castle, and bring back a reply; you, Aubrey, to the Castle of the Black Lady of Speen."

They looked astonished—as well they might—to be sent out for rides, of some fifteen miles each, at that hour.

But the ring—like the genii who were the slaves of the Lamp, so were they slaves of the Ring.

"And who will help me with the prisoners?" said Tustain.

"You are permitted to call in such of the men-at-arms as you please."

"Why did he not send men-at-arms? You are sure he said my sons were to go? Why, if we were suddenly called to put any of my lambs to the torture, these men-at-arms would hardly know how to do it."

"You could direct them," said Osric. Then to the sons, "Now, my men, haste speed."

In half an hour they were gone.

"A cup of sack for consolation—the best wine from our lord's own cellar. I have brought thee a flask."

"Wilt thou stay and help me discuss it?"

"For a few minutes only; I have much yet to do."

Osric produced the flask from the gypsire which hung from the belt of his tunic.

Then the old man took down two goblets, and Osric poured the wine.

The old man drank freely; Osric but sparingly. Soon the former began to talk incoherently, and at last he cried—

"What wine was that? Why, it was Old Nick's own brewing. I can't keep my eyes open."

Half suspecting something amiss, the old man rose, as if going to the door; but Osric threw his arms around him, and as he did so the old man gave way to the influence of the powerful narcotic which the youth had mingled with his drink, and fell like a log on the couch to which Osric had dragged him.

"I hope I have not killed him; but if I have it is only half his deserts. Now for my perilous task. How this ring has helped me!"

He went first and strongly barred the outer door, then traversed the upper corridor till he came to a room in the new buildings, which was a private den of the Baron. It was panelled with oak, and pressing a knob on the panel, a secret door opened, disclosing a flight of steps. These went down into the bowels of the earth; then a narrow passage opened at right angles to the corridor above, which Osric traversed. It was damp and slimy, and the air had a deathly odour; but it soon came to an end, and Osric ascended a similar flight of steps to the one by which he had descended; again he drew out the key and opened an iron door at the summit. He stood upon a terrace at the edge of the river, and just upon a level with the water.

The night was dark and stormy—not a star could be seen. The stream rippled by as Osric stood and listened. The clock struck twelve, or rather the man on duty with an iron hammer struck the bell in the tower of St. Peter's Church twelve times with his hammer to tell the midnight hour. A few minutes of feverish suspense—the night air fanned his heated brow—when he heard muffled oars close by, heard rather the splash of the water as it fell from the upraised blades. A large boat was at hand.

"Who comes?" said Osric in a low voice.

"Englishmen, good and true."

The outlaws stood on the terrace.

"Follow me," said Osric.

In a few minutes they were all assembled in the heart of the stronghold in the gaoler's room, where the gaoler himself lay snoring like a hog.

"Shall we slay him?" said they, naturally looking on the brute with abhorrence.

"No," said Osric; "remember our compact—no bloodshed save in self-defence. He will sleep till this time to-morrow night, when I fear Brian will do for him what he has done for thousands."

"What is that?"

"Hang him."

"He deserves it. Let the gaoler and the hangman hang."

"Amen."

"Now for the keys," said Thorold.

Osric knew them all, and taking them, led the liberators down below, into the gloomy corridor from which the dungeons opened on either side. The men shuddered as they stood between these dens of cruelty, from which moans, faint and low, from time to time issued like the sighing of the plaintive wind.

One by one they opened these dens, and took the prisoners out. Many were too weak, from torture and privation, to stand, and had to be supported. They hardly understood at first what it all meant; but when they knew their deliverers, were delirious with joy.

At last they came to the cell where the "crucet-box" was placed, and there they found Herwald. Osric opened the chest, of which the lid was only a framework of iron bars. He was alive, and that was all; his hair was white as snow, his mind almost gone.

"Are the angels come to take me out of Purgatory?" he said.

"Herwald, do you not know me?" said Thorold.

It was vain; they could evoke no memory.

Then they went to the torture-chamber, where a plaintive, whimpering cry struck their ears. In the corner stood a boy on tiptoes; a thin cord attached to a thumbscrew, imprisoning both his poor thumbs, was passed over a pulley in the ceiling, and then tied to a peg in the wall, so that the poor lad could only find firm footing at the expense of the most exquisite pain; and so he had been left for the night, the accursed iron eating into the flesh of his thumbs all the time.

"My boy! my boy!" said Thorold, and recognised his own son Ulric, whom he had only lost that week, and traced to the castle—hence his anxiety for Osric's immediate aid—and the poor father wept.

Happily Osric had the key of the thumbscrew, and the lad was soon set free.

"Break up all the instruments of torture," said Thorold.

Axes were at their girdles: they smashed all the hateful paraphernalia. No sound could possibly be heard above; the depth of the dungeons and the thickness of the walls gave security.

"Lock up all the cells, all the outer doors, and bring the keys; we will throw them into the river."

It took a long time to get the poor disabled victims through the passages—many had to be carried all the way; but they were safely brought to the large boat, and placed on beds of straw or the like; not one sentinel taking the alarm, owing to the darkness and the storm.

"Now for Dorchester Abbey," said Osric. "We must take sanctuary, before daybreak, for all these poor captives, they are incapable of any other mode of escape."

"And we will attend as an escort," said the outlaws.

"Then for the forest."

So Osric atoned for his residence in Wallingford Castle.

CHAPTER XXV

THE SANCTUARY

THE heavily-laden boat ascended the stream with its load of rescued captives, redeemed from their living death in the dungeons of Brian's stronghold.

The night continued intensely dark, a drizzling rain fell; but all this was in favour of the escape. Upon a moonlight night this large boat must have been seen by the sentinels, and followed.

There was of course no "lock" at Bensington in those days, consequently the stream was much swifter than now; and it was soon found that the load they bore in their barge was beyond the strength of the rowers. But this was easily remedied: a towing rope was produced, and half a dozen of Thorold's band drew the bark up stream, while another half-dozen remained on board, steered or rowed, or attended to the rope at the head of the boat, as needed.

Osric was with them: he intended to go to Dorchester and see his father, and obtain his approbation of the course he was pursuing and direction for the future.

All that night the boat glided up stream; their progress was, of necessity, slow. The groans of the poor sufferers, most of whom had endured recent torture, broke the silence of the night, otherwise undisturbed, save by the rippling of the water against the prow of the boat.

That night ever remained fixed in the memory of Osric, —the slow ascent of the stream; the dark banks gliding by; the occasional cry of the men on the shore, or the man at the prow, as the rope encountered difficulties in its course; the joy of the rescued, tempered with apprehension lest they should be pursued and recaptured, for they were, most of them, quite unable to walk, for every one was more or less crippled; the splash of the rain; the moan of the wind; the occasional dash of a fish,—all these details seemed to fix themselves, trifles as they were, on the retina of the mind.

Osric meditated much upon his change of life, but he did not now wish to recall the step he had taken. His better feelings were aroused by the misery of those dungeons, and by the approbation of his better self, in the contemplation of the deliverance he had wrought.

While he thus pondered a soft hand touched his; it was that of the boy, the son of Thorold, who had been chained to the wall by means of the thumbscrew locked upon his poor thumbs.[1]

"Do your thumbs pain you now?" asked Osric.

"Not so much; but the place where the bar crossed them yet burns—the pain was maddening."

"Dip this linen in the stream, and bind it round them; they will soon be well. Meanwhile you have the satisfaction that your brave endurance has proved your faithfulness: not many lads had borne as much."

"I knew it was life or death to my father; how then could I give way to the accursed Norman?"

"Pain is sometimes a powerful reasoner. How did they catch you?"

"I was sent on an errand by my father, and a hunting party saw and chased me; they questioned me about the outlaws, till they convinced themselves I was one, and brought me to the castle, where they put on the thumbscrew, and told me there it should remain till I told them all the secrets of the band—especially their hiding-places. I moaned with the pain, but did not utter a word; and

---

[1] This cruelly ingenious contrivance of thumbscrew, lock, and steel chain may be seen at the house of John Knox, at Edinburgh, amongst other similar curiosities.

they left me, saying I should soon confess or go mad; then God sent you."

"Yes, God had sent him." Osric longed no more for the fleshpots of Egypt.

Just as the autumnal dawn was breaking they arrived at the junction of Tame and Isis, and the Synodune Hills rose above them. They ascended the former stream, and followed its winding course with some difficulty, as the willows on the bank interfered with the proper management of the boat, until they came to the abbey-wharf. They landed; entered the precincts, bearing those who could neither walk nor limp, and supporting those who limped, to the hospitium.

They were in sanctuary.

In the city of refuge, and safe while they remained there. Whatever people may think of monasteries now, they thanked God for them then. It is quite true that in those dreadful days even sanctuary was violated from time to time, but it was not likely to be so in this instance. Brian Fitz-Count respected the forms and opinions of the Church, outwardly at least; although he hated them in his inward heart, especially when they came between him and his prey.

The good monks of Dorchester were just emerging from the service of Lauds, and great was their surprise to see the arrival of this multitude of impotent folk. However, they enacted their customary part of good Samaritans at once, under the direction of the infirmarer—Father Alphege himself—who displayed unwonted sympathy and activity when he learned that they were refugees from Wallingford dungeons; and promised that all due care should be taken of the poor sufferers.

There had been one or two Jews amongst the captives, but they had not entered the precincts, seeking refuge with a rabbi in the town.

When they had seen their convoy safe, the outlaws returned to their haunts in the forest, taking Ulric, son of Thorold, with them, but leaving poor Herwald in the hands of Father Alphege, secure of his receiving the very best attention. Poor wretch! his sufferings had been so great and so prolonged in that accursed den, or rather chest, that his reason was shaken, his hair prematurely gray, his whole gait and bearing that of a broken-down old man, trembling at the least thing that could startle him, anon with piteous cries beseeching to be let out, as if still in his "crucet-box."

"'Thou art out, my poor brother, never to return," said Alphege. "Surely, my Herwald, thou knowest me! thou hast ridden by my side in war and slept beside me in peace many and many a time."

Herwald listened to the tones of his voice as if some chord were struck, but shook his head.

"He will be better anon," said the Father; "rest and good food will do much."

While thus engaged the great bell rang for the Chapter Mass, which was always solemnly sung, being the choral Mass of the day; and the brethren and such guests as were able entered the hallowed pile. Osric was amongst them. He had not gone with the outlaws; he had done his duty by them; he now claimed to be at his father's disposal.

For the first time in a long period he felt all the old associations of his childhood revive—all the influences of religion, never really abjured, kindle again. He could hardly attend to the service. He did not consciously listen to the music or observe the rites, but he felt it all in his inmost soul; and as he knelt all the blackness of his sinful participation in deeds of cruelty and murder—for it was little else—all the baseness of his ingratitude in allowing, nay, nurturing, unbelief in his soul, in trying, happily very successfully, *not* to believe in God, came upon him.

He had come to consult his natural father, as he thought, and to offer himself to his direction as an obedient son: he now rather sought the priest, and reconciliation as a prodigal to his Heavenly Father as the first step necessary, for in those days penitence always found vent in such confession.

But both father and priest were united in Alphege; and after the Chapter Mass he sought the good infirmarer, and craved of his charity to make his confession.

Will it be believed? his father did not know him. It was indeed years since they had met, and it was perhaps difficult to recognise the child in this young warrior, now come to man's estate—at least to man's height and stature.

Alphege marked the tear-bedewed cheek, the choking voice; he knew the signs of penitence; he hesitated not for a moment.

"My son, I am not the *pœnitentiarius* who ordinarily receives strangers to Confession."

"But I wish to come to thee. Oh, father, I have fought against it, and almost did Satan conquer in me: refuse me not."

"Nay, my son; I cannot refuse thee."

And they entered the church.

Father Alphege had composed himself in the usual way for the monotonous recitation of human sin—all too familiar to his ears—but as he heard he became agitated in himself. The revelation was clear, none could doubt it: he recognised the penitent.

"My son," he said at the close, "thy sin has been great, very great. Thou hast joined in ill-treating men made in the image of God; thou art stained with blood; thy sin needs a heavy penance."

"Name it, let it be ever so heavy."

"Go thou to the Holy Land, take the Cross, and employ thy talents for war in the cause of the Lord."

"I could desire nothing better, father."

"On that condition I absolve thee;" and the customary formula was pronounced.

A hard "condition" indeed! a meet penance! Osric might still gratify his taste for fighting, without sin.

They left the church—Osric as happy as he could be.

A great weight was lifted off his mind. It was only in such an age that a youth, loving war, might still enjoy his propensity as a religious penance. *Similia similibus curantur*, says the old proverb.

The two walked in the cloisters.

"My father—for thou knowest thy son now—I am wholly in thy hands. Hadst thou bidden me, I had joined the outlaws, and fought for my country. Now thou must direct me."

"Were there even a *chance* of successful resistance, my son, I would bid thee stay and fight the Lord's battle here; but it is hopeless. What can such desultory warfare do? No, our true hope lies now in the son of the Empress —the descendant of our old English kings, for such he is by his mother's side—Henry Plantagenet. He will bridle these robbers, and destroy their dens of tyranny."

"But Brian is fighting on that side."

"And when the victory is gained, as it will be, it will cut short such license as the Lord of Wallingford now exercises,—destroy these robber castles, the main of them, put those that remain under proper control, drive these 'free lances' out of England, and restore the reign of peace."

"May I not then assist the coming of that day?"

"How couldst thou? Thou canst never return to Wallingford, or take part in the horrible warfare, which, nevertheless, is slowly working out God's Will. No; go abroad, as thou art now *bound* to do, and never return to England until thou canst do so with honour."

"Thou biddest me go at once?"

"Without wasting a day."

"What steps must I take?"

"Dost thou know a moated grange called Lollingdune, in the parish of Chelseye?"

"Well."

"It is an infirmary for Reading Abbey, and the Abbot is expected to-morrow; thou must go, furnished with credentials from our Abbot Alured. The Abbot of Reading is a mitred abbot, and has power to accept thy vows and make thee a knight of the Cross. I doubt if even Brian would dare touch thee then; but keep out of his way till that time; go not by way of Wallingford."

"That were madness. I will make across country."

"And now, dear son, come to noon-meat; I hear the refectory bell."

To the south-west of the village of Cholsey (Chelseye) the Berkshire downs sink into the level plain of the valley of the Thames. Here, therefore, there was that broken ground which always accompanies the transition from a higher to a lower level, and several spurs of the higher ranges stretch out into the plain like peninsulas; while in other places solitary hills, like islands, which indeed they once were, stand apart from the mainland of hills.

One of these hill islands was thickly clothed with wood in those days, as indeed it is now. And to the north-west there lay a "moated grange."

A deep moat, fed by streams which arose hard by, enclosed half an acre or less of ground. This had been laid out as a "pleasaunce," and in the centre was placed a substantial house of stone, of ecclesiastical design. It was a country residence of the monks of Reading Abbey, where they sent sick brethren who needed change of air, to breathe the refreshing breezes which blow off the downs.

Such a general sense of insecurity, however, was felt all over the country by clericals and laics alike, that they dug this deep moat, and every night drew up their drawbridge, leaving the enclosure under the protection of huge and faithful mastiffs, who had been taught to reverence a monk's cassock at night, but to distrust all parties wearing lay attire, whether of mail or otherwise.

A level plain, between outlying spurs of the downs, lay to the west, partly grazing land, partly filled with the primeval forest, and boggy and dangerous in places. Here the cows of the abbey grazed, which supplied the convalescents with the milk so necessary in their cases; but every night each member of the "milky herd" was carefully housed inside the moat.

There was great preparation going on at the grange of Lollingdune, so called from its peculiar position at the foot of the hill. The Abbot of Reading, as we have elsewhere learned, was expected on the morrow. He was a mighty potentate; thrice honoured; had a seat in the great council of the kingdom; wore a mitre; was as great and grand as a bishop, and so was reverenced by all the lesser fry.

So the cooks were busy. The fatted calf was slain, several fowls had to pay the debt of nature, carp were in stew; various wines were broached—Malmsey, Osey, Sack, and such like; devices in pastry executed, notably a pigeon-pie, with a superincumbent mitre in pie-crust; and many kinds of sweets were curiously and wonderfully made.

At the close of the day sweet tinkling bells announced the approach of the cavalcade over the ridge of the hill to the eastward; and soon a dozen portly monks, mounted on sleek mules, with silver bells on their trappings, for they did not affect the warlike horse, and accompanied meetly by lay attendants, laden with furniture and provisions for the Abbot's comfort, approached by the "under-down" road, which led from the gorge of the Thames at Streatley. The whole community turned out to meet them, and there was such an assembly of dark robes that the bailiff of the farm jocosely called it "Rook-Fair."

"*Pax vobiscum fratres omnes, clerici atque laici.* I have come to repose my weary limbs amongst you, but by St. Martin the air of these downs is fresh, and will make us relish the venison pasty, or other humble fare we may receive for the sustenance of our flesh. How are all the invalids?"

"They be doing well," said Father Hieronymus, the senior of the monks at Lollingdune; "and say that the sight of their Abbot will be a most salutary medicament."

The Abbot smiled; he liked to think himself loved.

"But who is this youth in lay attire?" and he smiled sweetly, for he liked to see a handsome youth.

"It is one Osric, who has brought letters commendatory from the Abbot of Dorchester."

"Our brother Alured—is he well?"

"He is well, my lord," replied Osric, as he bent the knee.

"And what dost thou seek, sweet son? dost wish to become a novice of our poor house of St. Benedict?"

"Nay, my good lord, it is in another vocation I wish to serve God."

"And that,—ah, I guess thou wishest to take the Cross and go to the Holy Land."

"I do with all my heart."

"And this letter assures me that thou art a fitting person, and skilled in the use of carnal weapons."

"I trust I am."

"Then thou shalt share our humble fare this night, and then thou shalt on the morrow take the vow and receive the Cross from my own hands, after the Mass which follows Terce."

Osric bowed in joyful assent. And that night he dined at the monastic table of Lollingdune Grange. The humble fare was the most sumptuous he had ever known; for at Wallingford Castle they paid small attention to the culinary art—quantity, not quality, was their motto; they ate of meat half raw, thinking it increased their ferocity; and "drank the red wine through the helmet barred."

But it was not so here; the weakness of the monastic orders, if it was a weakness, was good cooking.

"Why should we waste or spoil the good things God has given us?" they asked.

We wish our space permitted us to relate the conversation which had place at that table. The Abbot of Reading was devoted more or less to King Stephen, for Maude, in one of her progresses, had spoiled the abbey and irritated the brethren by exacting heavy tribute. So they told many stories of the misdeeds of the party of the Empress, and many more of the cruelties of Brian Fitz-Count, whose lordly towers were visible in the distance.

Osric sat at table next to the lord Abbot, which was meant for a great distinction.

"In what school, my son, hast thou studied the warlike art and the science of chivalry?" asked the Abbot.

"In the Castle of Wallingford, my lord."

"I could have wished thee a better school, but doubtless thou art leaving them in disgust with their evil deeds of which we hear daily; in fact, we are told that the townspeople cannot sleep for the shrieks of the captives in the towers."

"It is in order to atone for ever having shared in their deeds that I have left them, and the very penance laid on me is to fight for the Cross of Christ in atonement for my error."

"And what will Brian think of it?"

"I must not let him get hold of me."

"Then tarry here till I return to Reading, and assuming the palmer's dress, travel in our train out of his country; he will not dare to assail us."

It was wise counsel.

On the morrow Mass was said in the chapel, which occupied the upper story of the house, over the dormitories, under a high arched roof, which was the general arrangement in such country houses of the monks;[1] and at the offertory Osric offered himself to God as a Crusader, took the vow, and the Abbot bound the red cross on his arm.

---

[1] The author has twice seen the remains of such chapels in the upper stories of farmhouses—once monastic granges.

CHAPTER XXVI

SWEET SISTER DEATH [1]

THE reader may feel quite sure that such a nature as Evroult's was not easily conquered by the gentle influences of Christianity; indeed, humanly speaking, it might never have yielded had not the weapon used against it been *Love*.

One day, as he sat rapt in thought on the sunny bank outside the hermitage, the hermit and Richard talking quietly at a short distance, he seemed to receive a sudden inspiration,—he walked up to Meinhold.

"Father, tell me, do you think you can recover of the leprosy you have caught from us?"

"I do not expect to do so."

"And do you not wish we had never come here?"

"By no means; God sent you."

"And you give your life perhaps for us?"

"The Good Shepherd gave His life for me."

"Father, I have tried not to listen to you, but I can fight against it no longer. You are right in all you say, and always have been, only—only——"

A pause. The hermit waited in silent joy.

"Only it was so hard to flesh and blood."

"And can you yield yourself to His Will now?"

"I am trying—very hard; I do not even yet know whether I quite can."

"He will help you, dear boy; He knows how hard it is for us weak mortals to overcome self."

[1] So called by St. Francis of Assisi.

"I knew if I had kept well I should have grown up violent, wicked, and cruel, and no doubt have lost my soul. Do you not think so, father?"

"Very likely, indeed."

"And yet I have repined and murmured against Him Who brought me here to save me."

"But He will forgive all that, now you truly turn to Him and submit to His Will."

"I try to give myself to Him to do as He pleases."

"And you believe He has done all things well?"

"Yes."

"Even the leprosy?"

"Yes, even that."

"You are right, my dear son; we must all be purified through suffering, for what son is he whom the Father chasteneth not? and if we are not partakers thereof, then are we bastards and not sons. All true children of God have their Purgatory here or hereafter—far better here. He suffered more for us."

A few days passed away after this conversation, and a rapid change for the worse took place in poor Evroult's physical condition. The fell disease, which had already disfigured him beyond recognition, attacked the brain. His brother and the hermit could not desire his life to be prolonged in such affliction, and they silently prayed for his release, grievous although the pang of separation would be to them both—one out of their little number of three.

One day he had been delirious since the morning, and at eventide they stood still watching him. It had been a dark cloudy day, but now at sunset a broad vivid glory appeared in the west, which was lighted up with glorious crimson, azure, and gold, beneath the edge of the curtain of cloud.

"'At eventide it shall be light,'" quoted Meinhold.

"See, he revives," said Richard.

He looked on their faces.

"Oh brother, oh dear father, I have seen Him; I have

heard with the hearing of the ear, but now mine eye hath seen Him."

They thought he spake of a vision, but it may have been, probably *was*, but a revelation to the inward soul.

"And now, dear father, give me the Viaticum; I am going, and want my provision for the way."

He spoke of the Holy Communion, to which this name was given when administered to the dying.

Then followed the Last Anointing, and ere it was over they saw the great change pass upon him. They saw Death, sometimes called the grim King of Terrors, all despoiled of his sting; they saw the feeble hand strive to make the Holy Sign, then fall back; while over his face a mysterious light played as if the door of Paradise had been left ajar when the redeemed soul passed in.

"*Beati qui in Domino morinutur*," said Meinhold; "his Purgatory was here. Do not cry, Richard; the happy day will soon come when we shall rejoin him."

They laid him out before the altar in their rude chapel, and prepared for the last funeral rite.

Meanwhile disfigured forms were stealing through the woods, and finding a shelter in various dens and caves, or sleeping round fires kindled in the open or in woodcutters' huts, deserted through fear of them; as yet they had not found the hermit's cave or entered the Happy Valley.

On the morrow Meinhold celebrated the Holy Eucharist, and afterwards performed the burial service with simplest rites; they then committed the body to the earth, and afterwards wandered together, discoursing sweetly on the better life, into the forest, where the twilight was

"Like the Truce of God
With earthly pain and woe."

Never were they happier—never so full of joy and resignation—these two unfortunates, as the world deemed them; bearing about the visible sentence of death on themselves, but they had found the secret of a life Death could not touch.

And in their walk they came suddenly upon a man, who reposed under the shadow of a tree; he seemed asleep, but talked and moaned as if in a feverish dream.

"Father, he is a leper like us, look."

"God has sent him, perhaps, in the place of Evroult."

They woke him.

"Where am I?"

"With friends. Canst walk to our home; it is not far?"

"Angels from Heaven. Yes, I can walk—see."

But without their assistance he could never have reached the cave.

They gave him food; he took little, but drank eagerly.

"How did you come here?"

He told them of the plague at Byfield, and of the death of the Chaplain.

"Happy man!" said Meinhold; "he laid down his life for the sheep the Good Shepherd had committed to his care."

And so may we, he thought.

That night the poor man grew worse; the dark livid hue overspread him. Our readers know the rest.

Voices might have been heard in the cave the next day—sweet sounds sometimes as if of hymns of praise.

The birds and beasts came to the hermit's cave, and marvelled that none came out to feed them—that no crumbs were thrown to them, no food brought forth. A bold robin even ventured in, but came out as if affrighted, and flew right away.

They sang their sweet songs to each other. No human ear heard them; but the valley was lovely still.

Who shall go into that cave and wake the sleepers? Who?

Then came discordant noises, spoiling nature's sweet

harmony—the baying of hounds, the cries of men sometimes loud and discordant, sometimes of those who struggled, sometimes of those in pain.

Louder and louder—the hunt is up—the horse and hound invade the glen.

A troop of affrighted-looking men hasten down the valley.

Look, they are lepers.

They have cause to fear; the deep baying of the mastiffs is deepening, drawing near.

They espy the cave—they rush towards it up the slope—in they dash.

Out again.

Another group of fugitives follow.

"The cave! the cave! we may defend the mouth."

"There are three there already," said the first.

"*Three?*"

"*Dead of the Plague.*"

And they would have run away had not the hunters and dogs come upon them, both ways, up and down the glen.

They are driven in—some two score in all.

The leaders of the pursuing party pause.

"I think," says a dark baron, "I see a way out of our difficulty without touching a leper."

"Send the dogs in."

"In vain; they will not go; they scent something amiss."

"This cave has but one opening."

"I have heard that a hermit lived here with two young lepers."

"Call him."

"Meinhold! Meinhold!"

No reply.

"He is dead long ago, I daresay."

"If he does not come out it is his own fault."

"There were two young lepers who dwelt with him."

"What business had he with lepers?"

"All the world knew it, and he had caught it himself."

"Then we will delay no longer. God will know His own." And then he gave the fatal order.

"Gather brushwood, sticks, reeds, all that will burn, and pile it in the mouth of the cave."

They did so.

"Fire it."

The dense clouds of smoke arose, and as they hoped in their cruelty, were sucked inward.

"There must be a through draught."

"Can they get out?"

"No, lord baron."

"Watch carefully lest there be other outlets. We must stamp this foul plague out of the land."

Then they stood and watched.

The flames crackled and roared; dense volumes of smoke arose, now arising above the trees, now entering the cave; the birds screamed overhead; the fierce men looked on with cruel curiosity; but no sound was heard from within.

At this moment the galloping of horsemen was heard.

"Our brother of Kenilworth, doubtless."

But it was not. A rider in dark armour appeared at the head of a hundred horsemen.

"What are you doing?" cried a stern voice.

"Smoking lepers out."

"Charge them! cut them down! slay all!"

And the Wallingford men charged the incendiaries as one man. Like a thunderbolt, slaying, hewing, hacking, chopping, cleaving heads and limbs from trunks, with all the more deadly facility as their more numerous antagonists lacked armour, having only come out to slay lepers.

The Baron of Hanwell Castle was a corpse; so was the knight of Cropredy Towers; so was the young lord of Southam; others were writhing in mortal agony, but within a quarter of an hour more, only the dead and dying disputed the field with the Wallingford men. The rest had fled, finding the truth of the proverb, "There be many that come out to shear and go back shorn."

"Drag the branches away! pull out the faggots! extinguish the fire! scatter it! fight fire as ye have fought men!"

That was done too. They dispersed the fuel, they scattered the embers; and hardly was this done than Brian rushed in the cave, through the hot ashes. But scarce could he stay in a moment, the smoke blinded—choked him.

Out again, almost beside himself with rage, fear for his boys, and vexation.

In again. Out again.

So three or four abortive attempts.

At last the smoke partially dispersed, and he could enter.

The outer cave was empty.

But in the next subterranean chamber lay a black corpse—a full-grown man. Brian knew him not. He crossed this cave and entered the next one, and by the altar knew it was their rude chapel.

Before the altar lay two figures; their hands clasped in the attitude of prayer; bent to the earth; still—motionless.

Their faces, too, were of the same dark hue.

The one wore the dress of a hermit, the other was a boy of some sixteen years.

Brian recognised his younger son in the latter, rather by instinct and by knowledge of the circumstances than otherwise.

"It is my Richard. But where is Evroult?"

"Here," said a voice,—"read."

Upon the wall was a rude inscription, scratched thereon by Meinhold, his last labour of love—

EVROULT IN PACE.

Little as he possessed the power of reading, Brian recognised his son's name, and understood all. The strong man fell before that altar, and for the first time in many years recognised the Hand which had stricken him.

They dragged him away, as they felt that the atmosphere was dangerous to them all—as indeed it was.

"Leave them where they are—better tomb could they not have ; only wall up the entrance."

And they set to work, and built huge stones into the mouth of the cave—

> " Leaving them to rest in hope—
> Till the Resurrection Day."

And what had become of the other lepers ?

Driven by the smoke, they had wandered into the farthest recesses of the cave—once forbidden to Evroult by the hermit.

Whether they perished in the recesses, or whether they found some other outlet, and emerged to the upper day, we know not. No further intelligence of the poor unfortunates reached the living, or has been handed down to posterity.

And now, do my readers say this is a very melancholy chapter ? Do they pity, above all, the hermit and Richard, struck down by the pestilence in an act of which Christ would have said, " Inasmuch as ye did it to the least of these My brethren, ye did it unto Me " ?

The pestilence saved them from the lingering death of leprosy, and even had they lived to grow old, they had been dust and ashes seven centuries ago. What does it matter now whether they lived sixteen or sixty years ? The only point is, did they, through God's grace, merit to hear the blessed words, " Well done, good and faithful servant, enter into the joy of your Lord " ?

And we think they did.

CHAPTER XXVII

FRUSTRATED

HAD the Abbot of Reading seen fit, or rather had the business on which he came to Lollingdune allowed him to return home on the day in which he had decorated Osric with the red cross, it had been well for all parties, save the writer; for the entangled web of circumstance which arose will give him scope for another chapter or two, he trusts, of some interest to the reader.

As it was, Osric was thrown upon his own resources for the rest of that day, after the Mass was over; and his thoughts not unnaturally turned to his old home, where the innocent days of his childhood had been spent, and to his old nurse Judith, sole relict of that hallowed past.

Could he not bid her farewell? He had an eye, and he could heed; he had a foot, and he could speed—let Brian's spies watch ever so narrowly.

Yes, he *must* see her. Besides, Osric loved adventure: it was to him the salt of life. He loved the sensation of danger and of risk. So, although he knew that there must be a keen hunt on foot from Wallingford Castle after the fugitives, and that the old cottage might be watched, he determined to risk it all for the purpose of saying goodbye to his dear old nurse.

So, without confiding his purpose to any one, he started on foot. He passed the old church of Aston Upthorpe, where his grandfather lay buried, breathing a prayer for the old man, as also a thanksgiving for the teaching which had at last borne fruit, for he felt that he was reconciled to God and man, now that he had taken the Holy Vow, and abandoned his godless life at Wallingford Castle. Then passing between the outlying fort of Blewburton and the downs, he entered the maze of forest.

But as he approached the spot, he took every precaution. He scanned each avenue of approach from Wallingford; he looked warily into each glade; anon, he paused and listened, but all was still, save the usual sounds of the forest, never buried in absolute silence.

At length he crossed the stream and stood before the door of the hut. He paused one moment; then he heard the well-known voice crooning a snatch of an old ballad; he hesitated no longer.

"Judith!"

"My darling," said the fond old nurse, "thou hast come again to see me. Tell me, is it all right? Hast thou found thy father?"

"I have."

"Where? Tell me?"

"At Dorchester Abbey of course."

Judith sighed.

"And what did he say to thee?"

"Bade me go on the Crusades. And so I have taken the vow, and to-morrow I leave these parts perhaps, for ever."

"Alas! it is too bad. Why has he not told thee the whole truth? Woe is me! the light of mine eyes is taken from me. I shall never see thee again."

"That is in God's hands."

"How good thou hast grown, my boy! Thou didst not talk like this when thou camest home from the castle."

"Well, perhaps I have learnt better;" and he sighed, for there was a reproach, as if the old dame had said, "Is Saul also amongst the prophets?"

"But, my boy," she continued, "is this all? Did not Wulfnoth—I mean Father Alphege—tell thee more than this?"

"What more could he tell me?"

She rocked herself to and fro.

"I *must* tell him; but oh, my vow——"

"Osric, my child, my bonnie boy, thou dost not even yet know all, and I am bound *not* to tell thee. But I was here when thou wast brought home by Wulfnoth, a baby-boy; and—and I know what I found out—I saw—God help me; but I swore by the Black Cross of Abingdon I would not tell."

"Judith, what can you mean?"

"If you only knew, perhaps you would not go on this crusade."

"Whither then? I *must* go."

"To Wallingford."

"But *that* I can never do. I have broken with them and their den of darkness for ever."

"Nay, nay; it may be all thine own one day, and thou mayst let light into it."

"What can you mean? You distract me."

"I cannot say. Ah!—a good thought. You may look—I didn't say I wouldn't show. See, Osric, I will show thee what things were on thy baby-person when thou wast brought home. Here—look."

She rummaged in her old chest and brought forth—a ring with a seal, a few articles of baby attire, a little red shoe, a small frock, and a lock of maiden's hair.

"Look at the ring."

It bore a crest upon a stone of opal.

The crest was the crest of Brian Fitz-Count.

"Well, what does this mean?" said Osric. "How came this ring on my baby-self?"

"Dost thou not see? Blind! blind! blind!"

"And deaf too—deaf! deaf! deaf!" said a voice. "Dost thou not hear the tread of horses, the bay of the hound, the clamour of men who seek thee for no good?"

It was young Ulric who stood in the doorway.

"Good-bye, nurse; they are after me; I must go."

"What hast thou done?"

"Let all their captives loose. Farewell, dear nurse;" and he embraced her.

"Haste, Osric, haste," said the youthful outlaw, "or thou wilt be taken."

They dashed from the hut.

"This way," said Ulric.

And they crossed the stream in the opposite direction to the advancing sounds.

"I lay hid in the forest and heard them say they would seek thee in thine old home, as they passed my lurking-place."

"Now, away."

"But they may hurt Judith. Nay, Brian has not yet returned, *cannot* yet have come back, and without his orders they would not dare. He forbade them once before even to *touch* the cottage."

They pressed onward through the woods.

"Whither do we go?" said Osric, who had allowed his young preserver to lead.

"To our haunt in the swamp."

"You have saved me, Ulric."

"Then it has been measure for measure, for didst thou not save me when in direful dumps? Wilt thou not tarry with us, and be a merry man of the greenwood?"

"Nay, I am pledged to the Crusades."

Ulric was about to reply, when he stopped to listen.

"There is the bay of that hound again: it is one of a breed they have trained to hunt men."

"I know him—it is old Pluto; I have often fed him: he would not hurt me."

"But he would *discover* thee, nevertheless, and *I* should not be safe from his fangs."

"Well, we are as swift of foot as they—swifter, I should think. Come, we must jump this brook."

Alas! in jumping, Osric's foot slipped from a stone on which he most unhappily alighted, and he sank on the ground with a momentary thrill of intense pain, which made him quite faint.

He had sprained his ankle badly.

Ulric turned pale.

Osric got up, made several attempts to move onward, but could only limp painfully forward.

"Ulric, I should only destroy both thee and me by perseverance in this course."

"Never mind about me."

"But I do. See this umbrageous oak—how thick its branches; it is hollow too. I know it well. I will hide in the tree, as I have often done when a boy in mere sport. You run on."

"I will; and make the trail so wide that they will come after *me*."

"But will not this lead them to the haunt?"

"Water will throw them when I come to the swamps. I can take care."

"Farewell, then, my Ulric; the Saints have thee in their holy keeping."

The two embraced as those who might never meet again—but as those who part in haste—and Ulric plunged into the thicket and disappeared.

Osric lay hidden in the branches of the hollow tree. There was a comfortable seat about ten feet from the ground, the feet hidden in the hollow of the oak, the head and shoulders by the thick foliage. He did not notice that Ulric had divested himself of an upper garment he wore, and left it accidentally or otherwise on the ground. All was now still. The sound of the boy's passage through the thick bushes had ceased. The scream of the jay, the tap of the woodpecker, the whirr of an occasional flight of birds alone broke the silence of the forest day.

Then came a change. The crackling of dry leaves, the low whisper of hunters, and that sound—that bell-like sound—the bay of the hound, like a staunch murderer, steady to his purpose, pursuing his prey relentlessly, unerringly, guided by that marvellous instinct of scent, which to the pursued seemed even diabolical.

At last they broke through the bushes and passed beneath the tree—seven mounted pursuers.

"See, here is the trail; it is as plain as it can be," cried Malebouche; for it was he, summoned in the emergency from Shirburne, the Baron not having yet returned—six men in company.

But the dog hesitated. They had given him a piece of Osric's raiment to smell before starting, and he pointed at the tree.

Luckily the men did not see it; for they saw on the ground the tunic Ulric had thrown off to run, with the unselfish intention that that should take place which now happened, confident he could throw off the hound.

The men thrust it to the dog's nose, thinking it Osric's, —they knew not there were *two*—and old Pluto growled, and took the new scent with far keener avidity than before, for now he was bidden to chase one he might tear. Before it was a friend, the scent of whose raiment he knew full well. They were off again.

All was silence once more around the hollow tree for a brief space, and Osric was just about to depart and try to limp to Lollingdune, when steps were heard again in the distance, along the brook, where the path from the outlaws' cave lay.

Osric peered from his covert: they were passing about a hundred yards off.

Oh, horror! they had got Ulric.

"How had it chanced?"

Osric never knew whether the dog had overtaken him, or what accident had happened; all he saw was that they had the lad, and were taking him, as he judged, to Wallingford, when they halted and sat down on some fallen trees, about a hundred yards from his concealment. They had wine, flesh, and bread, and were going to enjoy a mediæval picnic; but first they tied the boy carefully to a tree, so tightly and cruelly that he must have suffered much unnecessary pain; but little recked they.

The men ate and drank, the latter copiously. So much the worse for Ulric—drink sometimes inflames the passions of cruelty and violence.

"Why should we take him home? our prey is about here somewhere."

"Why not try a little torture, Sir Squire—a knotted string round the brain? we will make him tell all he knows, or make the young villain's eyes start out of his forehead."

The suggestion pleased Malebouche.

"Yes," he said, "we may as well settle his business here. I have a little persuader in my pocket, which I generally carry on these errands; it often comes useful;" and he produced a small thumbscrew.

Enough; we will spare the details. They began to carry out their intention, and soon forced a cry from their victim—although, judging from his previous constancy, I doubt whether they would have got more—when they heard a sound—a voice—

"Stop! let the lad go; he shall not be tortured for me. I yield myself in his place."

"Osric! Osric!"

And the men almost leapt for joy.

"Malebouche, I am he you seek—I am your prisoner; but let the boy go, and take me to Wallingford."

"Oh, why hast thou betrayed thyself?" said Ulric.

"Not so fast, my young lord, for lord thou didst think thyself—thou bastard, brought up as a falcon. Why should I let him go? I have you both."

But the boy had been partially untied to facilitate their late operations, which necessitated that the hands cruelly bound behind the back should be released; and while every eye was fixed on Osric, he shook off the loosened cord which attached him to the tree, and was off like a bird.

He had almost escaped—another minute and he had been beyond arrow-shot—when Malebouche, snatching up a bow, sent a long arrow after him. Alas! it was aimed with Norman skill, and it pierced through the back of the unfortunate boy, who fell dead on the grass, the blood gushing from mouth and nose.

Osric uttered a plaintive cry of horror, and would have hurried to his assistance, but they detained him rudely.

"Nay, leave him to rot in the woods—if the wolves and wild cats do not bury him first."

And they took their course for Wallingford, placing their prisoner behind a horseman, to whom they bound him, binding also his legs beneath the belly of the horse.

After a little while Malebouche turned to Osric—

"What dost thou expect when our lord returns?"

"Death. It is not the worst evil."

"But what manner of death?"

"Such as may chance; but thou knowest he will not torture *me*."

"He may hang thee."

"Wait and see. Thou art a murderer thyself, for whom hanging is perhaps too good. God may have worse things in store for thee. Thou hast committed murder and sacrilege to-day."

"Sacrilege?"

"Yes; thou hast seized a Crusader. Dost not see my red cross?"

"It is easy to bind a bit of red rag crossways upon one's shoulder. Who took thy vows?"

"The Abbot of Reading; he is now at Lollingdune."

"Ah, ah! Brian Fitz-Count shall settle that little matter; he may not approve of Crusaders who break open his castle. Take him to Wallingford, my friends. I shall go back and get that deer we slew just before we caught the boy; our larder is short."

So Malebouche rode back into the forest alone.

Let us follow him.

It was drawing near nightfall. The light fleecy clouds which floated above were fast losing the hues of the departing sun, which had tinted their western edges with crimson; the woods were getting dim and dark; but Malebouche persisted in his course. He had brought down a fine young buck with his bow, and had intended to send for it, being at that moment eager in pursuit of his human prey; but now he had leisure, and might throw it across his horse, and bring it home in triumph.

Before reaching the place the road became very ill-defined, and speedily ceased to be a road at all; but Malebouche could still see the broken branches and trampled ground along which they had pursued their prey earlier in the day.

At last he reached the deer, and tying the horse to a branch of a tree, proceeded to disembowel it ere he placed it across the steed, as was the fashion; but as he was doing this, the horse made a violent plunge, and uttered a scream of terror. Malebouche turned—a pair of vivid eyes were glaring in the darkness.

It was a wolf, attracted by the scent of the butchery.

Malebouche rushed to the aid of his horse, but before he could reach the poor beast it broke through all restraint in its agony of fear that the wolf might prefer horse-flesh to venison, and tearing away the branch and all, galloped for dear life away, away, towards distant Wallingford, the wolf after it; for when man or horse runs, the savage beast, whether dog or wolf, seems bound to follow.

So Malebouche was left alone with his deer in the worst possible humour.

It was useless now to think of carrying the whole carcass home; so he cut off the haunch only, and throwing it over his shoulder, started.

A storm came drifting up and obscured the rising moon —the woods grew very dark.

Onward he tramped—wearily, wearily, tramp! tramp! splash! splash!

He had got into a bog.

How to get out of it was the question. He had heard there was a quagmire somewhere about this part of the forest, of bottomless depth, men said.

So he strove to get back to firm ground, but in the darkness went wrong; and the farther he went the deeper he sank.

Up to the knees.

Now he became seriously alarmed, and abandoned his venison.

Up to the middle.

"Help! help!" he cried.

Was there none to hear?

Yes. At this moment the clouds parted, and the moon shone forth through a gap in their canopy—a full moon, bright and clear.

Before him walked a boy, about fifty yards ahead.

"Boy! boy! stop! help me!"

The boy did not turn, but walked on, seemingly on firm ground.

But Malebouche was intensely relieved.

"Where he can walk I can follow;" and he exerted all his strength to overtake the boy, but he sank deeper and deeper.

The boy seemed to linger, as if he heard the cry, and beckoned to Malebouche to come to him.

The squire strove to do so, when all at once he found no footing, and sank slowly.

He was in the fatal quagmire of which he had heard.

Slowly, slowly, up to the middle—up to the neck.

"Boy, help! help! for Heaven's sake!"

The boy stood, as it seemed, yet on firm ground. And now he threw aside the hood that had hitherto concealed his features, and looked Malebouche in the face.

It was the face of the murdered Ulric upon which Malebouche gazed! and the whole figure vanished into empty air as he looked.

One last despairing scream—then a sound of choking—then the head disappeared beneath the mud—then a bubble or two of air breaking the surface of the bog—then all was still. And the mud kept its secret for ever.

CHAPTER XXVIII

FATHER AND SON

MEANWHILE Osric was brought back as a prisoner to the grim stronghold where for years his position had been that of the chartered favourite of the mighty Baron who was the lord thereof.

When the news had spread that he was at the gates, all the inmates of the castle—from the grim troopers to the beardless pages—crowded to see him enter, and perhaps to exult over the fallen favourite; for it is not credible that the extraordinary partiality Brian had ever shown Osric should have failed to excite jealousy, although his graceful and unassuming bearing had done much to mollify the feeling in the hearts of many.

And there was nought common or mean in his behaviour; nor, on the other hand, aught defiant or presumptuous. All was simple and natural.

"Think you they will put him to the torture?" said a youngster.

"They dare not till the Baron returns," said his senior.

"And then?"

"I doubt it."

"The rope, then, or the axe?"

"Perchance the latter."

"But he is not of gentle blood."

"Who knows?"

"If it were you or I?"

"Hanging would be too good for us."

In the courtyard the party of captors awaited the orders

of the Lady Maude, now regent in her stern husband's absence. They soon came.

"Confine him strictly, but treat him well."

So he was placed in the prison reserved for the captives of gentle birth, or entitled to special distinction, in the new buildings of Brian's Close; and Tustain gnashed his teeth, for he longed to have the torturing of him.

Unexpected guests arrived at the castle that night—that is, unexpected by those who were not in the secret of the letters Osric had written and the Baron had sent out when Osric last played his part of secretary—Milo, Earl of Hereford, and Sir Alain of St. Maur, some time page at Wallingford.

At the banquet the Lady Maude, sorely distressed, confided her griefs to her guests.

"We all trusted him. That he should betray us is past bearing."

"Have you not put him on the rack to learn who bought him?"

"I could not. It is as if my own son had proved false. We all loved him."

"Yet he was not of noble birth, I think."

"No. Do you not remember the hunt in which you took part when my lord first found him? Well, the boy, for he was a mere lad of sixteen then, exercised a wonderful glamour over us all; and, as Alain well knows, he rose rapidly to be my lord's favourite squire, and would soon have won his spurs, for he was brave—was Osric."

"Lady, may I see him? He knows me well; and I trust to learn the secret," said Alain.

"Take this ring; it will ope the doors of his cell to thee."

"And take care *thou* dost not make use of it to empty Brian's Close," said Milo ironically.

Alain laughed, and proceeded on his mission.

"Osric, my fellow-page and brother, what is the meaning of this? why art thou here?"

He extended his hand. Osric grasped it.

"Dost thou not know I did a Christlike deed?"

"Christlike?"

"Yes. Did He not open the prison doors of Hell when He descended thither, and let the captives out of Limbus? I daresay the Dragon did not like it."

"Osric, the subject is too serious for jesting."

"I am not jesting."

"But what led thee to break thy faith?"

"My faith to a higher Master than even the Lord of Wallingford, to whom I owed so much."

"The Church never taught me that much: if all we do is so wrong, why are we not excommunicated? Why, we are allowed our chapel, our chaplain—who troubles himself little about what goes on—our Masses! and we shall easily buy ourselves out of Purgatory when all is over."

Too true, Alain; the Church did grievously neglect her duty at Wallingford and elsewhere, and passively allow such dreadful dens of tyranny to exist. But Osric had learnt better.

"I do not believe you will buy yourselves out. The old priest who served our little church once quoted a Saint—I think they called him 'Augustine'—who said such things could only profit those whose lives merited that they should profit them. But you did not come here to discuss religion."

"No, indeed. Tell me what changed your mind?"

"Things that I heard at my grandfather's deathbed, which taught me I had been aiding and abetting in the Devil's work."

"Devil's work, Osric! The tiger preys upon the deer, the wolf on the sheep, the fox on the hen, the cat on the bird,—it is so all through creation; and we do the same. Did the Devil ordain the laws of nature?"

"God forbid. But men are brethren."

"Brethren are we! Do you think I call the vile canaille my brethren?—not I. The base fluid which circulates in their veins is not like the generous blood which flows in the veins of the noble and gallant. I have no more sympathy with such folk than the cat with the mouse. Her nature, which God gave, teaches her to torture, much as we torment our captives in Brian's Close or elsewhere; but knights, nobles, gentlemen,—they are my brethren. We slay each other in generous emulation,—in the glorious excitement of battle,—but we torture them not. *Noblesse oblige.*"

"I cannot believe in the distinction; and you will find out I am right some day, and that the blood of your victims, the groans of your captives, will be visited on your head."

"Osric, you are one of the conquered race,—is it not so? Sometimes I doubted it."

"I am one of your victims; and I would sooner be of the sufferers than of the tyrants."

"I can say no more; something has spoilt a noble nature. Do you not dread Brian's return?"

"No."

"Why not? I should in your place. He loved you."

"I have a secret to tell him which, methinks, will explain all."

"Wilt not tell it me?"

"No; I may not yet."

And Alain took his departure sorrowfully, none the wiser.

The sound of trumpets—the beating of drums. The Baron returns. He enters the proud castle, which he calls his own, with downcast head. The scene in the woods near Byfield has sobered him.

One more grievous blow awaits him,—one to wound him in his tenderest feelings, perhaps the only soft spot in that hard heart. What a mystery was hidden in his whole relation to Osric! What could have made the tiger love the fawn? Was it some deep mysterious working of nature?

Can the reader guess? Probably, or he has read our tale to little purpose.

Osric knows it is coming. He braces himself for the interview. He prays for support and wisdom.

The door opens—Brian enters.

He stands still, and gazes upon Osric for full five minutes ere he speaks.

"Osric, what means this?"

"I have but done my duty. Pardon me, my lord, but the truth must be spoken now."

"Thy duty! to break thy faith?"

"To man but not to God."

"Osric, what causes this change? I trusted thee, I loved thee, as never I loved youth before. Thou hast robbed me of my confidence in man."

"My lord, I will tell thee. At my grandfather's dying bed I learnt a secret I knew not before."

"And that secret?"

"I am the son of Wulfnoth of Compton."

"So thy grandfather told *me*—*I* knew it."

"But I knew not that thou didst slay my kindred—that my mother perished under thy hands in her burning house—and I alone escaped. Had I known it, could I have loved and served thee?—NEVER."

"And yet repenting of that deed, I have striven to atone for it by my conduct to thee."

"Couldst thou *hope* to do so? nay, I acknowledge thy kindness."

"And thou wouldst open my castle to the foe and slay me in return?"

"No; we shed no blood—only delivered the helpless. Thou hadst made me take part in the slaughter, the torture of mine own helpless countrymen, whose blood God will surely require at our hands, if we repent not. I have repented, but I could not harm thee. See, I had taken the Cross, and was on my way to the Holy Wars, when thy minions seized me and brought me back."

"Thou hast taken the Cross?"

"I have."

"I know not whether thou dost think that I can let thee go: it would destroy all discipline in my castle. Right and left, all clamour for thy life. The late-comers from Ardennes swear they will desert if such order is kept as thy forgiveness would denote. Nay, Osric, thou must die; but thy death shall be that of a noble, to which by birth thou art not entitled."

The choking of the voice, the difficulty of utterance which accompanied this last speech, showed the deep sorrow with which Brian spoke. Brutus sacrificing his sons may have shown less emotion. Osric felt it deeply.

"My lord, do what you think your duty, and behead your former favourite. I forgive you all you have done, and may think it right yet to do. I die in peace with you and the world."

And Osric turned his face to the wall.

The Baron left the cell, where he found his fortitude deserting him.

As he appeared on the ramparts he heard all round the muttered words—

"Death to the traitor! death!"

At last he spoke out fiercely.

"Stop your throats, ye hounds, barking and whining for blood. Justice shall be done. Here, Alain, seek the doomster Coupe-gorge and the priest; send the priest to your late friend, and tell the doomster to get his axe ready; tell Osric thyself he dies at sundown."

A loud shout of exultation.

Brian gnashed his teeth.

"Bring forth my steed."

The steed was brought.

He turned to a pitying knight who stood by, the deputy-governor in his absence.

"If I return not, delay not the execution after sunset. Let it be on the castle green."

A choking sensation—he put his hand to his mouth; when he withdrew it, it was tinged with blood.

He dashed the spurs into his steed; the drawbridges fell before him; he rode at full gallop along the route by the brook described in our second chapter. Whither was he bound?

For Cwichelm's Illawe.

It is a wonder that he was not thrown over and over again; but chance often protects the reckless while the careful die. He rides through the forest over loose stones—over protruding roots of trees—still he kept his seat; he flew like the whirlwind, but he escaped projecting branches. In an hour he was ascending the slope from Chiltune to the summit of the hill.

He reined his panting steed at the foot of the barrow.

"Hag, come forth!"

No reply.

He tied up his steed to a tree and entered her dread abode—the ancient sepulchre.

She sat over the open stone coffin with its giant skeleton.

"Here thou art then, witch!"

"What does Brian Fitz-Count want of me?"

"I seek thee as Saul sought the Witch of Endor—in dire trouble. The boy, old Sexwulf's grandson"—he could not frame his lips to say Wulfnoth's son—"has proved false to me."

"Why hast thou not smitten him, and ridden thyself of '*so frail an encumbrance*'?"

"I could not."

"Did I not tell thee so long syne? ah, ha!"

"Tell me, thou witch, why does the death of a peasant rend my very heart? Tell me, didst thou not give me a philter, a potion or something, when I was here? My heart burns—what is it?"

"Brian Fitz-Count, there is one who can solve the riddle—seek him."

"Who is he?"

"Ride at once to Dorchester Abbey—waste no time—

ask to see Father Alphege, he shall tell thee all. When is the boy to die?"

"At sundown."

"Then there is no time to be lost. It is now the ninth hour; thou hast but three hours. Ride, ride, man! if he die before thy return, thy heart-strings will crack. Ride, man, ride! if ever thou didst ride—Dorchester first, Father Alphege, then Wallingford Castle."

Brian rushed from the cavern—he gave full rein to his horse—he drove his spurs deep into the sides of the poor beast.

Upon the north-east horizon stood the two twin clumps of Synodune, about ten miles off; he fixed his eyes upon them; beyond them lay Dorchester; he descended the hill at a dangerous pace, and made for those landmarks.

He rode through Harwell—passed the future site of Didcot Station, where locomotives now hiss and roar—he left the north Moor-town on the right—he crossed the valley between the twin hills—he swam the river, for the water was high at the ford—he passed the gates of the old cathedral city. Every one trembled as they saw him, and hid from his presence. He dismounted at the abbey gates.

The porter hesitated to open.

"I have come to see Father Alphege—open!"

"This is not Wallingford Castle," said the daring porter, strong in monastic immunities.

Brian remembered where he was, and sobered down.

"Then I would fain see the Abbot at once: life or death hang upon it."

"Thou mayst enter the hospitium and wait his pleasure."

He waited nearly half an hour. They kept him on purpose, to show him that he was not the great man at Dorchester he was at Wallingford. But they were unwittingly cruel; they knew not his need.

Meanwhile the Abbot sought Father Alphege, and told him who sought him.

"Canst thou bear to see him?"

"I can; it is the will of Heaven."

"Then he shall see thee in the church; the sacred house of God will restrain you both. Enter the confessional; he shall seek thee there."

Then the Abbot sought Brian.

"Come with me and I will show thee him thou seekest."

Brian was faint with exhaustion, but the dire need, the terrible expectation of some awful secret, held him up. He had had no food that day, but he recked not.

The Abbot Alured led him into the church.

The confessional was a stone cell[1] in the thickness of the wall, entered by the priest from a side chapel. The penitent approached from the opposite side of the wall from the nave of the church.

"I am not come to make a confession—yes I am, though, yet not an ordinary one."

"Go to that aperture, and through it thou mayst tell your grief, or whatever thou hast to say, to Father Alphege."

Brian went to the spot, but he knelt not.

"Father Alphege, is it thou?" he said.

"It is I. What does Brian Fitz-Count seek of me? Art thou a penitent?"

"I know not. A witch sent me to thee."

"A witch?"

"Yes—Hertha of Cwichelm's Hlawe."

"Why?"

"Listen. I adopted a boy, the son of a man I had slain, partly, I think, to atone for a crime once committed, wherein I fired his house, and burnt his kith and kin, save this one boy. I loved him; he won his way to my heart; he seemed like my own son; and then he *betrayed* me. And now he is doomed to death."

"To die WHEN?" almost shrieked the priest.

"At sundown."

---

[1] The like may be still seen in the great church at Warwick.

"God of Mercy! he must not die. Wouldst thou slay thy son?"

"He is not my son by blood—I only meant by adoption."

"Listen, Brian Fitz-Count, to words of solemn truth, although thou wilt find them hard to believe. He is thine *own* son—the son of thy bowels."

Brian felt as if his head would burst beneath the aching brain. A cold sweat bedewed him.

"Prove it," he said.

"I will. Brian Fitz-Count, I am Wulfnoth of Compton."

"Thou? I slew thee on the downs in mortal combat."

"Nay, I yet breathed. The good monks of Dorchester passed by and brought me *here*. I took the vows, and here I am. Now listen: thou didst slay my loved and dearest ones, but I can forgive thee now. Canst thou in turn forgive me?"

"Forgive thee what?"

"In my revenge, I robbed thee of thy son and brought him up as my own."

"But Sexwulf swore that the lad was his grandson."

"He believed it. I wilfully deceived him; but the old nurse Judith has the proofs—a ring with thy crest, a lock of maiden's hair."

"Good God! they were his mother's, and hung about his little neck when we lost him. Man, how couldst thou?"

"Thou didst slay all mine, and I made thee feel *like* pangs. And when the boy came to me after his deadly breach with thee, although I had forgiven thee, I could not tell him the truth, lest I should send him to be a murderer like unto thee; but I did my best for him. I sent him to the Holy Wars, and——"

He discovered that he spake but to the empty air.

Brian was gone.

———

A crowd was on the green sward of the castle, which filled the interior between the buildings. In the centre rose a scaffold, whereon was the instrument of death, the block, the axe. A priest stood by the side of the victim, and soothed him with holy rite and prayer. The executioner leant on his axe.

From the courtyard—the green of the castle—the sun was no longer visible; but the watchman on the top of the keep saw him from that giddy height descending like a ball of fire towards Cwichelm's Hlawe. It was his to give the signal when the sun sank behind the hill.

Every window was full—every coigne of vantage to see the sight. Alas! human nature is ever the same. Witness the precincts of the Old Bailey on hanging mornings in our grandfathers' days!

The man on the keep saw the sun actually touch the trees on the summit of the distant hill, and bathe them in fiery light. Another minute and all would be over.

In the intense silence, the galloping of a horse was heard—a horse strong and powerful. Down went the drawbridges.

The man on the keep saw, and omitted to give the signal, as the sun disappeared.

"Hold! hold!" cried a commanding voice.

It was Brian on his foaming steed. He looked as none had ever seen him look before; but joy was on his face.

He was in time, and no more.

"Take him to my chamber, priest; executioner, put up thine axe, there will be no work for it to-day. Men of Wallingford, Osric is my son—my own son—the son of my bowels. I cannot spare you my son. Thank God, I am in time."

Into that chamber we cannot follow them. The scene is beyond our power of description. It was Nature which had all the time been speaking in that stern father's heart, and now she had her way.

On the following morning a troop left Wallingford Castle for Reading Abbey. The Baron rode at its head, and by his side rode Osric. Through Moulsford, and Streatley, and Pangbourne—such are their modern names—they rode; the Thames on their left hand, the downs on their right. The gorgeous abbey, in the freshness of its early youth, rose before them. Would we had space to describe its glories! They entered, and Brian presented Osric to the Abbot.

"Here, my lord Abbot, is the soldier of the Cross whom thou didst enroll. He is lame as yet, from an accident, but will soon be ready for service. Meanwhile he would fain be thy guest."

The Abbot was astonished.

"What has chanced, my son? We wondered that thou didst not rejoin us, and feared thou hadst faltered."

"He has found a father, who restrained his freedom."

"A father?"

"But who now gives his boy to thee. Osric is my son."

The Abbot was astonished; as well he might be.

"Go, my Osric, to the hospitium; let me speak to my lord Abbot alone."

And Brian told his story, not without strong emotion.

"What wilt thou do now, my Lord of Wallingford?"

"He shall fulfil his vow, for himself and for me. But, my lord, my sins have come home to me. What shall I do? Would I could go with him! but my duties, my plighted faith to my Queen, restrain me. Even to-morrow the leaders of our cause meet at Wallingford Castle."

"Into politics we enter not here. But thy sin, if thou hast sinned, God hath left the means of forgiveness. Repent—confess—thou shall be loosed from all."

"I have not been shriven for a long time, but I will be now."

"Father Osmund is a meet confessor."

"Nay, the man whom I wronged shall shrive me both as priest and man—so shall I feel forgiven."

They parted—the father and son—and Brian rode to

Dorchester, and sought Father Alphege again. Into the solemn secrets of that interview we may not enter. No empty form was there; priest and penitent mingled their tears, and ere the formal absolution was pronounced by the priest they forgave each other as men, and then turned to Him of Whom it is written—

> "Yea, like as a father pitieth his own children,
> Even so is the Lord merciful unto them that fear Him."

And taught by adversity, Brian feared Him now.

CHAPTER XXIX

IN THE HOLY LAND

"Last scene of all,
Which ends this strange eventful history."

OUR tale is all but told. Osric reached the Holy Land in safety, more fortunate than many of his fellows; and there, bearing Brian's recommendations and acknowledged as his son, joined the order of the Knights Templars,—that splendid order which was astonishing the world by its valour and its achievements, whose members were half monks, half warriors, and wore the surplice over the very coat of mail; having their chief church in the purified Mosque of Omar, on the site of the Temple of Jerusalem, and their mission to protect pilgrims and defend the Holy City.

He was speedily admitted to knighthood, a distinction his valour fully justified; and we leave him—gratifying both the old and the new man: the old man in his love of fighting, the new man in his self-conquest—a far nobler thing after all. It was a combination sanctioned by the holiest, best men of that age; such as St. Bernard, whose hymns still occupy a foremost place in our worship.[1]

Brian still continued his warlike career, but there was a great change in his mode of warfare. Wallingford Castle was no longer sullied by unnecessary cruelties. Coupe-gorge and Tustain had an easy time of it.

In 1152 Stephen again besieged Wallingford, but the skill and valour of Brian Fitz-Count forced him to retreat.

[1] As the admirers of Captain Hedley Vicars and other military Christians sanction the combination even now.

Again, having reduced the Castle of Newbury, he returned, and strove to reduce the place by famine, blocking them in on every side; so that they were forced to send a message to Henry Plantagenet to come to their aid from Normandy. He embarked in January 1153 with three thousand foot and a hundred and forty horse. Most of the great nobles of the west joined his standard in his passage through England, and he was in time to relieve Wallingford, besieging the besiegers in their Crowmarsh fort. Stephen came in turn to relieve them with the barons who adhered to his standard, accompanied by his son, the heir presumptive, Eustace, animated with strong emulation against Henry. On his approach, Henry made a sudden sally, and took by storm the fort at the head of the bridge, which Stephen had erected the year before, and following the cruel customs of the war, caused all the defenders to be beheaded on the bridge. Then leaving a sufficient force to bridle Crowmarsh, Henry marched out with great alacrity to offer Stephen a pitched battle and decide the war. He had not gone far when he found Stephen encamped on Cholsey Common, and both sides prepared for battle with eagerness.

But the Earl of Arundel, assembling all the nobility and principal leaders, addressed them.

"It is now fourteen years since the rage of civil war first infected the kingdom. During that melancholy period what blood has been shed, what desolation and misery brought on the people! The laws have lost their force; the Crown its authority; this great and noble nation has been delivered over as a prey to the basest of foreigners,—the abominable scum of Flanders, Brabant, and Brittany,— robbers rather than soldiers, restrained by no laws, Divine or human,—instruments of all tyranny, cruelty, and violence. At the same time our cruel neighbours the Welsh and the Scotch, taking advantage of our distress, have ravaged our borders. And for what good? When Maude was Queen, she alienated all hearts by her pride and violence, and made them regret Stephen. And when Stephen returned to power, he made them regret Maude. He discharged not his foreign hirelings; but they have lived ever since at free-quarters, plundering our houses, burning our cities, preying upon the very bowels of the land, like vultures upon a dying beast. Now, here are two new armies of Angevins, Gascons, and what not. If Henry conquer, he must confiscate our property to repay them, as the Conqueror that of the English, after Senlac. If Stephen conquer, have we any reason to think he will reign better than before? Therefore let us make a third party—that of peace. Let Stephen reign (with proper restraint) for life, and Henry, as combining the royal descent of both nations, succeed him."

The proposal was accepted with avidity, with loud shouts, "So be it: God wills it."

Astonishment and rage seized Eustace, thus left out in the cold; but his father, weary of strife, gave way, and Stephen and Henry met within a little distance from the two camps, in a meadow near Wallingford, the river flowing between the two armies—which had been purposely so disposed to prevent collision—and the conditions of peace were virtually settled on the river-bank.

Eustace went off in a great rage with the knights of his own household, and ravaged the country right and left, showing what an escape England had in his disappointment. His furious passion, coupled with violent exertion, brought on a brain fever, of which he died. Alas, poor young prince! But his death saved thousands of innocent lives, and brought peace to poor old England. The treaty was finally concluded in November 1153, in the fourteenth year of the war. Stephen died the following year, and Henry quietly succeeded; who sent the free-lances back to the continent, and demolished one thousand one hundred and fifteen robbers' castles.

"Peace and no more from out its brazen portals
The blasts of war's great organ shake the skies,
But beautiful as songs of the immortals,
The holy harmonics of peace arise."

And now Brian Fitz-Count could carry out his heart's desire, and follow Osric to the Crusades. His wife, Maude of Wallingford, had before retired into Normandy, weary of strife and turmoil, and taken the veil, with his consent, in a convent connected with the great monastery of Bec.

In the chamber overlooking the south terrace, the river, and the glacis, once the bower of Maude d'Oyley, sat the young King Henry. He was of ruddy countenance and well favoured, like David of old. His chest was broad but his stature short, his manners graceful and dignified.

Before him stood the lord of the castle.

"And so thou *wilt* leave us! For the sake of thy long and great services to our cause, I would fain have retained thee here."

"My liege, I wish to atone for a life of violence and bloodshed. I must save my poor soul."

"Hast thou sinned more than other men?"

"I know not, only that I repent me of my life of violence: I have been a man of blood from my youth, and I go to the tomb of Him Who bled for me that I may lay my sins there."

"And who shall succeed thee here?"

"I care not. I have neither kith nor kin save one—a Knight Templar. A noble soldier, but, by the rules of his stern order, he is pledged to poverty, chastity, and obedience."

"I have heard that the Templars abound in those virtues, but they are a monastic body, and can hold no property independently of their noble order; and I have no wish to see Wallingford Castle a fief of theirs."

"I leave it all to thee, my liege, and only ask permission to say farewell."

"God be with thee, since go thou must."

Brian kissed the royal hand and was gone.

Once he looked back at the keep of Wallingford Castle from the summit of Nuffield in the Chilterns, on his road to London *en route* for the sea. Ah! what a look was that!

He never saw it again.

And when he had gone one of the first acts of the king was to seize as an "escheat" the Castle and honour of Wallingford which Brian Fitz-Count and Maude his wife, having entered the religious life, had ceased to hold.

The sun was setting in the valley between Mount Ebal and Mount Gerizim—the mountains of blessing and cursing. In the entrance to the gorge, thirty-four miles from Jerusalem and fifteen south of Samaria, was the village of El Askar, once called Sychar.

An ancient well, surmounted by an alcove more than a hundred feet deep—the gift of Jacob to his son Joseph—was to be seen hard by; and many pilgrims paused and drank where the Son of God once slaked His human thirst.

The rounded mass of Ebal lay to the south-east of the valley, of Gerizim to the north-west; at the foot of the former lay the village.

As in that olden time, it yet wanted four months of harvest. The corn-fields were still green; the foliage of leafy trees afforded delicious shades, as when He sat weary by that well, old even then.

Oh what memories of blessing and cursing, of Jacob and Joseph, of Joshua and Gideon, clung to that sacred spot! But, like stars in the presence of a sun, their lustre paled at the remembrance that His sacred Feet trod that hallowed soil.

In a whitewashed caravansary of El Askar lay a dying penitent,—a pilgrim returning from Jerusalem, then governed by a Christian king. He seemed prematurely old,—worn out by the toils of the way and the change of climate and mode of life. He lacked not worldly wealth, which there, as elsewhere, commanded attention; yet his feet were blistered and sore, for he had of choice travelled barefoot to the Holy Sepulchre.

A military party was passing along the vale, bound from Acre to Jerusalem, clad in flexible mail from head to foot; armed, for the rules of their order forbade them ever to lay their arms aside. But over their armour long monastic mantles of scarlet were worn, with a huge white cross on the left shoulder. They were of the array of the Knights Templars. Soldiers, yet monks! of such high renown that scarcely a great family in Europe but was represented in their ranks. Their diet was simple, their discipline exact; they shunned no hardship, declined no combat; they had few ties to life, but were prepared to sacrifice all for the sake of the holy warfare and the Temple of God. Their homes, their churches, lacked ornament, and were rigidly simple, as became their vow of poverty. Never yet had they disgraced their holy calling, or neglected to bear their white banner into the heart of the foe; so that the Moslem trembled at the war-cry of the Templars—" God and His Temple."

Such were the Templars in their early days.

The leader of this particular party was a knight in the prime of life, of noble, prepossessing bearing; who managed his horse as if rider and steed were one, like the Centaur of old.

They encamped for the night in the open, hard by the Sacred Well.

Scarcely were the camp-fires lit, when a villager sought an audience of the commander, which was at once granted.

"Noble seigneur," he said, "a Christian pilgrim lies dying at the caravansary hard by, and craves the consolations of religion. Thou art both monk and soldier?"

"I am."

"And wilt visit the dying man?"

"At once."

And only draining a goblet of wine and munching a crust, the leader followed the guide, retaining his arms, according to rule; first telling his subordinate in command where he was going.

On the slopes of the eastern hill stood the caravansary, built in the form of a hollow square; the courtyard devoted to horses and cattle, chambers opening all round the inner colonnade, with windows looking outward upon the country.

There the Templar was taken to a chamber, where, upon a rude pallet, was stretched the dying man.

"Thou art ill, my brother; canst thou converse with me?"

"God has left me that strength."

"With what tongue dost thou adore the God of our fathers?"

"English or French. But who art thou?"

The dying man raised himself up on his elbows.

"Osric!"

"My father!"

It was indeed Brian Fitz-Count who lay dying on that couch. They embraced fervently.

"*Nunc dimittis servum tuum Domine in pace*," he said. "Osric, my son, is yet alive—I see him: God permits me to see him, to gladden my eyes. Osric, thou shalt close them; and here shalt thou bury thy father."

"Tell me, my sire, hast thou long arrived? why have we not met before?"

"I have been to Jerusalem; I have wept on Calvary; I have prayed at the Holy Sepulchre; and there I have received the assurance that He has cast my sins behind my back, and blotted them out, nailing them to His Cross. I then sought thee, and heard thou wert at Acre, at the commandery of St. John. I sought thee, but passed thee on the road unwittingly. Then I retraced my steps; but the malaria, which ever hangs about the ruins of old cities, has prostrated me. My hours are numbered; but what have I yet to live for? no, *Nunc dimittis, nunc dimittis, Domine; quia oculi mei viderunt salutare Tuum.*"

And he sank back as in ecstasy, holding still the hand of his son, and covering it with kisses.

The setting sun cast a flood of glory on the vale beneath, on Jacob's Well.

Once more the sick man rose on his bed, and gazed on the sacred spot where once the Redeemer sat, and talked with the woman of Samaria.

"He sat there, weary, weary, seeking His sheep; and I

am one. He has found me. Oh my God, Thou didst thirst for my soul; let that thirst be satisfied."

Then to Osric—

"Hast thou not a priest in thy troop, my son?"

"Our chaplain is with us."

"Let him bring me the Viaticum. I am starting on my last long journey, I want my provision for the way."

The priest arrived; the last rites were administered.

"Like David of old, I have been a man of blood; like him, I have repented that I have shed innocent blood," said the sick penitent.

"And like Nathan, I tell thee, my brother," said the priest, "that the Lord hath put away thy sin."

"And my faith accepts the blessed assurance."

"Osric, my son, let me bless thee before I die; thou dost not know, canst never know on earth, what thou didst for me."

"God bless thee too, my father. We shall meet before His throne when time shall be no more."

He fell back as if exhausted, and for a long time lay speechless. At last he raised himself on his elbow and looked steadfastly up.

"Hark! they are calling the roll-call above."

He listened intently for a moment, then, as if he had heard his own name, he answered—

"ADSUM."

And Brian Fitz-Count was no more.

THE END

A SELECTION

FROM THE

Recent Publications

OF

Messrs. RIVINGTON

*WATERLOO PLACE, PALL MALL
LONDON*

Woodford's Sermons.

Two Vols. Crown 8vo. 5s. each. Sold separately.

SERMONS.

By James Russell Woodford, D.D.,
Sometime Lord Bishop of Ely.

Vol. I.—OLD TESTAMENT SUBJECTS.

The Feast of Tabernacles—Man's Impatience of Things Supernatural—The Death of Moses—The Power of Christ's Presence in Restraining Evil—The Co-operation of Divine and Human Forces—The Sovereignty of God—The Noiseless Building of the House of God—The Power of Music—The Gentleness of God—The Silence of God—Man's Yearning for Safety, Satisfied in a Personal God—God's Use of Evil in Working out His Purposes—The Probation of Man Limited to this Life—The Arm of the Lord—Noah, Daniel, and Job and the Communion of Saints—The Church Designed to Embrace every Age and Character—Light at Eventide.

Vol. II.—NEW TESTAMENT SUBJECTS.

A City that is Set on a Hill—The Closed Door—The Peril of Playing with Spiritual Convictions—Misinterpretation of the Voice of God—The Resurrection Change—The Birthday of the Church—St. Peter's Shadow—The First Martyr—The Reign of the Son of Man—The Condition of the Disembodied Soul Imperfect—The Deposit of the Faith in Christ's Safe Keeping—Entrance through the Veil of Christ's Humanity—The Cloud of Witnesses—The Names of Individual Souls on the Breastplate of Christ—Absolute Obedience to the Guidance of Christ—The Many Crowns—The Rightful Entrance into the City of God.

Paget on Belief.

Crown 8vo. 6s. 6d.

FACULTIES AND DIFFICULTIES FOR BELIEF AND DISBELIEF.

By Francis Paget, D.D.,
Canon of Christ Church, Oxford.

Introductory Essay. Part I.—The Virtue of Self-assertion, in the Life of the Intellect—The Virtue of Self-assertion, in the Life of the Will—The Social Instinct—The Reasonableness of Life—The Love of Beauty in Nature—The Love of Beauty in Art—The Love of Beauty in Character—The Place of the Intellect—The Dignity of Man—Readiness. Part II.—The Need of Healing—The Miracle of Repair—The Reality of Grace—The Transformation of Pity—The Transformation of Hope—The Records of the Past—The Force of Faith—Discord and Harmony—The Inner Life.

Waterloo Place, London.

Armitage's Early Church History.

Crown 8vo. 5s.

SKETCHES OF CHURCH AND STATE IN THE FIRST EIGHT CENTURIES.

By the Rev. William Armitage, B.A.,

Vicar of Scotford, Lancaster; late Scholar of Emmanuel College, Cambridge.

Extension of the Roman Empire into Britain—Early Struggles of the Church with Jews and Gnostics—Heresies and Persecutions—Christian Apologists—Christianity established by the State—The Arian Heresy—Growing Power of Roman Bishops—Gothic Invasions—Growing Corruptions in the Church—The Miracles of Saints—Northumbrian Kings—The Easter Controversy—General Councils—Atilla, King of the Huns—Monastic Institutions—Mahomet—Mahometan Conquests—Image Worship—Irish Missionaries—Charlemagne.

Ottley on Revealed Truths.

Crown 8vo. 5s.

RATIONAL ASPECTS OF SOME REVEALED TRUTHS.

By Edward B. Ottley, M.A.,

Minister of Quebec Chapel; lately the Principal of Salisbury Diocesan Theological College.

Introductory—Modern Doubt and Unbelief: its Extent, Origin, and Causes—The Authority of the Holy Scriptures—The Divinity of Christ (I.): Witness of the Church, etc.—The Divinity of Christ (II.): Witness of Hebrew Scriptures—The Divinity of Christ (III.): Witness of the New Testament—Christianity and Culture.

Life of Bishop Bickersteth.

With Portrait. 8vo. 12s.

A SKETCH OF THE LIFE AND EPISCOPATE OF THE RIGHT REV. ROBERT BICKERSTETH, D.D., Bishop of Ripon, 1857-1884. With a Preface by the Lord Bishop of Exeter.

By his Son, Montagu Cyril Bickersteth, M.A.,

Vicar of St. Paul's, Pudsey, Leeds.

Waterloo Place, London.

Liddon's Easter Sermons.

Second Edition. Two Vols. Crown 8vo. 5s. each. Sold separately.

EASTER IN ST. PAUL'S. Sermons bearing chiefly on the Resurrection of our Lord.

By Henry Parry Liddon, D.D., D.C.L.,
Chancellor and Canon of St. Paul's.

Liddon's Bampton Lectures.

Eleventh Edition, revised. Crown 8vo. 5s.

THE DIVINITY OF OUR LORD AND SAVIOUR JESUS CHRIST; being the Bampton Lectures for 1866.

By Henry Parry Liddon, D.D., D.C.L.,
Chancellor and Canon of St. Paul's.

Liddon's Elements of Religion.

Fifth and Cheaper Edition. Small 8vo. 2s. 6d. Or in Paper Cover, 1s. 6d.

SOME ELEMENTS OF RELIGION. Lent Lectures.

By Henry Parry Liddon, D.D., D.C.L.,
Chancellor and Canon of St. Paul's.

The Crown 8vo (Fourth) Edition, 5s., may still be had.

Liddon's University Sermons.

Two Vols. Crown 8vo. 5s. each. Sold separately.

SERMONS PREACHED BEFORE THE UNIVERSITY OF OXFORD.

By Henry Parry Liddon, D.D., D.C.L.,
Chancellor and Canon of St. Paul's.

FIRST SERIES.—1859-1868.
SECOND SERIES.—1868-1882.

Waterloo Place, London.

Goulburn's Gospels for Sundays.
Second Edition. Two Vols. Crown 8vo. 16s.

THOUGHTS UPON THE LITURGICAL GOSPELS FOR THE SUNDAYS, ONE FOR EACH DAY IN THE YEAR. With an Introduction on their origin, history, the modifications made in them by the Reformers and by the Revisers of the Prayer Book, the honour always paid to them in the Church, and the proportions in which they are drawn from the Writings of the four Evangelists.

By **Edward Meyrick Goulburn, D.D., D.C.L.,**
Dean of Norwich.

Goulburn's Gospels for Holy Days.
Crown 8vo. 8s. 6d.

MEDITATIONS UPON THE LITURGICAL GOSPELS. For the minor Festivals of Christ, the two first week-days of the Easter and Whitsun Festivals, and the Red Letter Saints' Days. To which is prefixed some account of the origin of Saints' Days, and their Evens or Vigils; of the pruning of the Calendar of the English Church by the Reformers; and of the re-introduction of the Black-Letter Festivals, with separate notices of the Four which were re-introduced in the Prayer-Book of 1552.

By **Edward Meyrick Goulburn, D.D., D.C.L.,**
Dean of Norwich.

Goulburn's Holy Week Lectures.
Crown 8vo. 5s.

HOLY WEEK IN NORWICH CATHEDRAL; being Seven Lectures on the several Members of the Most Sacred Body of our Lord Jesus Christ. Delivered at Evensong on each Day of the Holy Week in the Cathedral Church of the Holy and Undivided Trinity of Norwich.

By **Edward Meyrick Goulburn, D.D., D.C.L.,**
Dean of Norwich.

Waterloo Place, London.

Welldon's Harrow Sermons.

Crown 8vo. 7s. 6d.

SERMONS PREACHED TO HARROW BOYS.

By the Rev. J. E. C. Welldon, M.A.,

Head Master of Harrow School.

The Future and the Past—Individuality—All Saints' Day—The Religious Value of Small Duties—The Promise of the Advent—The Bible—The Meetings with the Angels—The Sins of the Tongue—The Bearing of the Cross—Worldliness—The Keeping of Sunday—The Natural Body and the Spiritual Body—Balaam—The Animal World—The Blessing of Failure—Friendships—Spiritual Insight—The Lord's Prayer—The Uses of the Holidays.

The Altar Book.

With Rubrics in Red. Large Type. Royal 8vo. 10s. 6d.

THE ORDER OF THE ADMINISTRATION OF THE HOLY COMMUNION, AND THE FORM OF SOLEMNIZATION OF MATRIMONY, according to the Use of the Church of England.

May also be had bound in Morocco.

Knox Little's Hopes of the Passion.

Crown 8vo. 3s. 6d.

THE HOPES AND DECISIONS OF THE PASSION OF OUR MOST HOLY REDEEMER.

By the Rev. W. J. Knox Little, M.A.,

Canon Residentiary of Worcester, and Vicar of Hoar Cross, Burton-on-Trent.

Waterloo Place, London.

Woodford's Great Commission.

Crown 8vo. 5s.

THE GREAT COMMISSION. Twelve Addresses on the Ordinal.

By James Russell Woodford, D.D.,
Sometime Lord Bishop of Ely.

Edited, with an Introduction on the Ordinations of his Episcopate,

By Herbert Mortimer Luckock, D.D.,
One of his Examining Chaplains.

Luckock's Bishops in the Tower.

Crown 8vo. 6s.

THE BISHOPS IN THE TOWER. A Record of Stirring Events affecting the Church and Nonconformists from the Restoration to the Revolution.

By Herbert Mortimer Luckock, D.D.,
Canon of Ely, etc.

The Book of Church Law.

Fourth Edition, revised. Crown 8vo. 7s. 6d.

THE BOOK OF CHURCH LAW: being an Exposition of the Legal Rights and Duties of the Parochial Clergy and the Laity of the Church of England.

By the late Rev. John Henry Blunt, D.D.,

Revised by Sir Walter G. F. Phillimore, Bart., D.C.L.,
Barrister-at-Law, and Chancellor of the Diocese of Lincoln.

Waterloo Place, London.

Holland's Creed and Character.

Crown 8vo. 7s. 6d.

CREED AND CHARACTER. A Volume of Sermons.

By the Rev. H. S. Holland, M.A.,
Canon of St. Paul's.

Contents.

The Story of an Apostle's Faith—The Story of a Disciple's Faith—The Rock; The Secret; The Fellowship; The Witness; The Resources; The Mind; The Ministry of the Church—The Solidarity of Salvation—The Freedom of Salvation—The Gift of Grace—The Law of Forgiveness—The Coming of the Spirit—The Beauty of Holiness—The Energy of Unselfishness—The Fruit of the Spirit—Thanksgiving—The Activity of Service—Character and Circumstance.

Holland's Logic and Life.

Third Edition. Crown 8vo. 7s. 6d.

LOGIC AND LIFE, with other Sermons.

By the Rev. H. S. Holland, M.A.,
Canon of St. Paul's.

'Some of these sermons are as powerful as any preached in this generation, and, indeed, full of genius, original thought, and spiritual veracity. Of the three first, it would be hard to speak in terms too high.'—*Spectator.*

'These [two last-named] sermons exhibit at the full the real greatness of Mr. Holland's power—his originality, his insight, his range of experience, observation, and sympathies; and, above all, his never-failing elevation of spiritual feeling and judgment, speaking in language brilliant, forcible, copious, rising often to splendour and magnificence.'—*Church Quarterly Review.*

'The sermons are thoughtful, earnest, and often eloquent and powerful. They fully bear out the high reputation Mr. Holland has obtained as a preacher of considerable acceptableness and influence with hearers of education and culture.'—*Guardian.*

Holland's Good Friday Addresses.

Small 8vo. 2s.

GOOD FRIDAY: being Addresses on the Seven Last Words, delivered at St. Paul's Cathedral, on Good Friday 1884.

By the Rev. H. S. Holland, M.A.,
Canon of St. Paul's.

Waterloo Place, London.

Crake's Church History.

New Edition. Crown 8vo. 7s. 6d.

HISTORY OF THE CHURCH UNDER THE ROMAN EMPIRE, A.D. 30-476.

By the Rev. A. D. Crake, B.A.,

Fellow of the Royal Historical Society, Vicar of Cholsey, Berks.

Crake's Chronicles of Æscendune.

Three Vols. Crown 8vo. 3s. 6d. each. Sold separately.

By the Rev. A. D. Crake, B.A.,

Author of the 'History of the Church under the Roman Empire,' etc., etc.

EDWY THE FAIR; OR, THE FIRST CHRONICLE OF ÆSCENDUNE.
A Tale of the Days of St. Dunstan.

ALFGAR THE DANE; OR, THE SECOND CHRONICLE OF ÆSCENDUNE.
A Tale of the Days of Edmund Ironside.

THE RIVAL HEIRS; BEING THE THIRD AND LAST CHRONICLE OF ÆSCENDUNE.

Crake's House of Walderne.

Crown 8vo. 3s. 6d.

THE HOUSE OF WALDERNE: A Tale of the Cloister and the Forest in the Days of the Barons' Wars.

By the Rev. A. D. Crake, B.A.,

Fellow of the Royal Historical Society, Author of the 'Chronicles of Æscendune,' etc.

Waterloo Place, London.

Mozley on the Old Testament.

Third Edition. 8vo. 10s. 6d.

RULING IDEAS IN EARLY AGES AND THEIR RELATION TO OLD TESTAMENT FAITH. Lectures delivered to Graduates of the University of Oxford.

By J. B. Mozley, D.D.,

Late Canon of Christ Church, and Regius Professor of Divinity in the University of Oxford.

Contents.

Abraham—Sacrifice of Isaac—Human Sacrifices—Exterminating Wars—Visitation of the Sins of Fathers upon Children—Jael—Connection of Jael's Act with the Morality of her Age—Law of Retaliation—Retaliation: Law of Goël—The End the Test of a Progressive Revelation—The Manichæans and the Jewish Fathers.

Mozley's University Sermons.

Fifth Edition. Crown 8vo. 7s. 6d.

SERMONS PREACHED BEFORE THE UNIVERSITY OF OXFORD AND ON VARIOUS OCCASIONS.

By J. B. Mozley, D.D.,

Late Canon of Christ Church, and Regius Professor of Divinity, Oxford.

Contents.

The Roman Council—The Pharisees—Eternal Life—The Reversal of Human Judgment—War—Nature—The Work of the Spirit on the Natural Man—The Atonement—Our Duty to Equals—The Peaceful Temper—The Strength of Wishes—The Unspoken Judgment of Mankind—The True Test of Spiritual Birth—Ascension Day—Gratitude—The Principle of Emulation—Religion the First Choice—The Influence of Dogmatic Teaching on Education.

Waterloo Place, London.

Mozley's Essays.

Second Edition. Two Vols. 8vo. 24s.

ESSAYS, HISTORICAL AND THEOLOGICAL.

By J. B. Mozley, D.D.,
Late Canon of Christ Church, and Regius Professor of Divinity in the University of Oxford.

Contents.

VOLUME I.—Introduction and Memoir of the Author—Lord Strafford—Archbishop Laud—Carlyle's Cromwell—Luther.

VOLUME II.—Dr. Arnold—Blanco White—Dr. Pusey's Sermon—The Book of Job—Maurice's Theological Essays—Indian Conversion—The Argument of Design—The Principle of Causation considered in opposition to Atheistic Theories—In Memoriam—The Author's Articles and Works.

Mozley on Miracles.

Seventh Edition. Crown 8vo. 7s. 6d.

EIGHT LECTURES ON MIRACLES: being the Bampton Lectures for 1865.

By J. B. Mozley, D.D.,
Late Canon of Christ Church, and Regius Professor of Divinity in the University of Oxford.

Mozley's Parochial Sermons.

Second Edition. Crown 8vo. 7s. 6d.

SERMONS, PAROCHIAL AND OCCASIONAL.

By J. B. Mozley, D.D.,
Late Canon of Christ Church, and Regius Professor of Divinity in the University of Oxford.

Contents.

The Right Eye and the Right Hand—Temptation treated as Opportunity—The Influences of Habit on Devotion—Thought for the Morrow—The Relief of Utterance—Seeking a Sign—David Numbering the People—The Heroism of Faith—Proverbs—The Teaching of Events—Growing Worse—Our Lord the Sacrifice for Sin—The Parable of the Sower—The Religious Enjoyment of Nature—The Threefold Office of the Holy Spirit—Wisdom and Folly Tested by Experience—Moses, a Leader—The Unjust Steward—Sowing to the Spirit—True Religion, a Manifestation—St. Paul's Exaltation of Labour—Jeremiah's Witness against Idolatry—Isaiah's Estimate of Worldly Greatness—The Shortness of Life—The Endless State of Being—The Witness of the Apostles—Life a Probation—Christian Mysteries, the Common Heritage—Our Lord's Hour—Fear—The Educating Power of Strong Impressions—The Secret Justice of Temporal Providence—Jacob as a Prince Prevailing with God.

Waterloo Place, London.

Mozley's Lectures.

8vo. 10s. 6d.

LECTURES AND OTHER THEOLOGICAL PAPERS.

By J. B. Mozley, D.D.,
Late Canon of Christ Church, and Regius Professor of Divinity in the University of Oxford.

The Prayer Book in Latin.

With Rubrics in Red. Small 8vo. 7s. 6d.

LIBER PRECUM PUBLICARUM ECCLESIÆ ANGLICANÆ.

A Gulielmo Bright, S.T.P.,
Ædis Christi apud Oxon. Canonico, Historiæ Ecclesiasticæ, Professore Regio,

et

Petro Goldsmith Medd, A.M.,
Collegii Universitatis apud Oxon. Socio Seniore.

LATINE REDDITUS. Editio Tertia, cum Appendice.

[In hac Editione continentur Versiones Latinæ—1. Libri Precum Publicarum Ecclesiæ Anglicanæ; 2. Liturgiæ Primæ Reformatæ; 3. Liturgiæ Scoticanæ; 4. Liturgiæ Americanæ.]

Blunt's Household Theology.

New Edition. Small 8vo. 3s. 6d.

HOUSEHOLD THEOLOGY: a Handbook of Religious Information respecting the Holy Bible, the Prayer Book, the Church, the Ministry, Divine Worship, the Creeds, etc., etc.

By the Rev. John Henry Blunt, D.D.,
Editor of the 'Annotated Book of Common Prayer,' etc., etc.

Also a Cheap Edition. 16mo. 1s.

Waterloo Place, London.

Selections from Liddon.

New Edition. Crown 8vo. 3s. 6d.

SELECTIONS from the Writings of H. P. LIDDON, D.D., D.C.L.,
Chancellor and Canon of St. Paul's.

Selections from Keble.

Crown 8vo. 3s. 6d.

SELECTIONS from the Writings of JOHN KEBLE, M.A.,
Author of 'The Christian Year.'

Selections from Pusey.

Second Edition. Crown 8vo. 3s. 6d.

SELECTIONS from the Writings of EDWARD BOUVERIE PUSEY, D.D.,
Late Regius Professor of Hebrew, and Canon of Christ Church, Oxford.

Selections from Neale.

Crown 8vo. 3s. 6d.

SELECTIONS from the Writings of JOHN MASON NEALE, D.D.,
Late Warden of Sackville College.

Waterloo Place, London.

Corpus Christi.

With Red Borders. Royal 32mo. 2s.

CORPUS CHRISTI: A Manual of Devotion for the Blessed Sacrament.

With a Preface by the Rev. H. Montagu Villiers,
Vicar of St. Paul's, Wilton Place.

Also a Cheap Edition, without the Red Borders, 1s.

Williams on the Catechism.

New Edition. Two Vols. Crown 8vo. 5s. each. Sold separately.

PLAIN SERMONS ON THE CATECHISM.

By the Rev. Isaac Williams, B.D.,
Late Fellow of Trinity College, Oxford; Author of a 'Devotional Commentary on the Gospel Narrative.'

Bickersteth's Yesterday, To-day, and For Ever.

One Shilling Edition. 18mo.
With Red Borders. 16mo. 2s. 6d.

YESTERDAY, TO-DAY, AND FOR EVER: a Poem in Twelve Books.

By Edward Henry Bickersteth, D.D.,
Bishop of Exeter.

'This blank-verse poem, in twelve books, has made its way into the religious world of England and America without much help from the critics.'—*Times.*

'The most simple, the richest, and the most perfect sacred poem which recent days have produced.'—*Morning Advertiser.*

'A poem worth reading, worthy of attentive study; full of noble thoughts, beautiful diction, and high imagination.'—*Standard.*

'In these light Miscellany days there is a spiritual refreshment in the spectacle of a man girding up the loins of his mind to the task of producing a genuine epic. And it is true poetry. There is a definiteness, a crispness about it, which in these moist, viewy, hazy days is no less invigorating than novel.'—*Edinburgh Daily Review.*

'Mr. Bickersteth writes like a man who cultivates at once reverence and earnestness of thought.'—*Guardian.*

The Larger Edition, 5s., may be had.

Waterloo Place, London.

The Annotated Prayer Book.

In One Volume. Quarto. £1, 1s.
Or Half-bound in Morocco. £1, 11s. 6d.

THE ANNOTATED BOOK OF COMMON PRAYER: being an Historical, Ritual, and Theological Commentary on the Devotional System of the Church of England.

Edited by the Rev. John Henry Blunt, D.D., F.S.A.

The reception which the Annotated Book of Common Prayer has met with during an issue of eight editions in sixteen years has led the publishers to believe that a new edition, carefully revised and enlarged, in accordance with our advanced knowledge, would be acceptable. The present edition has therefore been prepared with, among others, the following improvements:—

1. A thoroughly trustworthy text of the whole Prayer Book, such as has not hitherto been accessible.
2. A much enlarged Introduction, embracing in a compact form all that is now known respecting the history of the Prayer Book.
3. The Epistles and Gospels, with all other portions of Holy Scripture, are now printed at length.
4. The Notes on the Minor Saints' Days have been carefully revised, and in most cases re-written.

À Kempis' Of the Imitation of Christ.

Large Type Edition. Crown 8vo. 3s. 6d.

OF THE IMITATION OF CHRIST. In Four Books.

By Thomas à Kempis.

Translated and Edited by the Rev. W. H. Hutchings, M.A.,
Rector of Kirkby Misperton, Yorkshire.

Waterloo Place, London.

Luckock on the Prayer Book.

Second Edition. Crown 8vo. 6s.

STUDIES IN THE HISTORY OF THE BOOK OF COMMON PRAYER. The Anglican Reform—The Puritan Innovations—The Elizabethan Reaction—The Caroline Settlement. With Appendices.

By Herbert Mortimer Luckock, D.D.,

Canon of Ely, etc.

'This able and helpful book—recommending it emphatically to all educated members of the entire Anglican community.' —*Church Quarterly Review.*
'We heartily commend this very interesting and very readable book.'—*Guardian.*
'Dr. Luckock's compact and clearly arranged volume is a valuable contribution to liturgical history, which will prove interesting to all readers and almost indispensable to the theological student who has to master the history and *rationale* of the Book of Common Prayer.'—*Notes and Queries.*

Knox Little's Mystery of the Passion.

Third Edition. Crown 8vo. 3s. 6d.

THE MYSTERY OF THE PASSION OF OUR MOST HOLY REDEEMER.

By the Rev. W. J. Knox Little, M.A.,

Canon Residentiary of Worcester and Vicar of Hoar Cross.

The Treasury of Devotion.

Fifteenth Edition. 18mo, 2s. 6d.; Cloth limp, 2s.; or bound with the Book of Common Prayer, 3s. 6d.

THE TREASURY OF DEVOTION : a Manual of Prayers for General and Daily Use.

Compiled by a Priest.
Edited by the Rev. T. T. Carter, M.A.

Also an Edition in Large Type. Crown 8vo. 5s.

Waterloo Place, London.

Williams's Female Scripture Characters.

New Edition. Crown 8vo. 5s.

FEMALE CHARACTERS OF HOLY SCRIPTURE. A Series of Sermons.

By the Rev. Isaac Williams, B.D.,
Formerly Fellow of Trinity College, Oxford.

Contents.

Eve—Sarah—Lot's Wife—Rebekah—Leah and Rachel—Miriam—Rahab—Deborah—Ruth—Hannah—The Witch of Endor—Bathsheba—Rizpah—The Queen of Sheba—The Widow of Zarephath—Jezebel—The Shunammite—Esther—Elisabeth—Anna—The Woman of Samaria—Joanna—The Woman with the Issue of Blood—The Woman of Canaan—Martha—Mary—Salome—The Wife of Pilate—Dorcas—The Blessed Virgin.

Blunt's Dictionary of Sects.

New Edition. Imperial 8vo. 36s.; or in half-morocco, 48s.

DICTIONARY OF SECTS, HERESIES, ECCLESIASTICAL PARTIES, AND SCHOOLS OF RELIGIOUS THOUGHT. By Various Writers.

Edited by the Rev. John Henry Blunt, D.D.,
Editor of the 'Dictionary of Theology,' 'Annotated Book of Common Prayer,' etc., etc.

Body's Life of Temptation.

Sixth Edition. Crown 8vo. 4s. 6d.

THE LIFE OF TEMPTATION. A Course of Lectures delivered in substance at St. Peter's, Eaton Square; also at All Saints', Margaret Street.

By the Rev. George Body, D.D.,
Canon of Durham.

Contents.

The Leading into Temptation—The Rationale of Temptation—Why we are Tempted—Safety in Temptation—With Jesus in Temptation—The End of Temptation.

Waterloo Place, London.

Knox Little's Manchester Sermons.

Second Edition. Crown 8vo. 7s. 6d.

SERMONS PREACHED FOR THE MOST PART IN MANCHESTER.

By the Rev. W. J. Knox Little, M.A.,
Canon Residentiary of Worcester, and Vicar of Hoar Cross.

Contents.

The Soul instructed by God—The Claim of God upon the Soul—The Supernatural Powers of the Soul—The Soul in its Inner Life—The Soul in the World and at the Judgment—The Law of Preparation—The Principle of Preparation—The Temper of Preparation—The Energy of Preparation—The Soul's Need and God's Nature—The Martyr of Jesus—The Secret of Prophetic Power—The Law of Sacrifice—The Comfort of God—The Symbolism of the Cross—The Beatitude of Mary, the Mother of the Lord.

Knox Little's Christian Life.

Third Edition. Crown 8vo. 3s. 6d.

CHARACTERISTICS AND MOTIVES OF THE CHRISTIAN LIFE. Ten Sermons preached in Manchester Cathedral in Lent and Advent 1877.

By the Rev. W. J. Knox Little, M.A.,
Canon Residentiary of Worcester, and Vicar of Hoar Cross.

Contents.

Christian Work—Christian Advance—Christian Watching—Christian Battle—Christian Suffering—Christian Joy—For the Love of Man—For the sake of Jesus—For the Glory of God—The Claims of Christ.

Knox Little's Witness of the Passion.

Crown 8vo. 3s. 6d.

THE WITNESS OF THE PASSION OF OUR MOST HOLY REDEEMER.

By the Rev. W. J. Knox Little, M.A.,
Canon Residentiary of Worcester, and Vicar of Hoar Cross.

Waterloo Place, London.

Williams's Devotional Commentary.

New Edition. Eight Vols. Crown 8vo. 5s. each. Sold separately.

A DEVOTIONAL COMMENTARY ON THE GOSPEL NARRATIVE.

By the Rev. Isaac Williams, B.D.,
Formerly Fellow of Trinity College, Oxford.

THOUGHTS ON THE STUDY OF THE HOLY GOSPELS.
A HARMONY OF THE FOUR EVANGELISTS.
OUR LORD'S NATIVITY.
OUR LORD'S MINISTRY (SECOND YEAR).
OUR LORD'S MINISTRY (THIRD YEAR).
THE HOLY WEEK.
OUR LORD'S PASSION.
OUR LORD'S RESURRECTION.

Voices of Comfort.

New Edition. Crown 8vo. 7s. 6d.

VOICES OF COMFORT.

Edited by the Rev. Thomas Vincent Fosbery, M.A.,
Sometime Vicar of St. Giles's, Oxford.

This Volume of prose and poetry, original and selected, aims at revealing the fountains of hope and joy which underlie the griefs and sorrows of life. It is so divided as to afford readings for a month. The keynote of each day is given to the title prefixed to it, such as: 'The Power of the Cross of Christ, Day 6. Conflicts of the Soul, Day 17. The Communion of Saints, Day 20. The Comforter, Day 22. The Light of Hope, Day 25. The Coming of Christ, Day 28.' Each day begins with passages of Holy Scripture. These are followed by articles in prose, which are succeeded by one or more short prayers. After these are poems or passages of poetry, and then very brief extracts in prose or verse close the section. The book is meant to meet, not merely cases of bereavement or physical suffering, but 'to minister specially to the hidden troubles of the heart, as they are silently weaving their dark threads into the web of the seemingly brightest life.'

Also a Cheap Edition. Small 8vo. 3s. 6d.

Waterloo Place, London.

The Star of Childhood.

Fourth Edition. Royal 16mo. 2s. 6d.

THE STAR OF CHILDHOOD: a First Book of Prayers and Instruction for Children.

Compiled by a Priest.
Edited by the Rev. T. T. Carter, M.A.

With Illustrations after Fra Angelico.

The Guide to Heaven.

New Edition. 18mo. 1s. 6d.; Cloth limp, 1s.

THE GUIDE TO HEAVEN: a Book of Prayers for every Want. For the Working Classes.

Compiled by a Priest.
Edited by the Rev. T. T. Carter, M.A.

An Edition in Large Type. Crown 8vo. 1s. 6d.; Cloth limp, 1s.

H. L. Sidney Lear's For Days and Years.

New Edition. 16mo. 2s. 6d.

FOR DAYS AND YEARS. A Book containing a Text, Short Reading and Hymn for Every Day in the Church's Year.

Selected by H. L. Sidney Lear.

Also a Cheap Edition. 32mo, 1s.; or Cloth gilt, 1s. 6d.

Williams on the Epistles and Gospels.

*New Edition. Two Vols. Crown 8vo. 5s. each.
Sold separately.*

SERMONS ON THE EPISTLES AND GOSPELS FOR THE SUNDAYS AND HOLY DAYS THROUGHOUT THE YEAR.

By the Rev. Isaac Williams, B.D.,
Author of a 'Devotional Commentary on the Gospel Narrative.'

Waterloo Place, London.

Moberly's Parochial Sermons.

Crown 8vo. 7s. 6d.

PAROCHIAL SERMONS, chiefly preached at Brighstone, Isle of Wight.

By George Moberly, D.C.L.,
Late Bishop of Salisbury.

Contents.

The Night is far spent, the Day is at hand—Elijah, the Warner of the Second Advent of the Lord—Christmas—Epiphany—The Rich Man and Lazarus—The Seventh Day Rest—I will arise and go to my Father—Confirmation, a Revival—Korah—The Law of Liberty—Buried with Him in Baptism—The Waiting Church of the Hundred and Twenty—Whitsun Day. I will not leave you comfortless—Whitsun Day. Walking after the Spirit—The Barren Fig Tree—Depart from me; for I am a sinful man, O Lord—Feeding the Four Thousand—We are debtors—He that thinketh he standeth—The Strength of Working Prayer—Elijah's Sacrifice—If thou hadst known, even thou—Harvest Thanksgiving—Jonadab, the Son of Rechab—The Transfiguration; Death and Glory—Welcome to Everlasting Habitations—The Question of the Sadducees.

Moberly's Plain Sermons.

New Edition. Crown 8vo. 5s.

PLAIN SERMONS, PREACHED AT BRIGHSTONE.

By George Moberly, D.C.L.,
Late Bishop of Salisbury.

Contents.

Except a man be born again—The Lord with the Doctors—The Draw-Net—I will lay me down in peace—Ye have not so learned Christ—Trinity Sunday—My Flesh is Meat indeed—The Corn of Wheat dying and multiplied—The Seed Corn springing to new life—I am the Way, the Truth, and the Life—The Ruler of the Sea—Stewards of the Mysteries of God—Ephphatha—The Widow of Nain—Josiah's discovery of the Law—The Invisible World: Angels—Prayers, especially Daily Prayers—They all with one consent began to make excuse—Ascension Day—The Comforter—The Tokens of the Spirit—Elijah's Warning, Fathers and Children—Thou shalt see them no more for ever—Baskets full of fragments—Harvest—The Marriage Supper of the Lamb—The Last Judgment.

Waterloo Place, London.

Luckock's Footprints of the Son of Man.

Third Edition. Two Vols. Crown 8vo. 12s.

FOOTPRINTS OF THE SON OF MAN AS TRACED BY SAINT MARK: being Eighty Portions for Private Study, Family Reading, and Instructions in Church.

By **Herbert Mortimer Luckock, D.D.**,
Canon of Ely; Examining Chaplain to the Bishop of Ely; and Principal of the Theological College.

With an Introduction by the late Bishop of Ely.

Goulburn's Thoughts on Personal Religion.

New Edition. Small 8vo. 6s. 6d.

THOUGHTS ON PERSONAL RELIGION: being a Treatise on the Christian Life in its two Chief Elements—Devotion and Practice.

By **Edward Meyrick Goulburn, D.D., D.C.L.**,
Dean of Norwich.

Also a Cheap Edition. 3s. 6d.

Presentation Edition, elegantly printed on Toned Paper.
Two Vols. Small 8vo. 10s. 6d.

Goulburn's Pursuit of Holiness.

Seventh Edition. Small 8vo. 5s.

THE PURSUIT OF HOLINESS: a Sequel to 'Thoughts on Personal Religion,' intended to carry the Reader somewhat farther onward in the Spiritual Life.

By **Edward Meyrick Goulburn, D.D., D.C.L.**,
Dean of Norwich.

Also a Cheap Edition. 3s. 6d.

Waterloo Place, London.

Goulburn on the Lord's Supper.

Sixth Edition. Small 8vo. 6s.

A COMMENTARY, Expository and Devotional, on the Order of the Administration of the Lord's Supper, according to the Use of the Church of England; to which is added an Appendix on Fasting Communion, Non-communicating Attendance, Auricular Confession, the Doctrine of Sacrifice, and the Eucharistic Sacrifice.

By **Edward Meyrick Goulburn, D.D., D.C.L.,**
Dean of Norwich.

Also a Cheap Edition, uniform with 'Thoughts on Personal Religion,' and 'The Pursuit of Holiness.' 3s. 6d.

Goulburn's Holy Catholic Church.

Second Edition. Crown 8vo. 6s. 6d.

THE HOLY CATHOLIC CHURCH: its Divine Ideal, Ministry, and Institutions. A short Treatise. With a Catechism on each Chapter, forming a Course of Methodical Instruction on the subject.

By **Edward Meyrick Goulburn, D.D., D.C.L.,**
Dean of Norwich.

Contents.

What the Church is, and when and how it was founded—Duty of the Church towards those who hold to the Apostles' Doctrine, in separation from the Apostles' fellowship—The Unity of the Church and its Disruption—The Survey of Zion's towers, bulwarks, and palaces—The Institution of the Ministry, and its relation to the Church—The Holy Eucharist at its successive Stages—On the Powers of the Church in Council—The Church presenting, exhibiting, and defending the Truth—The Church guiding into and illustrating the Truth—On the Prayer Book as a Commentary on the Bible—Index.

Waterloo Place, London.

Goulburn's Collects of the Day.

Third Edition. Two Vols. Crown 8vo. 8s. each. Sold separately.

THE COLLECTS OF THE DAY : an Exposition, Critical and Devotional, of the Collects appointed at the Communion. With Preliminary Essays on their Structure, Sources, and General Character, and Appendices containing Expositions of the Discarded Collects of the First Prayer Book of 1549, and of the Collects of Morning and Evening Prayer.

By Edward Meyrick Goulburn, D.D., D.C.L.,
Dean of Norwich.

Contents.

VOLUME I. BOOK I. *Introductory.*—On the Excellencies of the Collects—On the Origin of the word Collect—On the Structure of a Collect, as illustrated by the Collect in the Burial Service—Of the Sources of the Collects : Of the Sacramentary of Leo, of the Sacramentary of Gelasius, of Gregory the Great and his Sacramentary, of the Use of Sarum, and of S. Osmund its Compiler—On the Collects of Archbishop Cranmer—Of the Restoration Collects, and of John Cosin, Prince-Bishop of Durham—Of the Collects, as representing the Genius of the English Church. BOOK II. Part I.—*The Constant Collect.* Part II.—*Collects varying with the Ecclesiastical Season.*—Advent to Whitsunday.

VOLUME II. BOOK II. *contd.*—Trinity Sunday to All Saints' Day. BOOK III.—*On the Collects after the Offertory.* APPENDIX A.—*Collects in the First Reformed Prayer Book of* 1549 *which were suppressed in* 1552—The Collect for the First Communion on Christmas Day—The Collect for S. Mary Magdalene's Day (July 22). APPENDIX B.—*Exposition of the Collects of Morning and Evening Prayer*—The Second at Morning Prayer, for Peace—The Third at Morning Prayer, for Grace—The Second at Evening Prayer, for Peace—The Third at Evening Prayer, for Aid against all Perils.

Knox Little's Good Friday Addresses.

New Edition. Small 8vo. 2s. ; or in Paper Cover, 1s.

THE THREE HOURS' AGONY OF OUR BLESSED REDEEMER : being Addresses in the form of Meditations delivered in S. Alban's Church, Manchester, on Good Friday 1877.

By the Rev. W. J. Knox Little, M.A.,
Canon Residentiary of Worcester, and Vicar of Hoar Cross.

Waterloo Place, London.

Luckock's After Death.

Sixth Edition. Crown 8vo. 6s.

AFTER DEATH. An Examination of the Testimony of Primitive Times respecting the State of the Faithful Dead, and their relationship to the Living.

By Herbert Mortimer Luckock, D.D.,
Canon of Ely, etc.

Contents.

PART I.--The Test of Catholicity—The Value of the Testimony of the Primitive Fathers—The Intermediate State—Change in the Intermediate State—Prayers for the Dead: Reasons for Our Lord's Silence on the Subject—The Testimony of Holy Scripture—The Testimony of the Catacombs—The Testimony of the Early Fathers—The Testimony of the Primitive Liturgies—Prayers for the Pardon of Sins of Infirmity, and the Effacement of Sinful Stains—The Inefficacy of Prayer for those who died in wilful unrepented Sin.

PART II.—Primitive Testimony to the Intercession of the Saints—Primitive Testimony to the Invocation of the Saints—The Trustworthiness of the Patristic Evidence for Invocation tested—The Primitive Liturgies and the Roman Catacombs—Patristic Opinions on the Extent of the Knowledge possessed by the Saints—The Testimony of Holy Scripture upon the same Subject—The Beatific Vision not yet attained by any of the Saints—Conclusions drawn from the foregoing Testimony.

SUPPLEMENTARY CHAPTERS.—(*a.*) Is a fuller Recognition of the Practice of Praying for the Dead desirable or not?—(*b.*) Is it lawful or desirable to practise Invocation of Saints in any form or not?—Table of Fathers, Councils, etc.—Passages of Scripture explained or quoted—General Index.

S. Bonaventure's Life of Christ.

Crown 8vo. 7s. 6d.

THE LIFE OF CHRIST.

By S. Bonaventure.
Translated and Edited by the Rev. W. H. Hutchings,
Rector of Kirkby Misperton, Yorkshire.

'The whole volume is full of gems and rich veins of thought, and whether as a companion to the preacher or to those who seek food for their daily meditations, we can scarcely imagine a more acceptable book.'—*Literary Churchman.*

Waterloo Place, London.

Newman's Selection from Sermons.

Third Edition. Crown 8vo.

SELECTION, adapted to the Seasons of the Ecclesiastical Year, from the 'Parochial and Plain Sermons' of JOHN HENRY NEWMAN, B.D., sometime Vicar of S. Mary's, Oxford.

Edited by the Rev. W. J. Copeland, B.D.,
Late Rector of Farnham, Essex.

Contents.

Advent:—Self-denial the Test of Religious Earnestness—Divine Calls—The Ventures of Faith—Watching. *Christmas Day:*—Religious Joy. *New Year's Sunday:*—The Lapse of Time. *Epiphany:*—Remembrance of Past Mercies—Equanimity—The Immortality of the Soul—Christian Manhood—Sincerity and Hypocrisy—Christian Sympathy. *Septuagesima:*—Present Blessings. *Sexagesima:*—Endurance, the Christian's Portion. *Quinquagesima:*—Love, the One Thing Needful. *Lent:*—The Individuality of the Soul—Life the Season of Repentance—Bodily Suffering—Tears of Christ at the Grave of Lazarus—Christ's Privations a Meditation for Christians—The Cross of Christ the Measure of the World. *Good Friday:*—The Crucifixion. *Easter Day:*—Keeping Fast and Festival. *Easter-Tide:*—Witnesses of the Resurrection—A Particular Providence as Revealed in the Gospel—Christ Manifested in Remembrance—The Invisible World—Waiting for Christ. *Ascension:*—Warfare the Condition of Victory. *Sunday after Ascension:*—Rising with Christ. *Whitsunday:*—The Weapons of Saints. *Trinity Sunday:*—The Mysteriousness of our Present Being. *Sundays after Trinity:*—Holiness Necessary for Future Blessedness—The Religious Use of Excited Feelings—The Self-wise Inquirer—Scripture a Record of Human Sorrow—The Danger of Riches—Obedience without Love as instanced in the Character of Balaam—Moral Consequences of Single Sins—The Greatness and Littleness of Human Life—Moral Effects of Communion with God—The Thought of God the Stay of the Soul—The Power of the Will—The Gospel Palaces—Religion a Weariness to the Natural Man—The World our Enemy—The Praise of Men—Religion Pleasant to the Religious—Mental Prayer—Curiosity a Temptation to Sin—Miracles no Remedy for Unbelief—Jeremiah, a Lesson for the Disappointed—The Shepherd of our Souls—Doing Glory to God in Pursuits of the World.

Waterloo Place, London.

Jennings' Ecclesia Anglicana.

Crown 8vo. 7s. 6d.

ECCLESIA ANGLICANA. A History of the Church of Christ in England, from the Earliest to the Present Times.

By the Rev. Arthur Charles Jennings, M.A.,
Jesus College, Cambridge, sometime Tyrwhitt Scholar, Crosse Scholar, Hebrew University Prizeman, Fry Scholar of S. John's College, Carus and Scholefield Prizeman, and Rector of King's Stanley,

---

Bickersteth's The Lord's Table.

Second Edition. 16mo. 1s.; or Cloth extra, 2s.

THE LORD'S TABLE; or, Meditations on the Holy Communion Office in the Book of Common Prayer.

By E. H. Bickersteth, D.D.,
Bishop of Exeter.

'We must draw our review to an end, without using any more of our own words, except one parting expression of cordial and sincere thanks to Mr. Bickersteth for this goodly and profitable "Companion to the Communion Service." '—*Record*.

Manuals of Religious Instruction.

New and Revised Editions. Small 8vo. 3s. 6d. each. Sold separately.

MANUALS OF RELIGIOUS INSTRUCTION.

Edited by John Pilkington Norris, D.D.,
Archdeacon of Bristol and Canon Residentiary of Bristol Cathedral.

I. THE CATECHISM AND PRAYER BOOK.
II. THE OLD TESTAMENT.
III. THE NEW TESTAMENT.

Waterloo Place, London.

Aids to the Inner Life.

*Five Vols. 32mo, Cloth limp, 6d. each; or Cloth extra, 1s. each.
Sold separately.*

*These Five Volumes, Cloth extra, may be had in a Box, price 7s.
Also an Edition with Red Borders, 2s. each.*

AIDS TO THE INNER LIFE.

Edited by the Rev. W. H. Hutchings, M.A.,
Rector of Kirkby Misperton, Yorkshire.

These books form a series of works provided for the use of members of the English Church. The process of adaptation is not left to the reader, but has been undertaken with the view of bringing every expression, as far as possible, into harmony with the Book of Common Prayer and Anglican Divinity.

OF THE IMITATION OF CHRIST. In Four Books. By THOMAS À KEMPIS.

THE CHRISTIAN YEAR. Thoughts in Verse for the Sundays and Holy Days throughout the Year.

INTRODUCTION TO THE DEVOUT LIFE. From the French of S. FRANCIS DE SALES, Bishop and Prince of Geneva.

THE HIDDEN LIFE OF THE SOUL. From the French of JEAN NICOLAS GROU.

THE SPIRITUAL COMBAT. Together with the Supplement and the Path of Paradise. By LAURENCE SCUPOLI.

'We heartily wish success to this important series, and trust it may command an extensive sale. We are much struck, not only by the excellent manner in which the design has been carried out in the Translations themselves, but also by the way in which Messrs. Rivington have done their part. The type and size of the volumes are precisely what will be found most convenient for common use. The price at which the volumes are produced is marvellously low. It may be hoped that a large circulation will secure from loss those who have undertaken this scheme for diffusing far and wide such valuable means of advancing and deepening, after so high a standard, the spiritual life.'—*Literary Churchman.*

Blunt's Theological Dictionary.

Second Edition. Imperial 8vo. 42s.; or in half-morocco, 52s. 6d.

DICTIONARY OF DOCTRINAL AND HISTORICAL THEOLOGY.
By Various Writers.

Edited by the Rev. John Henry Blunt, D.D.,
Editor of the 'Annotated Book of Common Prayer,' etc., etc.

Waterloo Place, London.

Norris's Rudiments of Theology.

Second Edition, revised. Crown 8vo. 7s. 6d.

RUDIMENTS OF THEOLOGY. A First Book for Students.

By John Pilkington Norris, D.D.,
Archdeacon of Bristol, and Canon Residentiary of Bristol Cathedral.

Contents.

PART I.—FUNDAMENTAL DOCTRINES:—The Doctrine of God's Existence—The Doctrine of the Second Person of the Trinity—The Doctrine of the Atonement—The Doctrine of the Third Person of the Trinity—The Doctrine of The Church—The Doctrine of the Sacraments.

PART II.—THE SOTERIOLOGY OF THE BIBLE:—The Teaching of the Old Testament—The Teaching of the Four Gospels—The Teaching of S. Paul—The Teaching of the Epistle to the Hebrews, of S. Peter and S. John—Soteriology of the Bible (concluded).

APPENDIX—ILLUSTRATIONS OF PART I. FROM THE EARLY FATHERS:—On the Evidence of God's Existence—On the Divinity of Christ—On the Doctrine of the Atonement—On the Procession of the Holy Spirit—On The Church—On the Doctrine of the Eucharist—Greek and Latin Fathers quoted or referred to in this volume, in their chronological order—Glossarial Index.

Medd's Bampton Lectures.

8vo. 16s.

THE ONE MEDIATOR. The Operation of the Son of God in Nature and in Grace. Eight Lectures delivered before the University of Oxford in the year 1882, on the Foundation of the late Rev. John Bampton, M.A., Canon of Salisbury.

By Peter Goldsmith Medd, M.A.,
Rector of North Cerney; Hon. Canon of S. Alban's, and Examining Chaplain to the Bishop; late Rector of Barnes; Formerly Fellow and Tutor of University College, Oxford.

Waterloo Place, London.

H. L. Sidney Lear's Christian Biographies.

Eight Vols. Crown 8vo. 3s. 6d. each. Sold separately.

CHRISTIAN BIOGRAPHIES.

By H. L. Sidney Lear.

MADAME LOUISE DE FRANCE, Daughter of Louis xv., known also as the Mother Térèse de S. Augustin.

A DOMINICAN ARTIST: a Sketch of the Life of the Rev. Père Besson, of the Order of S. Dominic.

HENRI PERREYVE. By A. GRATRY. Translated by special permission. With Portrait.

S. FRANCIS DE SALES, Bishop and Prince of Geneva.

THE REVIVAL OF PRIESTLY LIFE IN THE SEVENTEENTH CENTURY IN FRANCE. Charles de Condren—S. Philip Neri and Cardinal de Berulle—S. Vincent de Paul—Saint Sulpice and Jean Jacques Olier.

A CHRISTIAN PAINTER OF THE NINETEENTH CENTURY: being the Life of Hippolyte Flandrin.

BOSSUET AND HIS CONTEMPORARIES.

FÉNELON, ARCHBISHOP OF CAMBRAI.

H. L. Sidney Lear's Five Minutes.

Third Edition. 16mo. 3s. 6d.

FIVE MINUTES. Daily Readings of Poetry.

Selected by H. L. Sidney Lear.

Pusey's Private Prayers.

Second Edition. Royal 32mo. 2s. 6d.

PRIVATE PRAYERS.

By the Rev. E. B. Pusey, D.D.
Edited, with a Preface, by H. P. Liddon, D.D., D.C.L.
Chancellor and Canon of St. Paul's.

Waterloo Place, London.

Half-a-Crown Editions of Devotional Works.

New and Uniform Editions.
Seven Vols. 16mo. 2s. 6d. each. Sold separately.

HALF-A-CROWN EDITIONS OF DEVOTIONAL WORKS.

Edited by H. L. Sidney Lear.

SPIRITUAL LETTERS TO MEN. By ARCHBISHOP FÉNELON.

SPIRITUAL LETTERS TO WOMEN. By ARCHBISHOP FÉNELON.

A SELECTION FROM THE SPIRITUAL LETTERS OF S. FRANCIS DE SALES, BISHOP AND PRINCE OF GENEVA.

THE SPIRIT OF S. FRANCIS DE SALES, BISHOP AND PRINCE OF GENEVA.

THE HIDDEN LIFE OF THE SOUL.

THE LIGHT OF THE CONSCIENCE. With an Introduction by the Rev. T. T. CARTER, M.A.

SELF-RENUNCIATION. From the French. With an Introduction by the Rev. T. T. CARTER, M.A.

H. L. Sidney Lear's Weariness.

Large Type. Fourth Edition. Small 8vo. 5s.

WEARINESS. A Book for the Languid and Lonely.

By H. L. Sidney Lear,
Author of 'For Days and Years,' 'Christian Biographies,' etc., etc.

Maxims from Pusey.

Third Edition. Crown 16mo. 2s.

MAXIMS AND GLEANINGS from the Writings of EDWARD BOUVERIE PUSEY, D.D.

Selected and arranged for Daily Use, by C. M: S.,
Compiler of 'Daily Gleanings of the Saintly Life,' 'Under the Cross,' etc.

With an Introduction by the Rev. M. F. Sadler,
Prebendary of Wells, and Rector of Honiton.

𝔚aterloo 𝔓lace, 𝔏ondon.

Body's Life of Justification.

Sixth Edition. Crown 8vo. 4s. 6d.

THE LIFE OF JUSTIFICATION. A Series of Lectures delivered in substance at All Saints', Margaret Street.

By the Rev. George Body, D.D.,
Canon of Durham.

Contents.

Justification the Want of Humanity—Christ our Justification—Union with Christ the Condition of Justification—Conversion and Justification—The Life of Justification—The Progress and End of Justification.

Keys to Christian Knowledge.

*Seven Volumes. Small 8vo. 1s. 6d. each. Sold separately.
The 2s. 6d. Edition may still be had.*

Edited by the Rev. John Henry Blunt, D.D.,
Editor of the 'Annotated Bible,' 'Annotated Book of Common Prayer,' etc., etc.

- THE HOLY BIBLE.
- THE BOOK OF COMMON PRAYER.
- CHURCH HISTORY (ANCIENT).
- CHURCH HISTORY (MODERN).
- CHRISTIAN DOCTRINE AND PRACTICE (founded on the Church Catechism).

Edited by John Pilkington Norris, D.D.,
*Archdeacon of Bristol, and Canon Residentiary of Bristol Cathedral.
Editor of the 'New Testament with Notes,' etc.*

- THE FOUR GOSPELS.
- THE ACTS OF THE APOSTLES.

Waterloo Place, London.

www.ingramcontent.com/pod-product-compliance
Lightning Source LLC
Chambersburg PA
CBHW022118230426
43672CB00008B/1426